Youth Violence and Delinquency

Youth Violence and Delinquency

Monsters and Myths

Volume 1
Juvenile Offenders and Victims

Edited by

MARILYN D. McSHANE
AND FRANK P. WILLIAMS III

Praeger Perspectives

Criminal Justice, Delinquency, and Corrections

PRAEGER

Westport, Connecticut
London

Library of Congress Cataloging-in-Publication Data

Youth violence and delinquency : monsters and myths / edited by Marilyn
D. McShane and Frank P. Williams III.
      p. cm. — (Criminal justice, delinquency, and corrections, ISSN 1535-0371)
    Includes bibliographical references and index.
    ISBN 978-0-275-99112-8 (set : alk. paper) — ISBN 978-0-275-99113-5
(v. 1 : alk. paper) — ISBN 978-0-275-99114-2 (v. 2 : alk. paper) —
ISBN 978-0-275-99115-9 (v. 3 : alk. paper) 1. Juvenile delinquency—
United States. 2. Juvenile justice, Administration of—United States. 3. Victims of
juvenile crime—United States. 4. Juvenile delinquency—United States—Prevention.
I. McShane, Marilyn D., 1956- II. Williams, Franklin P.
   HV9104.Y6854 2007
   364.360973—dc22   2007003047

British Library Cataloguing in Publication Data is available.

Library of Congress Catalog Card Number: 2007003047
ISBN-10: 0-275-99112-1 (set)
        0-275-99113-X (vol. 1)
        0-275-99114-8 (vol. 2)
        0-275-99115-6 (vol. 3)

ISBN-13: 978-0-275-99112-8 (set)
        978-0-275-99113-5 (vol. 1)
        978-0-275-99114-2 (vol. 2)
        978-0-275-99115-9 (vol. 3)

ISSN: 1535-0371

First published in 2007

Praeger Publishers, 88 Post Road West, Westport, CT 06881
An imprint of Greenwood Publishing Group, Inc.
www.praeger.com

Printed in the United States of America

The paper used in this book complies with the
Permanent Paper Standard issued by the National
Information Standards Organization (Z39.48-1984).

10 9 8 7 6 5 4 3 2 1

Contents

Preface

HERE THERE BE DRAGONS: THE UNKNOWN
AND DANGEROUS DELINQUENT

When ancient mapmakers worked their way to the edges of unchartered or unexplored territories, they marked the boundaries with the famous phrase, "beyond here monsters lie" or "here there be dragons," appealing to the common understanding that what was unknown must contain the dreaded or evil. Much the same can be said for the vast expanse of juvenile delinquency—the wild, unpredictable, and unrestrained tempers of youth are to be feared and often demonized. The media "mapmakers" often paint dramatic and terror-filled accounts of what are, in reality, rare events. Consequently, the routine parade of countless minor episodes of kids who shoplift, run away, and vandalize, and who are overlooked in the overcrowded and overworked juvenile courts, is far less attractive for the sound bites of the evening news.

The normal developmental tendencies of youth to talk, act, and dress in extreme and unique ways often contribute to these fearful images. The blue hair, Mohawk cuts, the cacophonic music, and elaborate piercings and tattoos often mark the borders of adult tolerance. Although generational misunderstandings and the inevitable rebellion of teenagers is nothing new, we seem to continue to approach each successive wave of youngsters with the same apprehension, fear, and readiness to suppress the wayward vestiges of individualism. So it is not surprising, then, that a crime committed by a spike-haired, nose-ringed, gothic-dressed, jack-booted young man is perhaps likely to draw more attention from the court and require longer supervision with more restrictions on activities. Anti-loitering and congregating statutes, as well as prohibitions against skateboarding, are viewed by critics as ways to cleanse business areas of unattractive nuisances. As a group of youth in Brattleboro, Vermont, gathering in downtown parking areas pushing the limits of municipal goodwill found out, no law prohibited them from stripping down to various levels of nudity, but there soon would be, as fast as the select board of town leaders could legislate one.

Today, theorists often spend as much time contemplating why youth do not commit crime as why youth do. We attempt to explain not only the overall decrease in juvenile crime, but also why, in the face of such a decrease, most people still have the impression that the juvenile crime rate is increasing. Media coverage of certain dramatic juvenile crimes tends to give people the wrong impression about current trends in delinquency. The terms "shocking crime" and "brutal violence" are often overplayed, creating a distorted and pessimistic view of youthful offenders. Although many people believe that juvenile delinquency is increasing, the truth is that the juvenile offending rate is fairly stable and that many youth are engaged in co-offending, which tends to make the amount of crime appear higher. That is, more offenders are arrested than actual crimes committed. Also, contrary to what some people seem to believe, juvenile offenders are not getting younger or engaging in more rapes and robberies.

Crime figures vary by whether you are talking about reports of crimes or arrests for crimes. As a consequence of better law enforcement techniques, arrests can increase even though the amount of reported crimes stays about the same. The accuracy of certain crime statistics and the likelihood of offenses being reported also vary by type, such as drug crime, violent crime, and status offenses, as well as by race and gender. We know that, overall, the juvenile arrest rate for property crimes has decreased. By 2003, the juvenile arrest rate for violent crime, particularly murder, had decreased to levels similar to those around the early 1980s. Some of the most recent government statistics indicate that arrests for simple assaults and aggravated assaults have increased, particularly for juvenile females.[1] So, although there is a great deal to be optimistic about, there is much to be done to enrich the lives of American youth and to improve their chances of success.

We know that the number of children living under the poverty limit is still dangerously high and that self-reported delinquency has always been associated with being poor. As in the past, data still suggest that most juvenile crime is intraracial, thus victims are likely to be the same race as their offenders. Children continue to be at higher risk for neglect and maltreatment in the home than they are for violent victimization in the streets. Schools are still one of the safest places for kids, and fewer kids drop out today than in the 1970s.

Although data seem to indicate a rise in lethality in some crimes, the casual ease with which juveniles access semiautomatic and automatic weapons can be used to explain trends in homicide. These explanations are as insightful and as full of implications for programs and policies as those that address deviant behavior. Although narrowing our focus to specific types of offenders only or certain types of offenses may be frustrating to those seeking a "one-size-fits-all" approach, it often gives us a greater, more accurate, albeit smaller, picture. Thus, readers who are looking for clear-cut answers to the problems of juvenile crime and violence will find that there are lots of little ones, plenty of pretty good ones, and certainly none that fit a broad range of behaviors and cultures. We believe that you will find the work in this volume is extremely informative and persuasive. It is evident that the field requires a wide range of research from many varied disciplines and involves not only environmental, social, legal, political, and economic change but also changes in our values, attitudes, and goals—the very fabric of our society.

The articles in this volume will provide readers with a picture of the current status of juvenile crime in this country. The realities are often far less dramatic and entertaining than the news clips on evening television reporting, but they represent the true focus of law enforcement, the courts, and youth services workers in corrections, treatment, and community outreach professions. Our tax dollars, our neighbor's children, our schools, and our police are all influenced by the way we view delinquency.

REFERENCE

Snyder, H. N., & Sickmund, M. (2006). *Juvenile offenders and victims: 2006 national report*. Washington, D.C.: U.S. Department of Justice, Office of Justice Programs.

CHAPTER 1

Myths and Realities: How and What the Public Knows about Crime and Delinquency

Marilyn D. McShane and Frank P. Williams III

We all know about crime and delinquency. It appears on television, it is featured in the newspapers, we talk about it with our friends. In fact, crime is such a constant in society that we can easily say that it is a part of our lives. Government reports and criminologists point out that most of us will be the victim of a crime at least once in our lives. That is a rather scary statistic.

What is not said is that most crimes are minor things such as vandalism and petty theft. They are inconveniences, but little else. Even "violent" crimes are mainly petty events—someone hits someone else, a police officer is pushed. As a result, our "chances" of being a victim of crime really describe the chances of being the victim of a minor incident. The serious crimes are much more rare.

We realize that you hear about serious crimes all of the time, so you are probably thinking that there *must* be a lot of violent crimes out there. The reality to this is both "yes, there is" and "no, there isn't." The yes is that there are a lot of people in the world, so even if something is a rare event, plenty of examples exist. The "no" is that you can think of your chances as something like hitting the lottery—most of the time you buy a lottery ticket and get nothing. When you do "win," it is likely to be a small amount. Larger winnings are progressively unlikely. On the whole, being the victim of a crime is like that: most of the time you get nothing, some of the time you get a petty crime, rarely you get a more serious crime, and, finally, there is the unlikely event that you will be the victim of a serious violent crime.

Having said this, you also need to recognize that your chances of being a victim of a crime will vary with your personal characteristics: age, race/

ethnicity, location, job, etc. Some people have a much higher probability of being a victim of serious crime than others. People will also tell you that a high percentage of the population are victims of serious crime, such as child abuse or rape. We will discuss the specifics of these claims later, but, for now, we'll just say that the truth of these statements depends on how you define these crimes.

Now for a relatively controversial statement: *the biggest problem is not crime and delinquent acts themselves, but rather how they affect us.* How crime affects us is not normally a product of our real-life experiences, but, instead, what we have been led to believe through the surrounding social environment. We refer to this as the *social reality of crime.*[1]

So what is this "surrounding social environment" that leads to the "social reality" of crime? It is what your family, your friends, and your coworkers tell you about crime. It is the news and stories you hear on television and read in the newspapers. It is the urban myths about crime. And more than knowing about crime, these provide the context for *explaining* crime. Simply having the knowledge of crime tells you what crimes are around you, how many occur, where they occur, who is a victim, who gets arrested, what happens in court, and so on. Explaining crime, on the other hand, is making sense of crime: why it occurs, why people commit criminal or delinquent acts, what we should do about it, and how you should live to avoid it. In short, your social environment produces your knowledge of crime and that, in turn, creates the way you interpret and explain crime. Thus, all of these assume that actual crime is directly related to your interpretation of crime—and that is rarely the case.

Social reality describes the difference between actual reality and socially interpreted reality. An early sociologist, W. I. Thomas, once said that what we perceive to be real is real in its consequences. By this he meant that what a person *thinks* is real might as well be truly real, because the person will actually behave *as if* it were real. Put another way, a child might believe that there is a monster under the bed. Adults know different, there are no monsters (at least of this variety . . .). That lack of actual reality still doesn't make any difference; the child will *behave* as if there were a monster under the bed. So, too, is the social reality of crime—people will act on what they "know" about crime, regardless of how close their knowledge is to true reality.

The social reality of crime, then, is the basis for the way the public thinks, acts, and makes pronouncements about crime. The "true" reality of crime is not at issue, the social reality is the critical component. Unfortunately, this social reality can be manipulated, and even created, by news media, politicians, or anyone with a special interest in crime (or the things it brings with it). This is why criminologists usually consider crime to be a *social problem*, rather than merely factual events. Social problems are constructed. That is, they are created by people who have a vested interest in them. The underlying reality of crime itself is actually unimportant to its existence as a social problem. Thus, our discussion of social reality fits in nicely with crime as a social problem. One criminologist has even referred to crime waves as "crime reporting waves"[2]—an adroit observation because individuals cannot possibly know how much crime is taking place around them or in the nation. When we become interested in crime, we experience a crime reporting wave that may or may not match the actual events of crime.

Another concept that applies to this problem is that of a "moral panic." Moral panics exist when people with a strong interest in a subject manage to convince the public that things have gotten out of hand and a huge problem exists. Almost universally, moral panics follow the same path:

- Someone notices a "problem"
- Someone becomes overenthusiastic about solving the problem
- Claims are made that the problem is widespread and serious
- The news media begins reporting on the "problem" and quotes the claims
- Politicians and special interest groups take up the claims and spread them
- The public begins to believe that the problem is serious and must be resolved
- The media engages in a problem-reporting wave
- People with actual information on the problem begin to question the claims
- The claims turn out to be highly exaggerated
- News-reporting declines, politicians and the public begins to lose interest
- The "problem" disappears

Examples of moral panics in recent times include child abuse, serial murderers, crack babies, missing children, and sex offenders. Each panic followed, almost to the letter, the above scheme. It is possible that, during a crime wave and the resulting public excitement, a moral panic actually is going on and the crime itself has not substantially changed.

HOW DO WE KNOW ABOUT CRIME AND DELINQUENCY?

The people who know the most about crime, criminologists and criminal justicians, have usually spent years of training and study in the subject. But because the amount of literature and research is quite large, even these people are reluctant to say that they know much about the entire subject. Normally, criminologists focus on one area of crime or delinquency (or the criminal/juvenile justice systems themselves) and reserve their judgments to that area. Conversely, most members of the public don't know much about crime but that doesn't stop them from thinking they do or from making pronouncements about crime and what to do with criminals and delinquents.

This leads us to our first "reality" statement:

Reality 1: Few people know much about crime, but almost everyone thinks they do.

The truth is that crime is one of those subjects about which everyone claims to be an expert. And because of this, much of our criminal and juvenile justice policy tends to be created by those who know little about both crime and the justice system. For a certainty, few people actually study crime and are aware of relevant research. This fact, coupled with the popular feeling that everyone "knows" about crime, raises the following question: "How *does* the public know about crime?" We believe there are four primary sources of crime information: personal experience, information from friends and relatives, government reports and pronouncements, and the media.

Information from Personal Experience

As noted above, most people have some experience with crime, but that experience is normally of a relatively minor sort. Such crimes as vandalism, petty theft, and a range of public disorder offenses are common experiences. So common, in fact, that you are likely to have experienced these multiple times. Thus, it is true that most people know crime from personal experience and therefore form opinions based on some degree of factual evidence. Conversely, when the public talks about crime, they don't actually refer to any of these common offenses. It is *real* crime—murder, rape, robbery, burglary, assault—to which they refer. Street crimes, or "index" crimes, are the offenses on everyone's mind. These crimes are far less commonly experienced and, even when experienced, may not produce similar effects (as we noted above, there are some people in certain areas who experience such crimes at much higher rates and *do* have factually informed opinions). Therefore, although some people are reasonably informed by personal experience, the crime experiences of most members of the pubic bear little resemblance to the crimes about which they make pronouncements.

Information from Family and Friends

One reasonable way to add to one's experiences is to draw from the experiences of others. Although these "anecdotal" incidents are emotionally powerful in their personal basis, they are not scientific nor can they be generalized—that is, they are not useful for prediction or for gauging trends. Those closest to us are the normal sources for this additional information. We know from research on social learning that, in addition to information, much of our attitudes and behaviors are formed by those around us. Consider, however, just how your family and friends learn about crime. Do they have any better sources of information than you do? Are their sources reliable? And, most of all, is it possible for their sources to even know the state of crime around us? After all, criminologists are themselves reluctant to talk about actual crime; they refer to those crimes we "know about."

Information from Government Reports and Pronouncements

Although the public receives much of its crime information from the government—including various crime-related agencies, the president's office, and Congress—it is also true that all this information is filtered through the media. Thus, the media is implicated in the delivery of virtually all crime information the public does not personally receive through their our own experiences or from people close to them. Assuming that much of this information is not "interpreted" for us by the media, the question then becomes how the government creates and conveys crime news.

The answer to this question is largely that, like all organizations, government agencies and personnel have agendas that either serve the agency or some moralistic or political purpose. This doesn't mean that government crime information is somehow part of an insidious plan, but merely that individual and agency beliefs, policies, and goals dictate the issues and questions they believe are important and therefore the type of information they provide the public. For instance, in the early years of the Reagan administration, there was a strong conviction that illicit drugs were a major threat to the United States. The problem was that the public didn't feel that drugs were a major social problem. President Reagan and members of his administration talked about the problem posed by drugs at every opportunity from 1982 to 1984. Finally, in 1984, a Gallup Poll indicated that Americans were listening and drugs showed up for the first time as one of the major problems facing the United States.[3] President Reagan promptly proclaimed that the American people wanted something done about drugs and he would obey their wishes. Of course, the truth was that Americans were simply reflecting the political emphasis and media hype on drugs. Every presidential administration has done similar things— they have agendas to push "for the good of the country." Why wouldn't they have such agendas? After all, isn't this why many people vote for them? Of course, no one ever knows the entire agenda.

Aside from obvious agenda items on crime, there are regular and routine government pronouncements. The Federal Bureau of Investigation (FBI) announces that the Uniform Crime Reports are showing a rise (or a decrease) in crime rates. The National Institute of Justice (NIJ) releases the latest victimization statistics or the findings from a specific subset of these statistics (such as victimization of the elderly). The NIJ and its various offices also release reports from funded research on a wide variety of crime and justice issues. To these can be added more than a thousand other national, state, and local agencies that are providing the public with crime-related information. In one sense, each of these organizations releases information that serves two noninformational purposes: (1) it serves to convey the importance of the agency, thus justifying the agency's budget; and (2) it serves to marshal public opinion around the "purpose" of the agency. In short, while informational, news releases from agencies serve their interests.

Such reports, news, and pronouncements help to create the social reality of crime to which we have been referring. For example, in 1996, political analyst John DiIulio compiled a highly publicized report that predicted that social circumstances were ripe to spawn a wave of serious juvenile superpredators who would plague American communities. Republican presidential candidate Bob Dole quickly adopted the "superpredator" scare scenario to propel legislators into passing The Violent Youth Predator Act of 1996, which allowed many young offenders to be tried and incarcerated as adults. In short time, of course, criminologists were able to demonstrate that the phenomenon was not going to occur and, in many areas, violent crime by juveniles decreased. Although DiIulio's pronouncements were widely discredited, the image lingers—as do many of the terms that continue to be resurrected during political campaigns and funding competitions.[4]

Information from the Media

Conceptions of crime, criminals, and delinquents are commonly derived from images presented by the popular media. The public acts on these images as certainly as if they were real. The truth is that popular images and criminological reality usually are in opposition. Here is another reality to keep in mind about crime and the media:

Reality 2: Crime pays—for the media!

The media sell crime because crime sells media. Imagine the mythological newsboy standing on the street corner hawking a newspaper: "Extra, extra, read all about it! Woman helps old man across street!" That is obviously a headline that wouldn't sell a dozen papers. Change the headline to "Woman shoots old man crossing street," and you have a sensational news item that will sell papers. The same concept applies to television and radio news (watch them to see how much crime they report during the hour or half-hour). Therefore, crime sells newspapers and increases the number of television news viewers. But not all crime is sensational enough to contribute to media sales. Thefts, for instance, are just not interesting. Here are the hard facts about crime and the media: the media report most often the crimes that happen the least, and the least-reported crimes are the ones that occur most frequently. Thus, the public is erroneously led to believe that violence is commonplace and, as a result, fear of crime is generated. Not all media crime information, however, comes from news sources. The standard fare of media involves crime images as well.

THE LONE RANGER, DIRTY HARRY, AND MEDIA IMAGES OF JUSTICE

One form of socially constructed reality can be found in popular film, television, and radio shows. For an example, we will use the old Lone

Ranger shows (available in all three forms of media). The Lone Ranger is particularly handy for our discussion because George Trendle, the creator of the show, acknowledged that he was as interested in sending moral messages as he was in entertaining. Every show had at least one major moral message. Realizing the importance of image, Trendle signed every actor playing the Lone Ranger to a contract that mandated that his off-stage behavior match his on-stage role. One of the actors, the late Clayton Moore, felt so strongly about the morality issue that, after playing the Lone Ranger for a half-dozen years, he maintained the role off stage for the rest of his life.

Almost 20 years ago, Quinney wrote an article about what the Lone Ranger had to say about criminology:

> What I am suggesting is that our understanding of crime in America is tied to a myth. Rather than basing our thought on social theory, whether of Emile Durkheim or of Max Weber, we have allowed our thinking to be shaped by the prevailing American frontier ideology. We have been party to a myth. *Law and order. Support your local sheriff. My country. To rule the world.*
>
> *And beware of evil.* What would a world look like that was not divided into the good and the bad? I can't say, can you? The reel spinning before me always shows men in white hats chasing men in black hats; cowboys and Indians; cops and robbers; Americans and Communists; believers and non-believers. To this day I cannot conceive of a world that does not pit the forces of good against those of evil.[5]

Perhaps another quotation, this time from the Lone Ranger himself, would make this concept more clear. In the following scene, the Lone Ranger is talking to his nephew Dan just after Grandma's death (the Lone Ranger left Dan with her to be raised while he was busy fighting crime). Dan has expressed a desire to go off with the Lone Ranger and Tonto to battle criminals, but the Lone Ranger tells Dan that he should first go to college (an important message in 1947 because of the number of unemployed young males after WWII). As he talks, the music of *America the Beautiful* begins quietly in the background and swells to a crescendo:

> She and your father left you a great heritage. They and others like them have handed down to you the right to worship as you choose. And the right to work and profit from your enterprise. They have given you a land where there is true freedom. True equality of opportunity. A nation that is governed by the people. By laws that are best for the greatest number. Your duty, Dan, is to preserve that heritage and strengthen it. That is the heritage and duty of every American. (At this point there is nothing to be heard but *America the Beautiful* playing which then fades into the Lone Ranger theme music.)[6]

From the various Lone Ranger episodes, we learned about the "*blinding light* of justice," the value of *silver* bullets (it seems that bullets from the good guy's gun had to be pure), the good guys riding a *white* horse, taking care of *defenseless* women, and so on. We also knew that the bad guys would always take advantage of the good guys, but never the reverse. The public learned that justice was pure and fair, and, where the Lone Ranger was concerned, it was swift and certain.

But the Lone Ranger imagery is now rather dated. What is the public now receiving as "justice" images? Perhaps the best answer is that reports of out-of-control crime and the "War on Crime," dating from the 1970s, begat a new type of media crime-fighter, one who gave evil its due without depending on a corrupt and ineffective justice system—Dirty Harry. In the first of Clint Eastwood's "Dirty Harry" movies, people literally cheered when the evil protagonist was illegally blown away. The young male movie-goers left the theater making comments about how to take care of justice. And, of course, Eastwood's Dirty Harry and his "Make my day, punk!" filtered into American consciousness and became an icon (Dirty Harry also became a name for a police stereotype[7]). Movie-goers received far more than entertainment from the movie—they learned a lesson in the ineffectual nature of formal justice and the "proper" way to achieve justice. They also learned that criminals are thoroughly evil and socially unredeemable creatures who are absolutely different from normal people. Of course, they already knew much of this—they had been to other movies, read other books, and watched other television shows that delivered the same messages. After Dirty Harry, a series of similarly themed movies staring Charles Bronson, Bruce Willis, and Mel Gibson were made. Television police programs such as *Nash Bridges, NYPD Blue, Miami Vice, Walker–Texas Ranger,* and *CSI* generally repeat these images. All find a way to cut corners and successfully "bring in the criminal" in spite of the legal technicalities standing in the way of "real" justice.

From other media sources, the public has learned that there is another type of criminal—a very devious, very intelligent, cold-blooded killer who requires much more than a Dirty Harry to bring him to justice. This criminal can only be caught by a superintelligent investigator who is capable of seeing and understanding the smallest nuances of evidence. Such villains are exemplified in the pages of writers such as Sir Arthur Conan Doyle (the *Sherlock Holmes* series), Agatha Christie, and, more recently, James Patterson. In fact, Patterson's best-sellers (such as *Along Came a Spider* and *Kiss the Girls*) trade on the public's concept of serial murder, painting a picture of murderers as genius sociopaths who kill over and over again. Patterson's detective requires a doctorate in clinical psychology to win the battle of wits. Furthermore, expensive labs with high-tech equipment and genius technicians turn tiny microscopic traces of fibers and skin cells into damning evidence resulting in iron-clad convictions. Ironically, materials are never lost, compromised, or piled up on the desk of someone who is taking extended leave.

The truth is there is not much reality in the television crime-reality shows. These shows demonstrate the exciting and tough nature of the police job and the general stupidity of average criminals. Although other stereotypical cops and robbers exist, all of these cater to, and help create, public perceptions of "real" police work. Moreover, they all serve to focus the public attention on the "front end of the justice system." Surette, in an excellent work on media and crime, has this to say about such emphases:

These images of society and criminality, combined with the emphasis on the front end of the justice system, investigations and arrests, ultimately promote pro-law enforcement and crime control policies. Crime shows may be about law and order, but they are light on law and heavy on order.[8]

In short, the Lone Ranger and others of his ilk (Superman, Batman, Spider Man, Wonder Woman, Teen-Age Mutant Ninja Turtles, Power Rangers, the Avengers, and the Fantastic Four, to name a few) have not just entertained us by providing action and adventure every week, they have intentionally and unintentionally provided moral messages and pictures of proper social reaction for impressionable minds, both young and old. These popular figures help construct the way justice is viewed and crime-fighting is done.

Media Affects Our Lives

Without spending much more time on the subject, it should now be obvious that media coverage of crime affects our lives. Imagine how it might affect which politicians we vote for (Richard Nixon "invented" the modern-day political use of candidates "being against crime"—after all, who is going to come out *for* crime?) and what we do on a daily basis. Fear of crime is largely a product of media reporting, political maneuvering, and the work of special interest groups. Thus, we come to another truism:

Reality 3: Crime pays—for politicians and special interest groups!

CONCLUSION

To couch this message in other terms, perception is a critical ingredient in what humans know and how they behave. Moreover, it is not merely perception that is important, but also *selective* perception. The world around us is too complex. A person simply cannot perceive all that he or she sees at any moment for the very reason that the complexity of the information would be too difficult to process and therefore result in paralysis. So, humans rely on selective perception to resolve the problem of filtering out all but the most important factors. Of course, those factors that humans define as "most important" are a product of preexisting belief systems or ideologies that tell us what we should observe and how we should process these observations (what is defined as important may even be a product of evolution ...). Reality is, of necessity, a selectively perceived reality. Popular media, the government, and our friends assist in that selection process.

Crime, justice, and the justice system are all interpreted through the filter of perception. Because the information we receive is, on the whole, lacking in accuracy, the public believes and acts on a version of crime and justice that is largely in the mind. This social reality of crime is the essence of the myths and misinterpretations that abound among the public. And, this reality is the source of most of our criminal and juvenile justice policies.

NOTES

1. See Richard Quinney's *The Social Reality of Crime* (1970) for the first elaborated statement on this concept.
2. Fishman, 1978.
3. Goode & Ben-Yehuda, 1994.
4. Schiraldi, 2001.
5. Quinney, 1973, p. 60.
6. Quinney, 1973, p. 57.
7. Klockars, 1980.
8. Surette, 1998, p. 50.

REFERENCES

Fishman, M. (1978). Crime waves as ideology. *Social Problems, 25*, 531–543.

Goode, E., & Ben-Yehuda, N. (1994). The American drug panic of the 1980s. *Moral panics: The Social Construction of Deviance, 12*, 205–223. Ames, IA: Blackwell Publishing.

Klockars, C. (1980). The Dirty Harry problem. *Annals of the American Academy of Political and Social Science, The Police and Violence, 452*, 33–47.

Patterson, J. (1993). *Along came a spider.* Boston: Little, Brown.

Patterson, J. (1995). *Kiss the girls.* Boston: Little, Brown.

Quinney, R. (1970). *The social reality of crime.* Boston: Little, Brown.

Quinney, R. (1973). There are a lot of folks grateful to the Lone Ranger: With some notes on the rise and fall of American Criminology. *The Insurgent Sociologist, 5*(1), 56–64.

Schiraldi, V. (2001, February 5). Will the real John DiIulio please stand up. *Washington Post.* Retrieved February 6, 2001, from www.cjcj.org/jpi/washpost020501.html and September 1, 2006, from www.commondreams.org/views01/0205-02.htm.

Surette, R. (1998). *Media, crime and criminal justice: Images and realities.* Belmont, CA: West/Wadsworth.

CHAPTER 2

Age, Gender, Race, and Rep: Trends in Juvenile Offending and Victimization

Richard McWhorter

The costs to society of juvenile offending are both direct and indirect. Direct costs include incarceration, damages, and injuries, as well as replacement of stolen property and treatment. Indirect costs are things like community fear, the purchase of security, and the loss of potentially productive citizens to a life of crime and institutionalization. Likewise, the direct and indirect affects of victimization can also be quantified, and these numbers provide significant motivation to address the causes of delinquency, identify those at greatest risk, and implement solutions that, at face value, seem to be a small fraction of the estimated costs of later interventions.

In 1999, a government study estimated that the cost to the public of one youth dropping out of school and becoming involved in crime and drug abuse was in excess of $2 million.[1] Over time, however, the estimates are projected much higher as the costs are adjusted for inflation.

Learning more about those who not only will become offenders but who also will persist in offending is as critical as determining what treatments and programs show the most promise for success. Long-held beliefs about the effects of age, gender, and race must be scrutinized in light of our demographically changing society and with the newer and more sophisticated statistical techniques available to analyze crime.

AGE, RACE, AND GENDER: WHAT REALLY COUNTS?

One of the problems with attempting to profile offenders or victims is that characteristics can be too broad or too narrow to be useful in predicting who is at risk. For example, the Federal Bureau of Investigation's

(FBI's) attempt to link certain traits to school shooters, based on a small number of previous incidents, is notably weak. The traits they listed, such as externalizing blame, inappropriate humor, narcissism, and access to violent videos, could be generalized to most adolescents and were unlikely to predict a homicidal teen. Conversely, prediction instruments that look for previous violent attacks, as well as mutilating small animals, may be a bit narrow and likely to overlook some who eventually do commit serious crimes.

Traditionally, variables like age, race, and gender have been considered the most consistent predictors of both criminality and victimization. Over time, age and gender remain powerful factors in any analysis, but race has been clarified by more complex relationships, such as socioeconomics, criminal history, neighborhoods, and education. Other variations in research outcomes can be attributed to different sampling locations. Official statistics gathered by the FBI from individual police jurisdictions is often criticized for overemphasizing the importance of street crimes to the exclusion of other serious offenses, such as white collar crimes, environmental crimes, and drug crimes. In addition, official statistics tend to underreport rape and domestic violence crimes, while overemphasizing those crimes requiring police reports for insurance purposes. They are also subject to the reluctance of both victims and witnesses to go to the police about certain offenses or offenders.

Conversely, self-report surveys, in particular the National Crime Victimization Survey (NCVS), tend to rely on respondents' recollections and their tendency to admit to certain types of victimizations and suppress others, to emphasize stranger-based crimes, and to downplay any behavior on their own part that might have originated or aggravated the criminal incidents. Studies taking place over a long period of time and with multiple observations, called longitudinal studies, may give us different types of research findings than those assessed at one specific point in time (cross-sectional studies). It was a well-known longitudinal study, The Wolfgang-Sellin Philadelphia Birth Cohort, that demonstrated the presence of a small group of persistent or chronic offenders, roughly 6 percent of the boys, were responsible for half of the area's juvenile crime.[2] This finding has since been replicated in many areas and has led to specific strategies being developed to address this high-rate offender.

Age, Race, and Gender

Although the age at which juveniles can be found criminally responsible varies from state to state, age is one of the most consistent predictors of crime—that is, criminality is young and male. Clarifying the exact function of the age variable, however, has been made somewhat difficult by the different ways age is defined and data on it are categorized and collected. For instance, the federal government defines a juvenile as a person under the age of 18. Sixteen states have legislated the minimum age of criminal responsibility. North Carolina has the youngest age, which is 6 years. For three other states, the minimum age is 7 years, in Arizona it is 8, and 11 other states, including Texas, have set the youngest age at 10 years.[3] This made the headlines recently when Houston prosecutors tried a youth who was only 10 years old when he shot his father during his parents' contentious and often violent divorce. Lohstroh, who was being given Prozac at the time, gained access to his mother's gun and pulled it from his backpack after entering his father's vehicle for a planned custody visit. The jury found the boy guilty of juvenile misconduct, an offense that could result in 40 years of incarceration with the first 10 years in juvenile facilities.

The upper age limit used in courts also differs among the states. For three states, a juvenile becomes an adult (for court purposes) at 15 years, for 10 states it is 16 years, and for the remaining states, and the District of Columbia, it is 17 years.[4] In addition, exceptions may exist to the upper age. Juvenile court jurisdictions can be extended for disposition (that is, sentencing in an adult court) reasons. For 33 states, this could extend through the age of 20 years or as old as 24 years, such as in California, Montana, Oregon, and Wisconsin. Juveniles can be transferred by statute to the adult criminal justice jurisdiction by certification, which is legislatively determined based on the level of crime committed by a juvenile.

The following sections will present the demographics of juveniles, juvenile delinquency, juvenile offenders, and juvenile victims. This analysis can be problematic because the various major database sources are not consistent in the way they define age. Because no uniform age range exists for juveniles, there are limitations on describing individuals in this status. Additionally, one of our major information sources, the NCVS, does not record any information on victims younger than 12 years of age. Therefore, in the discussions that follow, specific ages or age ranges will be identified when possible.

JUVENILE POPULATION DEMOGRAPHICS

In the United States in 2004, there were an estimated 73 million juveniles age 17 and under. Of these, 60 percent were white non-Hispanic, 16 percent were blacks, and 19 percent were Hispanics. Of the youth under 18 years of age, 17 percent lived in poverty. Of these, 10 percent were whites, 33 percent were blacks, and 29 percent were Hispanics.[5] Furthermore, 68 percent lived in two-parent family households and approximately three-quarters of these were whites and 35 percent blacks.[6] Of those who lived in one-parent households, 3 million had males as head of household. In addition, more than 95 percent of juveniles of school age were enrolled in public or private schools.[7]

Juvenile Delinquency

The early American criminal justice system was greatly influenced by Cesare Beccaria's (1764) treatise on crime and punishment and many of his principles of punishment were adopted in the Declaration of Independence and the U.S. Constitution. Along with disenchantment with the earlier, more theological, view of crime, many people began to focus on the causes of crime. With these efforts came a growing awareness of the significance of a criminal's childhood background.

The early focus was more on strengthening social stability and social controls to address the more problematic issues of childhood. Endeavors were initiated to "correct" criminal behaviors and to prevent future ones. This meant that the focal point became providing better environments for children. To accomplish this, houses of refuge and orphan asylums began to appear to protect and to provide for children. According to Empey, "Either the house of refuge or the orphan's asylum was to become an instrument of the new social order whose purpose it was to produce the ideal child."[8]

During the nineteenth century, efforts were made to strengthen children and to better prepare them for adulthood. These changes included school attendance laws and labor laws, which addressed the minimum ages for, and time limits on, work days for children over 12 years of age. Eventually, the struggle to improve living conditions and provide a better future for the nation's children, and a separate justice system, were established.[9]

With the enactment of the Illinois Juvenile Court Act (1899), a law was passed that officially defined the ages of children and adults. Those under 16 years of age were separated from adulthood and were identified as children. Not only did this act serve to define the concept of childhood, but Empey argued that it also served to invent the concept of delinquency. Others have also argued the definition of delinquency itself depended on a definition of childhood,[10] which was partially an attempt to extend the ages of childhood.[11]

Additionally, during the last few decades of the nineteenth century, there was an increase in the scientific study of the teen years. This effort to study teens culminated during the enactment of the Juvenile Court Act and with the publication of the work on adolescence by G. Stanley Hall.[12] These changes promoted the concept of children, adolescents, and juveniles as "fundamentally different from adults."[13]

Since the turn of the twentieth century, the constructs of childhood, adolescence, and juveniles continued to be influenced by an increased awareness of the developmental stage of adolescence. With a separate stage established, many developmental psychology scholars saw a critical need to establish the developmental differences of adolescence from childhood and adulthood.[14] As a result, separating adolescents from adulthood became the focus of much social posturing. Preoccupation with controlling children who were perceived to be a threat to the social order, by virtue of their physical size and lack of maturity, resulted in the expansion of the defined length of childhood and the consequent economic dependency of teenagers, which created even greater demands for formal social control.[15]

Hanawalt argued this was an attempt at control in which adults "manipulated access to the economic advantages of the adult world."[16] She further suggested that, in earlier times, apprenticeships were used to control this access. A major disruption of this control mechanism occurred during the Industrial Revolution when wages available for child labor provided a means for young people to achieve freedom. Eventually, by the turn of the nineteenth century, an adolescent working class existed alongside the adult working class.

Therefore, Hanawalt argued that control and freedom of children has revolved around an economic motivation. Control was required to continue the child's or later adolescent's role of physically or economically supporting the family. In addition, control was needed as society became more industrialized to control job and wage competition between adolescents and adults.

English law had declared that children less than 7 years old were incapable of a serious crime, therefore, there was no category for child offenders. Children from 7 to 14 years of age were treated the same as those under 7 years of age, unless it could be established that the child was aware of the wrongfulness or sinfulness of the act they committed. If this was established, their punishment could be as extreme as for an adult, including capital punishment. For those over 14 years of age, the English courts deemed them adults and, as such, they were treated accordingly.[17]

As it is today, in the past, there were behaviors and actions exclusive to children that were considered crimes. Some of these crimes could even be capital offenses, such as "rebelliousness against parents."[18] Other child crimes could receive corporal punishments. With the Juvenile Court Act, the framework had been more formally stated and structured, with the goal of juvenile rehabilitation.

Various descriptions and discussions have attempted to defend these judicial limits placed on juveniles. The very foundation of the juvenile justice system was based on the philosophy of aiding the juvenile to change his or her behavior and to make a positive entrance into adulthood. Through this separate and special handling, reformers hoped to avoid the stigmatizing of a juvenile who had entered the system. For these reasons, the informality and confidentiality of the juvenile justice process was established.

The basis of this separate system was the belief that juveniles lacked the development and cognitive ability to understand the consequences of various actions and activities and, therefore, deserved different handling by the court. Since the court's creation, this belief has been both supported and challenged. Studies have suggested that adolescents over 14 years old of an average intelligence have shown little difference than adults of average intelligence. Paradoxically, adolescents with lower-than-average intelligence were not similar to adults with lower-than-average intelligence.[19] Other issues that separated adolescents from adults were risk interpretations and impulse control. Oftentimes, these issues may go together. The impulse drive did not allow an adolescent to adequately measure the risk potential of an action, either as the result of improper evaluation or impulsivity.[20]

In addition, it has been that suggested delinquent behavior was a normal function of adolescent development.[21] The majority of the time, an adolescent appeared to "age out" of these behaviors.[22] Indeed, Riemer argued that certain behaviors would be hedonistic and spontaneous, suggesting "all persons are deviant at least some of the time."[23] Scott suggested these decisions to "act out" by adolescents may be developmental evidence of "cognitive and psychosocial immaturity."[24] Margaret Mead and G. Stanley Hall have described adolescence as a phase of "storm and stress."[25]

Adolescents gather into rather homogeneous groups, with the majority of friends tending to be of similar social status, ethnicity, and race.[26] Likewise, families are more harmonious than not. Also, as adolescents matured into adulthood, they would adopt the majority of values and beliefs of their parents.

Complicating the discussion of delinquency of juveniles are the status offenses, those offenses if committed by an adult would not be viewed as criminal. In the past, when a juvenile was adjudicated as a delinquent, he or she could have been guilty of a serious act, such as homicide, or could have been guilty of something as minor as truancy. In this discussion, the focus will be on those acts that would be criminal whether committed by a juvenile or an adult.

Beginning in the 1970s, the rates of juveniles committing more delinquent acts began to increase, and became more violent. This led some researchers to predict the coming of the superpredator. At about the same time this pronouncement was being made in the 1990s, the rates began to decrease—until in the early 2000s the rate was approximately the level it was in the 1970s. Unfortunately, in reaction to these pronouncements about juvenile crime, legislatures responded with a more "get tough" philosophy. This philosophy led to lowering the upper age range for adjudicating youth, certifying and transferring to the adult criminal system, and exclusionary laws. Even for those who remained within the juvenile system, there were changes in sentencing. These changes included blended sentences, mandatory minimums, and extended sentences.

Fritsch, Caeti, and Hemmens have argued, "the primary purpose of judicial waiver is to impose more severe sanctions than are permitted in juvenile court."[27] This statement suggested more severe sanctions became available in the adult system. As a result, research indicated more violent juveniles were transferred more often to the adult system. Yet, there was other research questioning the reality of this occurrence.

Poulos and Orchowsky suggested that certain factors would increase the possibility of transfer out of the juvenile system. Those factors included current offense, prior record, education, age, and previous treatment, especially mental health. If a juvenile was certified to be tried as an adult, many states adopted a "once an adult, always an adult" position. A few states did provide methods of being returned to the juvenile system, although this was left to the juvenile to pursue.[28]

Reports on Offending

Approximately 80 percent of all nonfatal violent crimes to juveniles reportedly have been committed by juvenile offenders.[29] Many of the violent types of crimes committed by juveniles have been mainly stable since 1980. Yet, today's homicide rates remains higher than in 1980.[30] The majority of violent crimes committed by juveniles were by males between 15 and 17 years old (we also know that the most common time is around 3 P.M.).[31]

In 2004, 1,578,893 arrests were reported by the FBI for crimes committed by juveniles under 18 years of age, ranging from running away and curfew violations to murder.[32] This figure can be misleading for this range of ages. The majority of those arrested were 15- to 17-year-old juveniles (1,075,514 arrests), which was more than twice as many as those arrested under 15 years of age (503,379).[33]

Under 18-year-old juveniles accounted for more than 18.5 percent of the total arrests made in 2004. Of these arrests, more than 69 percent were committed by males. Furthermore, almost 70 percent of those under 18 years of age were white males.[34]

Snyder and Sickmund reported the ranges in times of crime committed as well as whether the crimes occurred at school or nonschool locations. Sexual assaults and aggravated assaults most frequently occur at school at about 3 P.M. Shoplifting most often occurs at 5 P.M. and robbery at 9 P.M. Drug crimes appear to peak at noon at school and at 11 P.M. at nonschool location. More than 7 percent of 12- to 17-year-old juvenile offenders were reported selling drugs. Less than one-fourth used alcohol, which was divided nearly equally between male and females juveniles. More than 9 percent used marijuana and more than 7 percent used alcohol and marijuana.[35]

Snyder and Sickmund also counted nearly 8,500 homicides of juvenile victims committed by juvenile offenders. In 2002, there were more than 960 juvenile male homicide offenders compared with less than a hundred female offenders. More than 490 were white juvenile offenders and more than 530 were black juvenile offenders. Less than 370 of the 1,068 homicides involved a firearm. Approximately 50 percent of the homicides were committed by acquaintances and less than 14 percent were committed by a relative.[36]

Both national and international studies on delinquency note that the true picture of delinquent offending is distorted by the fact that most juvenile crimes are committed in groups, that is, that crime is a product of co-offending. This means that you cannot assume from the crime reports that one crime is equal to one offender. If more than one youth is arrested for a single offense, than the arrest information will distort the crime picture. For criminologists, this is not a surprising phenomenon as most theories stress the way the delinquent behavior is learned and valued in social groups. Peer pressure and status influence the likelihood that certain negative behaviors will be reinforced and rewarded. Data indicate that approximately 82 percent of juveniles committed their offense as members of a group and 44 percent of murders had more than one perpetrator. Nonwhites are more likely to offend in groups as are offenders under the age of 14. For 16- to 17-year-olds, violent crimes are twice as likely to take place in a co-offense. As age increases, single actors are more likely to commit crimes, particularly property offenses. We also know that those who are younger at the time of their first arrest have higher recidivism rates and those with long criminal histories eventually move from group to solo offending.[37]

In summary, the most frequently reported juvenile arrest is of a white male between 15 and 17 years old. He most likely would be arrested for a property crime or larceny theft. Of the property crime arrests, less than 55 percent would be petitioned to a juvenile court and just over two-thirds would be adjudicated delinquent. The majority of those adjudicated would be 16-year-old white males.[38]

Looking beyond Race and Delinquency

Research over time has indicated that a number of other factors may be much better predictors of delinquency than the controversial notion of race. Many people have argued that any true effect or influence of race would be hard to detect because race and economic status are so hard to separate in analysis. In a more recent series of studies in which multiple measures of socioeconomic status are used, strong correlations exist between lower socioeconomic status (SES) and delinquency. These studies also showed that poor parental supervision, low parental reinforcement, and males with low levels of family activity were all related to increased levels of delinquency.[39]

Another example of how our efforts to improve statistical analysis have resulted in different findings about the causes of delinquency is found in the impact of religion on youth. In the past, findings were mixed on the effect of religion and delinquency, particularly in situations in which religion was measured by church attendance or identification with a particular religious affiliation. More recent studies that have assigned the variable religion to particular values and spiritual ethics have found more of a negative relationship between religiosity and delinquency. In particular when both mothers and children have strong religious beliefs, youths may be more insulated against delinquency.

Juvenile Victims

For every crime, at least one person was a victim, excluding the somewhat special category of victimless crimes—prostitution, gambling, and illicit drug use. It has only been within the last 40 years or so the focus has been placed on victims. In the previous centuries, victims had received a diminishing concern by society, as the majority of concern and study had been on crimes and offenders. As rules and laws were formulated, the responsibility still remained with the victim to seek restitution. This period was often considered the age of a victim justice system. Near the end of the Middle Ages victims began to recede into the background as crimes were seen as being committed against the rulers, such as the feudal barons.

In the American Colonies and post-American Revolution, the victim in the United States became the state, as a crime was seen to be a challenge to social order. Therefore, it became the responsibility of public prosecutors who represented the government to begin the determination of whether to process a crime and, if so, how. The primary victim was responsible for filing charges and possibly to provide evidence through his or her testimony, but ultimately the state was the victim.

The 1950s and 1960s were the beginning of the civil rights movement, which began other movements, culminating in the victims' rights movement. With this movement, the role of the victim began to change in the criminal justice system, as well as his or her treatment. This was especially true of studying victimization and victims.

The study of victims began in the 1940s with the work of Hans von Hentig, a criminologist who had studied how criminals became criminals. He then applied the process to how victims became victims. Then, Benjamin Mendelsohn, an attorney, followed with his typology of classifying victims on the level of responsibility for a crime. With each decade, there appeared another typology or theory. In the twenty-first century, opportunity, lifestyle, and routine activities theories are in vogue.

The primary source of victim data in the United States is the NCVS. This annual survey of more than 40,000 households represents more than 90,000 individuals who are 12 years old or older. The survey was first conducted in 1973 as the National Crime Survey and was redesigned and renamed in 1992.

The data produced by this survey from 1992 to 2003, indicate that the frequency of violent crimes and theft at school shows a decreasing trend since 1993, with an occasional elevation in frequency. For nonschool locations, this has been true since 1992 for violent crime and since 1993 for theft.[40] During the decade beginning in 1993, nonfatal violence occurred approximately two and a half times more often to juveniles (12 to 17 years old) than to adults.[41] This age group was responsible for about three-quarters of juvenile victimizations reported to the police. More than half of the 12- to 14-year-old victims were more likely be a victim of an acquaintance, who was a nonrelative, and more likely to be a victim of nonviolence than the 15- to 17-year-old victims. The 12- to 17-year-old victims were also more likely to be a victim of violence than were adults.[42]

Finkelhor and Hashima developed a typology of juvenile victims, and in this typology, the first category was *pandemic victimization*. These types of victimization were the most common victim experiences and were potentially experienced at some point during a juvenile's life. The second category is *acute victimization*, which is experienced by fewer juveniles. These types were potentially more violent and destructive. The final category was *extraordinary victimization*. These were the more rare forms of victimizations, were more violent, and are experienced by few juveniles.[43]

Two characteristics of juvenile victims and victimizations were closely related to one another. These were locations and times of day. According to routine activities theory,[44] three elements must converge for a crime to take place. Those are a motivated offender, an attractive target, and the absence of guardian. For juveniles, offenders, and victims alike, school was the most common location and activity. It would be assumed that with teachers and other adults present there would be adequate guardianship. Upon review of NCVS data, however, schools and school grounds were the most frequent location for juvenile victimizations.

Theft was more common for juveniles than violence and generally occurred more frequently at school than at nonschool locations. This held true for both genders. In addition, the majority of juvenile victimization occurred at 3:00 P.M., which is the time most schools end their days.[45]

The peak time for aggravated assaults and sexual assaults was 3:00 P.M. For nonschool locations, the most frequent time aggravated assault occurred was 8:00 P.M. The most frequent offender was an acquaintance, who was not a relative. For sexual assaults by an acquaintance, the times were noon followed by 3:00 P.M. When the offender was a family member, the most common time for 12- to 14-year-old juveniles was 4:00 P.M. and for older juveniles it was 9:00 P.M. When aggravated assault was perpetrated by a family member, the crime most often occurred at 9:00 P.M.[46]

Three locations other than school identified were residences, outdoors, and commercial locations. In time order, outdoors incidents occurred most frequently at 3:00 P.M. For residences, the time was 4:00 P.M., and for commercial locations the time was 9:00 P.M.[47]

Racially, all juvenile races are victimized, but black and white juveniles have the higher frequencies of victimization. More than 13 percent of juvenile sexual assaults were black juveniles, which was more than twice as many as white juveniles. In addition, black juvenile victims experienced more physical assaults or witnessed violence more than white victims. The rates of violent victimizations were closer to the same rates. For younger juvenile victims of violence, white juveniles had a higher rate than black juveniles, but older juvenile blacks had a slightly higher rate than white juveniles.[48]

Socioeconomic status is also related to juvenile victimization. The majority of victimizations occurred more frequently in poor urban areas.[49] In addition, numerous categories of victimization were more frequent for victims who lived in a household of less than $20,000.[50] For younger juveniles, this was at a lower rate than the older juveniles. Suburban communities had the second highest rate, followed by rural areas.[51] One significant category of victimization of juveniles from households of more than $50,000 was bullying.[52]

Finally, juvenile victims of homicide were more than five times more likely to be 15 to 17 years of age than 12 to 14 years old. Slightly more victims were white than black and they were almost twice as often male rather than female. These homicides were least likely to be committed using a firearm. Additionally, these demographics were descriptive of victims and offenders of serious violent victimizations.[53]

According to Finkelhor and Ormrod, of all crimes reported to the police, more than 11 percent were juvenile victims and these accounted for more than 70 percent of all sexual crimes.[54] More than one-fourth of the violent crimes perpetrated on juvenile victims were reported to police, which was less than half of those of an adult victim. Of the in-school crimes, more than one-third were reported to a school official instead of the police.[55] When the offender was a juvenile, the victimization of a juvenile was often reported less frequently.[56]

Bullying was a major victimization experienced in schools and was more common for boys.[57] According to Haynie and colleagues in a World Health Organization Survey, almost 17 percent of juveniles reported having been bullied three or more times in a year. Also, approximately three-quarters of teenagers have been bullied once during their school years,[58] although more frequently for younger school age children.[59]

CONCLUSION

Much like the type of friends selected by a juvenile, a similarity exists between the juvenile victims selected by the juvenile offenders. The most frequent relationship between the juvenile offender and the juvenile victim was an acquaintanceship, which possibly could be an aspect of routine activities theory that is not often addressed. This would involve the approachability of an offender to a victim. An explanation of this dynamic would be that the victims and their offenders were members of a similar class or status, such as classmates.

The most frequent delinquent event was property crime and was committed most frequently by a black male, 15 to 17 years old, who lived in an urban area. He would commit this crime most frequently between 3:00 P.M. and 4:00 P.M., most likely on school grounds and without a firearm. The victim of this event was comparable. He, too, was a black 15- to 17-year-old male living in an urban area in a household with an income most likely less than $20,000.

Even with what is known about juveniles, questions persist as to who they are and what their roles are in society. Still, according to Mohr, Gelles, and Schwartz, they "continue to occupy a position in a no-man's-land between chattel and constitutionally protected citizen."[60] Despite the fact that they are citizens of the United States, they are denied the full rights granted a citizen under the Fourteenth Amendment of the U.S. Constitution.

In many ways, they continue to function under property rights laws of the past. They do not have the right to choose or decide for themselves in many life situations. In other life situations, it appears that explanations for certain actions are ignored. On the one hand, society puts forth juveniles who are not yet able to understand the full ramifications of their decisions. On the other hand, if one of these juveniles commits a serious enough crime, society flips its position and declares they should be treated as an adult.[61]

Society accepts that a juvenile can choose to join the military and die for his or her country, but does not let them purchase alcohol. In the juvenile justice system, for decades juveniles were denied adequate counsel, under the belief the court had the welfare of the juvenile as its focus. When this began to change, courts attempted to persuade juveniles to waive counsel.

As a result of Supreme Court rulings over the years, the differences between the juvenile justice system and the adult system have been reduced. In addition, the requirements to certify a juvenile as an adult for more serious crimes have been reduced. One of the earliest attempts to facilitate this and modify the juvenile systems jurisdiction was in 1935 in Illinois (that any juvenile over the age of 10 would be tried in the adult system for all felonies).[62] As a result of the changes and challenges, and because the juvenile system is losing its uniqueness, some have suggested the dissolution of the two justice systems.

It could be argued that this faction of the population is discriminated against in many ways on the basis of age. As a result of age, juveniles can suffer curfews, be denied voting for those who make laws that affect them and juries of their peers, and be subject to mandatory school attendance.

When born in this country, children's nationality is established, yet they are a special class of citizens, that is, one who may enjoy fewer rights than noncitizens in this country. Juveniles do not enjoy the same rights or privileges of those over a certain age. And the laws governing juveniles lack consistency, both in determining who is a juvenile and what society's expectations are for juveniles. If they are a protected citizenry, who are they being protected from, and why is there a need?

NOTES

1. Snyder & Sickmund, 1999.
2. Wolfgang, Figlio, & Sellin, 1972.
3. Office of Juvenile Justice and Delinquency Prevention, hereafter OJJDP, 1999.
4. OJJPD, 1999.
5. Federal Interagency Forum on Child and Family Statistics, 2006, pp. 5–6.
6. Snyder & Sickmund, 2006.
7. U.S. Census Bureau, 2004.
8. Empey, 1978, p. 82.
9. Platt, 1977.
10. Harris, Welsh, & Butler, 2000.
11. Repucci, 1999.
12. Demos & Demos, 1969; Furstenberg, 2000; Steinberg & Lerner, 2004.
13. Geraghty & Drizin, 1997, p. 2.
14. Harris et al., 2000; Reppucci, 1999.
15. Harris et al., 2000, p. 368.
16. Hanawalt, 1992, p. 10.
17. Empey, 1978; Reppucci, 1999.
18. Empey, 1978, p. 75.
19. Reppucci, 1999.
20. Reppucci, 1999.
21. Dornbusch, 1989; Reppucci, 1999; Scott & Grisso, 1997.
22. Scott & Grisso, 1997.
23. Riemer, 1981, p. 42.
24. Scott & Grisso, 1997, p. 139.
25. Demos & Demos, 1969; Dornbusch, 1989; Repucci, 1999.
26. Dornbusch, 1989.

27. Fritsch, Caeti, & Hemmens, 1996, p. 595.
28. Poulos & Orchowsky, 1994.
29. Baum, 2005.
30. Grinberg, Dawkins, Dawkins, & Fullilove, 2005.
31. Grinberg et al., 2005; Lerner & Galambos, 1998.
32. Federal Bureau of Investigation, hereafter FBI, 2006, p. 296.
33. FBI, 2006, p. 296.
34. FBI, 2006.
35. Snyder & Sickmund, 2006.
36. Snyder & Sickmund, 2006.
37. Conway & McCord, 2005.
38. Pastore & Maguire, 2003.
39. Farrington, Loeber, Yin, & Anderson, 2002.
40. Snyder & Sickman, 2006.
41. Baum, 2005.
42. Baum, 2005.
43. Finkelhor & Hashima, 2001, p. 58.
44. Cohen & Felson, 1979.
45. Snyder & Sickmund, 2006.
46. Snyder & Sickmund, 2006.
47. Snyder & Sickmund, 2006.
48. Kilpatrick, Saunders, & Smith, 2003.
49. Baum, 2005.
50. Finkelhor, Ormrod, Turner, & Hamby, 2005.
51. Baum, 2005.
52. Finkelhor et al., 2005.
53. Snyder & Sickmund, 2006.
54. Finkelhor & Ormrod, 2000.
55. Finkelhor & Ormrod, 2001.
56. Finkelhor et al., 2005.
57. Finkelhor et al., 2005.
58. Haynie et al., 2001.
59. Finkelhor et al., 2005.
60. Mohr, Gelles, & Schwartz, 1999, p. 37.
61. Mohr et al., 1999.
62. Alper, 1941.

REFERENCES

Alper, B. S. (1941). Forty years of the juvenile court. *American Sociological Review,* 6(2), 230–240.

Baum, K. (2005). Juvenile victimization and offending, 1993–2003. *Bureau of Justice Statistics Special Report.* Washington, D.C.: U.S. Department of Justice.

Beccaria, C. (1996). *Of crimes and punishments* (J. Grigson, Trans.). New York: Marsilio Publisher. (Original work published 1764).

Cohen, L. E., & Felson, M. (1979). Social change and crime rate trends: A routine activity approach. *American Sociological Review,* 44, 588–608.

Conway, K. P., & McCord, J. (2005). Co-offending and patterns of juvenile crime. Washington, D.C.: National Institute of Justice, Research in Brief.

Demos, J., & Demos, V. (1969). Adolescence in historical perspective. *Journal of Marriage and the Family,* 31(4), 632–638.

Dornbusch, S. M. (1989). The sociology of adolescence. *Annual Reviews of Sociology, 15*, 233–259.

Empey, L T. (1978). *American delinquency: Its meaning and construction.* Homewood, IL: The Dorsey Press.

Farrington, D. P., Loeber, R., Yin, Y., & Anderson, S. (2002). Are within-individual causes of delinquency the same as between-individual causes? *Criminal Behavior and Mental Health, 12*, 53–68.

Federal Bureau of Investigation. (2006). *Crime in the United States: Persons arrested* (Uniform Crime Report). Washington, D.C.: U.S. Government Printing Office.

Federal Interagency Forum on Child and Family Statistics. (2006). *America's Children: Key National Indicators of Well-Being 2006.* Retrieved August 1, 2006, from www.Childstats.gov.

Finkelhor, D., & Hashima, P. (2001). The victimization of children and youth: A comprehensive overview. Chpt. 4, 49–78. In S. O. White (Ed.), *Law and Social Science Perspectives on Youth and Justice.* New York: Plenum Publishing.

Finkelhor, D., & Ormrod, R. K. (2000, June). Characteristics of crimes against juveniles. *Juvenile Justice Bulletin.* Washington, D.C.: Office of Juvenile Justice and Delinquency Prevention.

Finkelhor, D., & Ormrod, R. K. (2001). Factors in the underreporting of crimes against juveniles. *Child Maltreatment, 6*(3), 219–229.

Finkelhor, D., Ormrod, R., Turner, H., & Hamby, S L. (2005). The victimization of children and youth: A comprehensive, national survey. *Child Maltreatment, 10*(1), 5–25.

Fritsch, E. J., Caeti, T. J., & Hemmens, C. (1996). Spare the needle but not the punishment: The incarceration of waived youth in Texas prisons. *Crime and Delinquency, 42*(4), 593–609.

Furstenberg, F. F. (2000). The sociology of adolescence and youth in the 1990s: A critical commentary. *Journal of Marriage and the Family, 62*(4), 896–910.

Geraghty, T. F., & Drizin, S. A. (1997). Symposium on the future of the juvenile court: Forward—the debate over the future of juvenile courts: Can we reach consensus? *The Journal of Criminal Law & Criminology, 88*(1), 1–13.

Grinberg, I., Dawkins, M., Dawkins, M P., & Fullilove, C. (2005, Fall). Adolescents at risk for violence: An initial validation of the life challenges questionnaire and risk assessment index. *Adolescence, 40*, 573–599.

Hanawalt, B. A. (1992). Historical descriptions and prescriptions for adolescence. *Journal of Family History, 17*(4), 341–352.

Harris, P. W., Welsh, W. N., & Butler, F. (2000). A century of juvenile justice. In G. LaFree (Ed.), *Criminal Justice 2000, Volume 1: The nature of crime: Continuity and change* (pp. 359–425). Washington, D.C.: National Institute of Justice.

Haynie, D. L., Nansel, T., Eitel, P., Crump, A. D., Saylor, K., & Yu, K. (2001). Bullies, victims, and bully/victims: Distinct groups of at-risk youth. *Journal of Early Adolescence, 21*(1), 29–49.

Kilpatrick, D. G., Saunders, B. E., & Smith, D. W. (2003). *Youth victimization: Prevalence and implications.* Washington, D.C.: National Institute of Justice. (NCJ 194972)

Lerner, R. M., & Galambos, N. L. (1998). Adolescent development: Challenges and opportunities for research, programs, and policies. *Annual Review of Psychology, 49*, 413–446.

Mohr, W., Gelles, R. J., & Schwartz, I. M. (1999). Shackled in the land of liberty: No rights for children. *The Annals of the American Academy of Political and Social Science, 564,* 37–55.

Office of Juvenile Justice and Delinquency Prevention. (1999). Juvenile justice: A century of change. *1999 National Report Series: Juvenile Justice Bulletin.* Washington, D.C.: Office of Juvenile Justice and Delinquency Prevention.

Pastore, A. L., & Maguire, K. (Eds.). (2003). *Sourcebook of criminal justice statistics.* Retrieved August 6, 2006, from www.albany.edu/sourcebook.

Platt, A. M. (1977). *The child savers: The invention of delinquency* (2nd ed.). Chicago, IL: The University of Chicago Press.

Poulos, T. M., & Orchowsky, S. (1994). Serious juvenile offenders: Predicting the probability of transfer to criminal court. *Crime and Delinquency, 40,* 3–17.

Repucci, N. D. (1999). Adolescent development and juvenile justice. *American Journal of Community Psychology, 27,* 307–321.

Riemer, J. W. (1981). Deviance as fun. *Adolescence, 16,* 39–43.

Scott, E. S., & Grisso, T. (1997). The evolution of adolescence: A developmental perspective on juvenile justice reform. *Journal of Criminal Law & Criminology, 88,* 137–189.

Snyder, H. N., & Sickmund, M. (1999). *Juvenile offenders and victims: 1999 national report.* Washington, D.C.: Office of Juvenile Justice and Delinquency Prevention.

Snyder, H. N., & Sickmund, M. (2006). *Juvenile offenders and victims: 2006 national report.* Washington, D.C.: Office of Juvenile Justice and Delinquency Prevention.

Steinberg, L., & Lerner, R. M. (2004). The scientific study of adolescence: A brief history. *Journal of Early Adolescence, 24,* 45–54.

U.S. Census Bureau. (2004). *SO902: Teenager's characteristics.* 2004 American Community Survey. Retrieved August 4, 2006, from http://factfinder.census.gov/servlet.

U.S. Department of Justice, Bureau of Justice Statistics. (n.d.). *National Crime Victimization Survey, 1992–2004* (Computer file). Conducted by U.S. Dept. of Commerce, Bureau of the Census. ICPSR04276-v3. Ann Arbor, MI: Inter-university Consortium for Political and Social Research [producer and distributor], 2006-06-08.

Wolfgang, M. E., R. M. Figlio and T. Sellin (1972). *Delinquency in a birth cohort.* Chicago: University of Chicago Press.

CHAPTER 3

Home Is Where the Hurt Is: Child Abuse and Delinquency

Robert L. Bing III

Parents ... always remember that you represent the window by which your kids view the world.

—Ray Wright, former Dallas Cowboy

The relationship between child abuse and delinquency has been the subject of debate throughout the years. It is generally assumed, for instance, that exposure to abuse as a child will predispose an individual to acts of aggression and delinquency. The importance of the problem is evidenced through allegations that serial killers, rapists, substance abusers, and juvenile superpredators have histories of mistreatment. These are best viewed as direct effects of abuse. Other, more indirect effects may result in children running away from home or being pushed out of the home and ultimately engaging in survival crimes like petty theft and prostitution, as well as drug and alcohol abuse, which may result in greater health and safety risks.

What follows is a look at issues and case studies exploring the relationship between child abuse and delinquency, beginning with an examination of themes and trends in the empirical literature. It is hoped that this chapter will enhance one's knowledge about the complex relationship between child abuse and delinquency. At the end of this chapter, recommendations to problems identified in the research are offered.

A LOOK AT ISSUES IN THE LITERATURE

The literature on child abuse can be divided into two categories: first-generation and second-generation research. The first-generation studies tend to be retrospective in nature with weak research designs. The second-generation studies have more rigorous research designs. We begin with findings and issues that emerge in the first-generation literature.

First-Generation Research

In this research, there are many different findings: Some researchers found physically abused children more aggressive.[1] Several other studies examining juvenile court and medical records reveal that a sizeable number of delinquents have been abused.[2] Similarly, two studies relying on self-reports found that juveniles in trouble with the law had been abused, in percentages ranging from 51 to 69 percent.[3] In a systematic review of existing studies on delinquency, Loeber and Dishion found parental family management techniques such as the inconsistent use of discipline to be strongly predictive of delinquency.[4] In all, a number of these first-generation studies point toward strong relationships between delinquency and child maltreatment.

Second-Generation Research

In the 1990s, many of the newer studies had more rigorous research designs. In this category of new research, many findings and observations parallel the earlier research. For example, Zingraff and others in a comparison study suggest that the overall rate of arrest was highest among maltreated children and next highest among low income groups.[5] Second, Smith and Thornberry report that a history of maltreatment significantly affects the prevalence and frequency of police arrests.[6] Similarly, Widom and Ames found that child neglect was a strong predictor of delinquency.[7] In addition, Ireland and others found that abused kids have higher rates of offending than nonabused youth.[8] Interestingly, this relationship holds for both official and self-report measures. These few examples point toward a complex yet undeniable relationship between abuse and delinquency.

What follows are a series of discussions based on major themes that appear in the literature, ranging from sex abuse, social status, and family conflict.

WHAT IS THE ROLE OF SEX ABUSE IN DELINQUENCY?

Much research confirms the devastating impact of child sexual abuse. Indeed, research reveals that children who have been sexually abused are at higher risk for delinquency, adolescent aggression, and suicidal thoughts. It should be recognized that sexual abuse varies in practice and content. For example, it can occur in the form of rewarding a child for sexual behavior that is inappropriate for his or her age. Sexual abuse can also include an unwarranted touch or forcible penetration. It is estimated that 1 in 10 boys and 1 in 3 girls have been the victim of some form of sexual exploitation. The impact of sexual abuse can be profound, affecting the mind, personality, and emotional development of the child. Sexual abuse may damage the emotional development of the individual, resulting in a child with little appreciation for what constitutes *normal* sexual behaviors.

One of the difficulties in prosecuting cases of child sexual abuse is the difficulty that jurors may have in understanding child sex abuse accommodation syndrome. The psychological symptoms of victims of repeated abuse by those they trust can result in a form of pathological bonding with the offender that may delay disclosure and reporting. Often, it is difficult to understand the complex emotions faced by victims who are violated by those they trust. The feelings of powerlessness, helplessness, and entrapment can lead to not only accommodation but also to false testimony, retractions, and defense of their abusers.

Child sexual abuse can cause many different behaviors. Long-term effects include confused boundaries, dissociative states, self-injury, memory repression, and even multiple personalities. Some victims or survivors (in adult life) find themselves sexualizing their own children. Other studies have found a strong relationship between sexual abuse and adolescent prostitution. Siegel and Williams found that juvenile offenders with past histories of sexual abuse fall into two arrest categories: (1) arrests for violent crimes and (2) arrests for running away.[9] Individuals who run away are at a greater risk of involvement in more serious behavior, such as drug use, prostitution, or exploitation by people they meet on the street.[10]

Last, but not least, Swanston and others provide compelling research to illustrate the fact that there is a cogent relationship between delinquency and a history of child sexual abuse. They state, "A history of child sexual abuse is clearly associated with self reported criminal behavior ... and should be seen as an independent risk factor for criminal offending."[11]

The following list captures the realities for women as *victims* and as *survivors* of sexual abuse.[12]

- Sexual abuse is related to mental health problems, school problems, and risky sexual behaviors.
- Young girls who experience sexual abuse may *perceive* greater barriers to counseling and service.
- The juvenile justice system is not well designed to respond to the myriad problems associated with sexual abuse.
- Women affected by sexual abuse must be seen as both *victims* and *survivors.*
- Focusing on sexually abused women as victims only perpetuates paternalistic attitudes.
- New intervention efforts should seek greater input from women who have been abused.
- Interventions should focus not only on the individual, but also on the entire family, community, and institutional level.

WHAT IS IT ABOUT SERIAL KILLERS?

Do many of the notorious serial killers, like Ted Bundy and John Wayne Gacy, have histories of child abuse? Ted Bundy was born out of wedlock, and law enforcement officials believe that he is responsible for more than 25 murders. He was eventually convicted of three murders and later executed in the state of Florida. According to Egger, many believe that "learning the circumstances of his 'out of wedlock birth' had a decided impact upon his behavior."[13] John Gacy, who was convicted of killing 33 young men and boys, had a father who drank excessively. It is said that the father would call him a "sissy and mamma's boy."[14]

Hickey conducted an analysis of female serial killers and found that many of these killers were from economically deprived backgrounds and had been severely abused as children.[15] The serial killer literature consistently includes some type of child mistreatment. In citing past research,[16] Egger identifies additional risk factors related to the childhood histories of serial killers. These include brutal or almost violent punishment, lack of love and genuine affection within the family structure, and a home known for physical abuse and neglect.

A Closer Look

The most common correlate among children who go on to murder is parental abuse.[17] These children who go on to commit homicide have learned their behaviors through the years of victimization suffered as a child. Said another way, abusive parents become powerful and negative role models for their children. Following are limited case studies of juveniles who are in prison for committing homicides:

- *Case 1:* John was sentenced to die for robbing and shooting a store clerk as she begged for life. Abandoned by his dad at the age of three, he was raised by a mother—a drug addict—who beat him often.
- *Case 2:* Sarah, with the help of a female friend, killed an elderly lady with a butcher knife. Court records reveal that Sarah had been sexually abused by her father and uncle. Her accomplice had been beaten and raped throughout her childhood.
- *Case 3:* Jerry and his sister Pam shot and killed their father. In this instance, court records reveal a history of sexual abuse of Pam and physical abuse by the father of both son and daughter.

It can be easily argued that those who have been abused or those who witness abuse are at increased risk for lashing out and retaliating later in life. Next, we examine the relationship between child maltreatment and drug use.

WHAT IS THE RELATIONSHIP AMONG SUBSTANCE ABUSE, CHILD ABUSE, AND DELINQUENCY?

Substance abuse is a major societal concern. Some of the available research points toward strong correlations between child abuse and alcoholism. One study, for example, found that children who grow up with

parents abusing alcohol were more likely to suffer adverse childhood experiences, such as delinquency.[18] Similarly, a standard textbook in the field
identifies research showing parallels between cocaine or heroin use and
child abuse.[19]

Yet another study concluded after highly structured interviews with 20
female abuse survivors that these women went on to commit delinquent
acts and later in life were presented with myriad health problems.[20] As
teenagers, the females in this same study had many behavioral problems in
school, frequently resulting in expulsion. Many of the females who were
sexually abused turned to substance abuse as a form of escapism. One
woman stated that drugs were "used to minimize emotional intensity—to
put memories on the back burner." Sadly, the use of drugs to abate feelings of sexual assault often resulted in opportunities for abuse by others,
providing evidence of the very vicious cycle linked with sexual abuse and
delinquency.

WHAT IS THE RELATIONSHIP AMONG SOCIAL CLASS, CULTURE, AND ABUSE?

Low-income families are heavily represented in the literature of crime
and delinquency. One can speculate that low-income families, especially
single-parent households are barely meeting the needs of their families.
Stated differently, poor people struggle to survive on a daily basis. It is
speculated that undue stressors and frustrations lead to unwise parental
decisions that result in child abuse. The issue of child abuse or neglect and
income seem to go hand and hand.

Slack and others in their analyses of an economically disadvantaged sample, found that "poverty and parenting are more strongly associated with
physical child neglect reports than others."[21] They also found a direct
relationship between parenting style and employment. Parents without
jobs were more likely to brutally spank their kids. The nature of the spanking or discipline is believed to be related to financial frustration. In contrast, these same researchers found that "more frequent work is also
associated with higher household incomes, suggesting that work may help
relieve financial stress, which could indirectly affect a parenting technique
such as a spanking."[22] With respect to mid- or high-income families, however, there are no guarantees that families from even the highest income
levels will possess good parenting skills.[23]

Examining the issue of race, Schuck found in a Florida study that
"higher child maltreatment reporting rates for black children were associated with more black female-headed families in poverty."[24] This overrepresentation is highest in urban areas and reverses itself when rural
communities are examined. Why are the rates lower for impoverished
black female-headed families in rural areas? Schuck conjectures that rural
blacks may live a more stable existence—with well-developed social networks and a stronger sense of community, absent in some urban locations.
Schuck goes on to suggest that "differences in parenting practices, cultural

aspects of child rearing, and discrimination by child welfare workers may also contribute to overrepresentation"[25] of poor black families. In all, many other studies provide additional support for the notion that there is far more abuse and neglect in poor homes.[26]

The following list contains risk factors associated with child abuse and delinquency. These variables increase the likelihood that maltreatment will result in adolescent or juvenile delinquency.

- Poor parental control
- Parental disinterest
- Inconsistent discipline
- Poor communication
- Absence of at least one biological parent
- Living at or below poverty level
- Education level of parent
- Sexual abuse

These variables lay the foundation for social and mental health agencies that are concerned with abuse and delinquency. Mandatory reporting laws require those in contact with children, primarily physicians, day care workers, and teachers to report suspected cases of child abuse. Over the years, differences in rates of child abuse may be traced to the perceived risks and benefits of reporting as viewed by these professional service groups. Critics argue that the potential political and economic dangers of reporting cases involving middle-class and upper-class clients guarantees that statistics will unfairly represent the poor. In other words, traits such as poverty do not represent those who are most likely to abuse, only those who are most likely to be caught.

WHAT IS THE ROLE OF THE FAMILY AND FAMILY SERVICES?

If the child is introduced to a loving relationship from both parents, the stability necessary for a life free of delinquency is enhanced. It is widely assumed that warmth exhibited by both parents will insulate the child from inappropriate conduct. Rosenbaum, for example, found that "the family background of incarcerated female delinquents was almost universally dysfunctional."[27] Love, consistent discipline, and nurturing behavior especially from the mother will reaffirm the positive identity of the child and go a long way to insulate kids during their development.[28]

Because of the various ways that domestic violence cases and families identified as negligent are processed or managed, it is often difficult for the criminal justice system or child protective services to respond effectively. High rates of mobility and short-term custody arrangements often make it difficult for service and protection agencies to monitor children at risk for abuse. Although Child Protective Services workers receive more than 50,000 maltreatment referral calls weekly, less than 20 percent are ever substantiated.[29] This does not mean that calls are not valid or contain accurate information. The problem is that agencies, underfunded and understaffed, are unable to follow up and investigate in enough depth to bring a case to court. Also, with families moving and children being shifted between caretakers, it is often difficult to locate those named in referrals, particularly if a significant period of time has elapsed.

IS THERE A RELATIONSHIP BETWEEN CHILD ABUSE AND AGGRESSIVE BEHAVIOR?

From a 1977 interview with John DiIulio, Cromartie reports that, if we want to understand the increased incidence of violence by kids, we need to look no farther than their treatment as kids. It is said that child maltreatment will increase the chances of delinquency by nearly 40 percent. To reaffirm this finding, DiIulio has said that every superpredator child that he has ever seen has been the victim of child abuse.

Because DiIulio is relatively famous for creating the "superpredator" myth of the 1990s and his connection between superpredators and child abuse, it is appropriate to list some of the myths related to these discussions about child abuse and delinquency. They are as follows:

Myth 1: There is a *direct* relationship between child abuse and delinquency and low-income status.
Myth 2: Child abuse is committed exclusively by men. The truth is that mothers and fathers are equally likely to be abusers, although fathers are more likely to be reported.
Myth 3: Child abuse will not have an indelible impact on the overall mental development of children.
Myth 4: Child abuse is mostly an American phenomenon.
Myth 5: Many allegations of child abuse are wrong and represent a tendency to overreport the offense.

Taken together, these myths espouse long-held beliefs that have not been empirically proven. The data that follow highlight significant research findings; please note that there may be variations in the data and research.[30]

- During 2004, an estimated 3 million children were alleged to have been abused or neglected. Approximately 872,000 children were determined to be victims of child maltreatment.
- Having a nonbiological parent in the household may place the child at greater risk.
- The number of individuals estimated to die annually from child abuse is around 1,000.
- Neglect is the most underrecorded form of fatal maltreatment.
- In 2002, one or both parents were involved in 79 percent of child abuse or neglect cases.
- There is no single profile of a perpetrator of fatal child abuse, although certain characteristics appear and reappear in many studies.

- Of the various types of maltreatment reported in recent years, more than 60 percent of all cases were neglect cases, 18 percent were physical abuse cases, and 10 percent were sexual abuse cases.
- The average age of an abused child is about 7 years old, a slight majority are females, and most are white.
- Infants younger than 1 year old accounted for 10 percent of child maltreatment victims in 2003.

Although neglect may be perceived by some to be a less serious form of child abuse (one that may be harder to define and detect), researchers are convinced that neglect frequently results in a continued cycle of violence. Over time, officials have made distinctions between physical neglect, medical neglect, and emotional neglect. As the research on child abuse in general reveals, the prevalence of child neglect is also largely underreported.

SOLUTIONS

In 1974, Congress passed the Child Abuse Prevention and Treatment Act, which provides money to increase and enhance services to maltreated children and their parents. This Act has provided the impetus for all 50 states to improve legal services for abused kids.

The complex dynamics of domestic violence suggests that society needs to explore nontraditional as well as traditional models of abuse intervention and treatment. A strict criminal justice response will not work. One idea promulgated by DiIulio, President George Bush's former director of Faith-Based Programs, is that the church become involved. His motto is to "build more churches, not jails." His idea is that the church must rally around juveniles who have been victimized as children by their parents or presumed loved ones.

Second, it has been suggested by Lemmon that treatment programs examine the role and influence of neglect, relative to abuse. He maintains that when types of maltreatment are separated, neglect is a stronger indicator of delinquency.[31] Although child neglect is the most common form of maltreatment, a strategy needs to be implemented that focuses equally on child neglect and child abuse.

Third, child protective service agencies and their counselors need to conduct more thorough investigations and to be more skilled and knowledgeable of different cultures. One way to achieve this is through the concept of child advocacy centers, which are multidisciplinary organizations that focus on the needs of the child. Although not necessarily a means of prevention, they represent a way to respond differently to the needs of abused children. The child advocacy center concept calls for greater coordination between various agencies, resulting in fewer meetings (and interviews) with the abused child. This paradigm may reduce the number of times an abused child has to repeat factual information to different people.

Fourth, Gellert offers a variety of methods to improve on the existing system.[32] He suggests, for example, establishing better coordination of data and resources to child care providers. He is also an advocate of the timely collection of information from well-qualified workers. Gellert believes that one way to achieve success in the response to child abuse problems is through creation of interagency child abuse teams (detailed below). These teams would establish links between agencies and improve identification of intervention opportunities, while decreasing the incidence of misdiagnosis and error.

In addition, data should not only be collected but should be analyzed and interpreted by researchers so that consumers clearly understand the information in a meaningful context. This often means focusing on trends rather than a single year's incidences and looking at an issue in comparison to other related problems or issues. For example, a major controversy in the past decade has been the actual number of stranger abductions and the realization that a more realistic interpretation of unaccounted for children was actually the problem of family-related disputes and custody battles. Concern over the disproportionate resources spent on the relatively rare occurrence of stranger-abducted children led the government to address the larger scope of potential abuse by sponsoring the National Incidence Studies of Missing, Abducted, Runaway and Throwaway (NISMART) children. These reports, available online (www.ojjdp.ncjrs.org) are funded through the Missing Children's Assistance Act and provide detailed analysis of the number of children in these different categories based on surveys of juvenile residential facilities, law enforcement, and households. Over time, researchers have come to understand much more about the nature of these problems and to report the data in ways that accurately depict the problem. In this manner, regularly updated and regional child abuse registries should be deployed everywhere to facilitate rapid data collection, improve coordination of agencies, and expedite preventive interventions for child abuse victims.

Fifth, Haugaard and Feerick bluntly state that more money is needed to address this problem.[33] They argue that the government and society must provide the resources to effectively *prevent* child abuse nationwide. This effort would be tantamount to a declaration of war on child abuse in much the same way we have the drug war and the terrorism war.

Sixth, Websdale offers recommendations as they relate to the prevention of child abuse.[34] He talks about the importance of a holistic perspective, that is, more frequent home visits by qualified counselors. Websdale calls for parenting programs for first-time parents and some parents with newborn children. He also identifies a need to break down the social isolation that at-risk families may experience in highly urban and densely populated communities.

Seventh, consistent with the observation of Websdale, and as mentioned earlier, child protection service agencies remain not only understaffed and underfunded, but the attrition rates of employees also remain high. If we are serious about eradicating child abuse, this society must not balk at the opportunity to adequately fund needed personnel and to provide the financial incentives that are essential to retain competent staff as well as the resources needed to abate burn out (which results in attrition).

Eighth, increased use of home visit programs may have limited utility; child care workers should look closely at a home visit program in Dallas, Texas, for parents with children at risk for child abuse and other forms of victimization. The program under evaluation is called the Parent Aid Program at the Child Abuse Center in Dallas. The researcher, Harder, shares the following results:[35]

- 76 percent of the parents who participated in the program did not receive subsequent referrals to Child Protective Services.
- 52 percent of those parents who dropped out of the program did not receive subsequent referrals to Child Protective Services.
- 62 percent of the parents who refused to participate in the program had subsequent referrals to Child Protective Services.

In all, Harder's study of the Dallas program revealed that home visits reduced the number of subsequent referrals to child protective services. However, the success rate for those who refused participation was close to the success rate of those who completed the program. This finding is not fully explained by the researcher, but one observation does become clear— it is a challenge to engage and retain the parents who participate. Harder indicates that retention problems abound in visitation programs across the country. The challenge, then, behind any recommendation to implement family visit programs, is to provide assurances that they will appeal to the *entire* family and that said programs are culture based.

Ninth, Dorne argues that privatization of child protective service agencies could potentially enhance services for abused children.[36] But is this really the answer? The argument is that the private agencies would perform well, because they would be motivated by profit. The truth, however, is that many of these agencies already contract out with the private sector to perform counseling and other services. It is this author's view that the idea of privatization is reprehensible. The government should never abdicate the responsibility of its children to a private entity; it would certainly result in disparate response systems and further fragment a system that needs better coordination.

Tenth, a massive advertising campaign is needed to engender increased public awareness. The campaign would carry slogans with facts that would have educational benefits. The public service announcement campaign would also include information about the extent of the problem, "do's and don'ts" with regard to parenting, the value of open dialogue, the importance of consistent discipline, and reminders to parents that consequences for inappropriate behavior must be fair and calibrated—not uneven or heavy-handed. This massive information and education campaign may result in increased public support for the expenditure of funds to improve the system, especially if policy makers can convince individuals from all income strata that everyone benefits (not just the poor) from additional funding and resources.

CONCLUSION

Many studies support the widespread assumption that a causal relationship exists between child abuse and delinquency. This relationship is a complex one. And while it is true that a great majority of maltreated children do not commit delinquent acts, research reveals that many delinquent youth have histories of child abuse. Consequently, there is clearly a need for identification of early intervention strategies.[37]

We know what some of the solutions are, but there are no moral imperatives to make a difference in the lives of children. Perhaps it is because the problem of child abuse has been mostly relegated to low-income families. It is the author's belief that there is no genuine interest in reducing child abuse and its potential devastating effects. Lastly, it is likely that child abuse will never be completely removed, *but we can do better* by investing in meaningful primary and secondary prevention initiatives. One start to achieve this would be to address the root causes of poverty in today's society. Such a strategy, if implemented, would go a long way toward reducing child abuse and neglect.

NOTES

1. Spivack, 1983.
2. See, e.g., Shanok & Lewis, 1981.
3. Kratcoski & Kratcoski, 1982; Rhoades & Parker, 1981.
4. Loeber & Dishion, 1984.
5. Zingraff, Leiter, Myers, & Johnson, 1993.
6. Smith & Thornberry, 1995.
7. Widom & Ames, 1994.
8. Ireland, Smith, & Thornberry, 2002.
9. Siegel & Williams, 2003.
10. Chesney-Lind, 1997.
11. Swanston et al., 2003, p. 743.
12. Goodkind, Ng, & Sarri., 2006.
13. Egger, 1998, p. 9.
14. Egger, 1998, p. 9.
15. Hickey, 1991.
16. Hazelwood & Douglas, 1980; Ellis & Gullo, 1971.
17. Ewing, 1990.
18. Dube et al., 2001.
19. Siegel & Senna, 1991.
20. Hall, 2000.
21. Slack, Holl, McDaniel, Yoo, & Bolger, 2004, p. 403.
22. Slack et al., 2004, p. 403.
23. Julian, 2006.
24. Schuck, 2005, p. 547.
25. Schuck, 2005, p. 551.
26. See Wexler (1995) for an excellent review of those studies.
27. Rosenbaum, 1989, p. 40.
28. Julian, 2006.

29. Snyder & Sickmund, 2006.
30. Snyder & Sickmund, 2006.
31. Lemmon, 1999.
32. As cited in Kiyohara, 1995.
33. Haugaard & Feerick, 2002.
34. Websdale, 2003.
35. Harder, 2005.
36. Dorne, 2002.
37. Grisson, 2002.

REFERENCES

Chesney-Lind, M. (1997). *The female offender: Girls, women and crime*. Thousand Oaks, CA. Sage Publications.

Cromartie, M. (1997, January 1). Kids who kill: A conversation with John DiIulio. *Ethics and Public Policy Center*. Retrieved August 1, 2006, from www.eppc.org/publications/pubID.89./pub_detail.asp.

Dorne, C. K. (2002). *An introduction to child maltreatment in the United States: History, public policy and research*. Monsey, NY: Criminal Justice Press.

Dube, S., Anda, R., Felitti, V., Croft, J., Edwards, V., & Giles, W. (2001). Growing up with parental alcohol abuse: Exposure to childhood abuse, neglect, and household dysfunction. *Child Abuse and Neglect, 25*, 1627–1640.

Egger, S. A. (1998). *The killers among us*. Upper Saddle River, NJ: Prentice Hall.

Ellis, A., & Gullo, J. (1971). *Murder and assassination*. New York: Lyle Stuart.

Ewing, C. P. (1990). *Kids who kill*. Boston: Lexington Books.

Gellert. As cited in Kiyohara.

Goodkind, S., Ng, I., & Sarri, R. (2006). The impact of sexual abuse in the lives of young women involved or at risk of involvement with the juvenile justice system. *Violence Against Women, 12*, 456–477.

Grisson, T. (2002). Using what we know about child maltreatment and delinquency. *Children Services: Social Policy, Research, and Practice, 5*, 299–305.

Hall, J. (2000). Core issues for female child abuse survivors in recovery from substance misuse. *Qualitative Health Research, 10*, 612–631.

Harder, J. (2005). Prevention of child abuse and neglect: An evaluation of a home visitation parent aide program using recidivism data. *Research on Social Work Practice, 15*, 246–256.

Haugaard, J., & Feerick, M. (2002). Interventions for maltreated children to reduce their likelihood of engaging in childhood delinquency. *Children Services: Social Policy, Research and Practice, 5*, 285–297.

Hickey, E.W. (1991). *Serial killers and their victims*. Pacific Grove, CA: Brooks/Cole.

Ireland, T., Smith, C. A., & Thornberry, T. (2002). Developmental issues in the impact of child maltreatment on later delinquency and drug abuse. *Criminology, 40*, 359–396.

Kiyohara, S. M. (1995). Child abuse detection: A mandate for refinement, *Journal of Child Sexual Abuse, 4*, 105–108.

Lemmon, J. (1999). How child maltreatment affects dimensions of juvenile delinquency in a cohort of low income urban youths. *Justice Quarterly, 16*, 357–376.

Loeber, R., & Dishion, T. (1984). Boys who fight in school and home: Family conditions influencing cross setting consistency. *Journal of Consulting and Clinical Psychology, 52*, 759–68.

Rhoades, P. W. & Parker, S. L. (1981). *The connections between youth problems and violence in the home.* Portland, OR: Oregon Coalition against Domestic and Sexual Violence.

Rosenbaum, J. (1989). Family dysfunction and female delinquency. *Crime and Delinquency, 35,* 31–44.

Schuck, A. M. (2005). Explaining black white disparity in maltreatment: Poverty, female headed families, and urbanization. *Journal of Marriage and Family, 67,* 543–551.

Shanok, S. S., & Lewis, D. O. (1981). Medical histories of abused delinquents. *Child Psychiatry and Child Development, 11,* 222–231.

Siegel, J., & Williams, L. (2003). The relationship between child sexual abuse and female delinquency and crime: A prospective study. *Journal of Research in Crime and Delinquency, 40,* 71–94.

Siegel, L., & Senna, J. (1991). *Juvenile delinquency: Theory, practice and law.* St. Paul: West Publishing Company.

Slack, K. S., Holl, J. L., McDaniel, M., Yoo, J., & Bolger, K. (2004). Understanding the risks of child neglect: An exploration of poverty and parenting characteristics. *Child Maltreatment, 9,* 395–408.

Smith, C., & Thornberry, T. (1995). The relationship between childhood maltreatment and adolescent involvement in delinquency. *Criminology. 33,* 451–481.

Snyder, H. N., & Sickmund, M. (2006). *Juvenile offenders and victims: 2006 national report.* Washington, D.C.: U.S. Department of Justice, Office of Justice Programs.

Spivack, G. (1983). *High risk early behaviors indicating vulnerabilities to delinquency in the community and the school.* Washington, D.C.: National Institute of Juvenile Justice and Delinquency Prevention.

Swanston, H., Parkinson, P., O'Toole, B., Plunkett, A., Shrimpton, S., & Oates, R. K. (2003). Juvenile crime, aggression and delinquency after sexual abuse. *British Journal of Criminology, 43,* 729–749.

Websdale, N. (2003). Child abuse. In M. D. McShane & F. P. Williams, III (Eds.), *Encyclopedia of Juvenile Justice* (pp. 50–54). Thousand Oaks, CA: Sage Publications.

Wexler, R. (1995). *Wounded innocents: The real victims of the war against child abuse.* Buffalo, NY: Promethus Books.

Widom C. & Ames, M. A. (1994). Criminal consequences of childhood sexual victimization. *Child Abuse and Neglect,* 18 (4), 303–318.

Zingraff, M., Leiter, J., Myers, K., & Johnson, M. C. (1993). Child maltreatment and youthful problem behavior. *Criminology, 31,* 173–202.

CHAPTER 4

Youth Street Gangs

Lorine A. Hughes

Youth street gangs[1] have been an enduring social problem that has defied effective amelioration and control. Despite numerous interventions and police crackdowns, street gangs have proliferated rapidly and continue to shock public sensibilities.[2] Between 1975 and 2000, gangs increased almost sevenfold, from 4,481 to 30,818.[3] Today, there are an estimated 24,000 gangs in the United States, with approximately 760,000 active members in 2,900 jurisdictions.[4] Gangs have spread beyond the boundaries of early gang cities, such as Los Angeles, Chicago, and New York, to cities in such states as Arkansas, Idaho, Kansas, Nebraska, Washington, Wisconsin, and even Hawaii.[5] They also have been documented on reservations as well as in both rural and suburban areas.[6] Specific reasons for the growth of gangs in these nontraditional places are unclear, but explanations that focus on migration undertaken to expand drug distribution markets appear to be less popular and empirically valid than those that point to internal community dynamics, media effects, and the influence of individual "cultural carriers" who relocate to a new area and bring with them their prior gang experiences.[7]

The failure of policies to combat gangs has baffled even the most astute social observers. From detached worker programs to police gang task forces, nothing has worked very well. The problem, it seems, is not just a matter of good policies being implemented poorly, but also a reflection of inadequate policies. Especially since the beginning of the conservative "get tough" era, in which gangs and gangbanging were assumed to be the result of individual free will and the existence of a "culture of poverty" among the lower classes of society, government agencies and government-funded responses have emphasized police crackdowns and enhanced penalties over community investment and provision of legitimate opportunities. For example, in 1988, California became the first of five states to enact the Street Terrorism Enforcement and Prevention (STEP) Act, patterned after the Racketeer Influenced and Corrupt Organizations (RICO) Act, which has been used primarily to deal with organized crime by means of enhanced police and legislative power as a form of deterrence.[8] The most recent, and perhaps most controversial, in a long line of antigang measures is the Gang Deterrence and Community Protection Act of 2005, otherwise known as the "Gangbusters Bill." This piece of legislation was introduced by Virginia lawmakers in response to a media-driven panic over gang violence, the alleged involvement of gangs in human and drug trafficking, and concerns over the growth of Mara Salvatrucha (MS-13), an El Salvadorian gang that is believed to be especially violent, organized, and spreading rapidly from Los Angeles to other parts of the country. The Bill authorizes increased federal funds to investigate and prosecute gang members; it also "expands the range of gang crimes punishable by death, establishes mandatory minimum sentences, authorizes the prosecution of 16- and 17-year-old gang members in federal court as adults, and extends the statute of limitations for all violent crimes from 5 to 15 years."[9] Although it is now evident that such suppression policies are misguided and ineffective, they remain a popular choice among legislatures and other policy makers. Surely, there must be something else we can (and should) do.

Papachristos argues that "[b]efore we can figure out what to do about gangs or what types of policies and interventions might be most effective, we need to devise analytic strategies that help us chart the real gang landscape and not just distorted images of it."[10] Criminologists are beginning to do this in the form of network analyses, which map the position of gangs and their members in social space, thus providing valuable information about the connectedness that exists between and among gangs.[11] Too often, however, findings from network analyses and other gang studies are simply incorporated into the reactionary "get tough" policy model and used to boost suppression tactics.[12] Although targeting central gang members for arrest and prosecution may shake the existing organizational structures of gangs and provide a measure of relief from gang-related crime and violence, such an approach is unlikely to solve the gang problem, because it neglects other critical points of intervention, such as gang formation and the enlisting of new members, and fails to address the underlying causes of gangs and gangbanging.[13]

Based on our personal experiences with gangs and gang research, my colleague and long-time gang scholar, Jim Short, and I are convinced that young people form and become involved in gangs as compensation for deficits in their lives. Gangs are not distributed equally across the country, nor do their members adequately represent the nation's youth population. Instead, gangs are found primarily in disadvantaged neighborhoods and draw the bulk of their membership from among the most powerless groups in society, that is, poor minorities between the ages of 12 and 24.[14] Policy makers and practitioners must attend to these social contexts and accept the failure of singular suppression strategies to adequately address them. However, throwing money at poverty-stricken and gang-infested communities will not work either. As Vigil's comparative study of Los Angeles gangs demonstrates, the gang problem is complex and involves "multiple marginalities," at home, in school, and in relation to other social institutions.[15] Here, I argue that the gang problem reflects not just poverty, but also is a function of the difficulties that many young people face in securing all forms of capital—economic, human, cultural, political, and social. Policies that neglect this reality are unlikely to produce or to sustain benefits and, in fact, may make the problem worse.

GANGS AND CAPITAL

Economic Capital

Although no two gangs are exactly alike, a common theme running through decades of gang research centers on the relationship between economic disadvantage and gang formation and involvement. From Thrasher's classic study of gangs in Chicago during the 1920s to more contemporary investigations in that city and elsewhere, gangs have been located primarily within the poorest neighborhoods in the country. Characteristic of these areas are unemployment and poverty rates that are much higher than the national average, as well as rows of dilapidated housing, a disproportionate share of liquor establishments and other shady businesses (e.g., check cashing), and a high concentration of immigrants or other racial and ethnic minorities living together in proximity. The most infamous examples include New York's Chinatowns, the Hispanic barrios of Los Angeles, and the ghetto areas surrounding the massive public housing projects that have long been home to some of Chicago's most economically marginalized blacks (e.g., Robert Taylor Homes).

Structural changes in the national economy facilitated the entrenchment of gangs in these three "chronic" gang cities and encouraged their proliferation to other places throughout the country.[16] The rapid departure of relatively high-paying and secure manufacturing jobs from the nation's urban centers helped turn these places into areas plagued by persistent joblessness, poverty and welfare dependency, female-headed households, family disruption, illegitimate births, crime, and other related social ills.[17] Gangs also flourished in this context. Although some gangs formed anew, other gangs—such as the Gangster Disciples, Latin Kings, Vice Lords, 18th Street Gang, Maravilla, and White Fence—continued their transformation into institutionalized "supergangs," complete with a complex web of affiliated but geographically distinct "sets" and a history spanning multiple generations.[18]

For youth growing up in such conditions, gangbanging often becomes a natural course of action. The reasons they cite for joining gangs—acceptance, love, identity, status, money, protection, and excitement—strongly suggest that they see in gangs a chance to recapitalize their lives.[19]

The reality, we now know, is that gangs often are exploitative and only rarely provide their members with the opportunity for substantial financial gains.[20] Moreover, everyday gang life tends to be fairly boring, with much of the time spent doing nothing but hanging out and getting high (or looking for something on which to get high).[21] Gangs may exacerbate their members' problems, placing them at increased risk of violent victimization and greater contact with police and prison. To the young men and women who join gangs, however, what matters is the meaning that gangbanging brings to their lives.

Human Capital

The gang problem is more than one of poverty; it is also a problem of insufficient human capital, which consists of the education, skills, and experiences that "influence future monetary and psychic income."[22] Gangs draw their membership primarily from among society's most unskilled and uneducated populations. Once absorbed by manufacturing jobs, these people now find themselves lacking the credentials needed to compete successfully in today's service- and information-based economy.[23] Exacerbating this already difficult situation, globalization of the world's economy continues to push more and more good jobs overseas. Although some affected youth manage to escape the vicious cycle of poverty and despair, many are not so fortunate. Most do not possess natural artistic or athletic ability; of those that do, few have the opportunity and support needed to fully develop their talents. College tends not to be a realistic option for these youth. The costs of higher education are often prohibitive, and the application and enrollment processes can be especially daunting to young people who have grown up on the streets, even if someone more knowledgeable happens to be there to help. Moreover, the secondary schools they attend are often substandard, unable to meet the needs of students—many of whom have only limited English proficiency—or they are oriented more toward remedial education for immigrant children and other academically challenged students than toward college preparation. The adoption of a "zero tolerance" policy by many schools may increase the already high dropout rates among gang members and other minority youth,[24] furthering their alienation through quasi-military security mechanisms and the transformation of the traditional role of teacher from mentor to detached bystanders.[25]

Faced with such limited prospects, gang youth are easily recruited into the illicit economy. Although most gangs are not involved in drug distribution *as gangs*, individual gang members are more likely than their non-gang counterparts to participate in such behavior and most other types of crimes, oftentimes as part of a clique.[26] They appear to do so more to supplement their income than in lieu of conventional activities, and many genuinely hope some day to be able to "go legit."[27] Instead, however, many wind up spending time in prison and returning to the streets with even fewer opportunities than before.[28] Even for those who manage to escape a criminal record and related problems (e.g., ineligibility for federal student aid), the only available jobs tend to be "in the fast-food industry or service work in hotels, malls, and restaurants," none of which provides decent wages and benefits.[29] Because these jobs offer no real hope for advancement in society, gang members may see them as a waste of time and effort, especially if transportation is an issue or if street activities promise more lucrative returns.[30] Thus, although gang members might at first seem like bad kids who are too lazy to do anything productive with their lives, the real problem may be that they typically have few opportunities to accumulate the human capital needed to overcome their disadvantaged backgrounds.

Political Capital

Youth occupy a precarious position in today's society. Their activities and actions are circumscribed and regulated by their parents, schools, and the law. Politically, they have few rights and wield limited power. Because gang youth typically belong to populations with muted political voices, they have even fewer opportunities to accumulate the political capital needed to influence the decisions that affect their lives. Historically, gangs have emerged among racial minorities and immigrants, two of the most politically powerless groups in society. Depending on the source of information, estimates of the racial composition of contemporary gangs range from 75 to 95 percent minority.[31] No comparable estimates of immigration status exist, but research suggests that first- and second-generation immigrants make up a sizable proportion of recently emerging Asian and Hispanic gangs,[32] just as they did among early white gangs.[33] Unlike the "ethnic Europeans of the gangs of the 1920s, whose marginality lasted only one generation,"[34] however, today's gang youth tend to be systematically excluded from the mainstream.

Although gangs typically are loosely organized and lack effective leadership, group cohesion, and the ability to mobilize effectively, they nevertheless provide their members with a sense of empowerment and the opportunity to transcend the limits of their lives, if only symbolically. Owing to their placement at the bottom of society's sociopolitical hierarchy, minority and immigrant youth are especially vulnerable to the allure of gangs. Despite greater societal awareness and tolerance of diversity, these youth continue to experience the effects of widespread racism and anti-immigrant sentiment. They also must contend with the fallout from community disinvestment and massive cutbacks in government welfare programs.[35] In addition, legislation intended to better the life situation of minorities and immigrants to this country (e.g., civil rights, affirmative action, Voting Rights Act, and Immigration Act of 1990) often have produced uneven results, benefiting those with relatively more resources while leaving the less fortunate largely untouched. In some cases, such legislation has given impetus to the flight of the middle and working classes from disadvantaged communities, depriving those left behind of their most promising political leaders and the ability to affect public policy.[36] The policies that then develop are often insensitive, if not detrimental, to the plight of these people. As Geis notes,

> It is no longer acceptable in American society to demonstrate prejudice overtly. But the same end can be achieved by pinpointing activities that are very largely those of the socially disenfranchised and inventing special kinds of laws that will bring persons who violate them to grief.[37]

Consider, for example, the disproportionate impact of the war on drugs, particularly crack cocaine, on black men and their communities. Under the draconian laws established as part of this war, thousands of young black men have been sent to prison for extended periods of time and at a rate much higher than white men.[38] These men often leave behind a community already devastated by other factors contributing to high rates of female-headed households, poverty, crime and violence, and male joblessness. Upon entering prison, they confront a system notorious for being a hotbed of gang formation and activity.[39] While in prison,[40] they are locked out of political participation by felon disenfranchisement laws, further limiting their communities' ability to influence legislation.[41] Even if the right to vote is restored upon release from prison, which in many states it is not, they reenter their communities with limited job skills and prospects, and face a larger society hostile to ex-convicts.[42] Many then turn to gangs and street hustles, placing themselves at risk of rearrest and added time in prison.

There is no end in sight for gang youth caught in this cycle. After a long period in which gang problems remained a low priority on the nation's domestic policy agenda,[43] gangs and gang members now find themselves at the center of a moral panic, confronting hardened approaches to gang control. Policies already on the books or now in the works threaten the civil liberties of gang members and promise to crack down on gangs like never before.[44] Although gangs and gang crime are serious problems demanding tough solutions, policies that further the political vulnerability of gang youth and their communities are misguided at best. Few gangs fit the assumptions on which most antigang laws and policies are based. Gangs generally are not sophisticated criminal or terrorist organizations, nor do they spend the majority of their time conspiring to commit violence or trafficking in drugs.[45] They "typically develop in marginalized contexts, and most gang members participate in small-time and relatively unorganized street hustles."[46]

Instead of challenging images popularized by the media (and often by gang members themselves), criminological research has often fueled them.[47] Partly because of the interest and demands of government funding agencies, recent gang studies have focused primarily on documenting the prevalence of gangs, the characteristics of gang members, and their participation in crime and violence.[48] To the extent that these studies obscure the diversity among gangs, they reinforce the tendency to conflate gangs with organized crime and to treat both accordingly. Less evident on the scholarly agenda are studies of the everyday realities faced by individual gang members, the causal significance of gangs to their members' behaviors, and the nature of the relationship between gangs and their communities.[49] Such research is needed to better inform gang policy and thus avoid further alienation of vulnerable youth. The development of sound policy may help gangs develop a healthy political voice and overcome the negative influences that hindered the attempts of earlier gangs to become legitimate organizations and catalysts for positive social change.[50]

Cultural Capital

Deficits in the other forms of capital are brought about by some of the same factors that limit opportunities for these young people to acquire cultural capital.[51] All too often, youth in poor areas see their own cultures devalued in the larger society and that they are denied the benefits that accrue to those whose lives bear a closer resemblance to the American ideal. These youth rarely experience the world beyond their immediate surroundings and must live day to day amid poverty, weakened primary social institutions (e.g., family and school), persistent unemployment, and drugs and crime. Few are exposed to the "finer things" in life—such as appreciation of art history, classical music and literature, foreign cuisines, travel abroad, and so forth—and most are not encouraged to go to college or taught how to be professional workers.[52] Many also are not shown what it means to be a good parent, because their own are caught up in drugs or are in prison, have abandoned or abused them, are dependent on them for money or other types of help (e.g., language or child care), or are simply too busy trying to make ends meet.

Urban ethnographies suggest that gangs are a manifestation of the alternate culture or street code that emerges in response to economic depression and marginalization. "At the heart of the code is the issue of respect," as reflected in the behavior of young men and in their artistic and symbolic expression.[53] Especially in "chronic" gang cities, where gangs have become institutionalized and are passed from one generation to the next,[54] young boys learn early on that being viewed as a "real man" requires the acquisition of various forms of street capital, including wads of cash, women, flashy cars, jewelry, guns, and a willingness to resort to violence. The exaggerated importance placed on each of these things is evident in the esteem accorded to those who possess them and in the graffiti spattered throughout the community. It can be seen, as well, in popular gang movies, such as *Boys 'N the Hood*, *Colors*, and *Menace II Society*. Perhaps nowhere is the street culture more apparent than in hip-hop and the music of rap artists Dr. Dre, Snoop Doggy Dogg, Tupac Shakur, 50 Cent, and others. Lyrics that glorify and glamorize thug life and the gangsta' identity also speak of the hard realities of life in ghetto projects. Along with all the talk about dope, 40s and other types of liquor, money, gold, guns, pimping and "pimped out" cars, there are numerous references to poverty, racism, police repression, drive-bys, murders, and body bags.

Although alternative cultures may have survival value for life on the streets or in prisons and jails, they do not translate well in mainstream society. Despite growing acceptance of rap music and ghetto styles in the cultural mainstream, the "code of the streets" may exacerbate the isolation of impoverished neighborhoods and the breakdown of traditional institutions.[55] When suburban and rural youth groups adopt gang names, sport gang clothing and tattoos, and flash gang signs, they, too, are likely to experience negative adult attention and develop factional rivalries among themselves.[56] It is in the nation's inner cities, however, that the numbers of alienated and deprived people have reached the "critical mass necessary for a viable subculture"[57] and where the emphasis on street capital is most widespread and problematic.

The prevalence of violent crime in the inner cities is especially troubling. Despite long-term declines in crime and violence in the United States since the 1980s, the rate of serious violent crime in cities with a population more than 250,000 is 932.6 per 100,000 population, including rates of murder, rape, robbery, and aggravated assault equaling 12.5, 41.8, 358.1, and 520.8, respectively.[58] Because rates of violent crime tend to be even higher in the inner cities, young people in these areas are at an increased risk of exposure to violence. A recent study funded by the National Institute of Mental Health (NIMH) reported that of 792 inner-city youth surveyed, 92.5 percent had been exposed to violence in the previous six months, 73.2 percent "knew of neighborhood shootings," 55.4 percent had seen a person "seriously beaten or killed," "half had heard of neighborhood murders," 22 percent said "there were shootings and knifings in their school," and 20 percent had been "hurt or threatened with physical violence in their own homes."[59] With violence such a prominent part of their lives, it is not surprising that many urban youth become involved in gangs and participate in violent activities.[60]

Although the nature of the relationship between gangs and violence is unclear, multiple data sources suggest the existence of a causal link. For example, of the 312,402 homicides recorded by police between 1976 and 2002 in the nation's largest cities, roughly 70 percent were classified as gang-related crimes, compared with 12.9 percent in small cities, 16.6 percent in the suburbs, and 0.8 percent in rural locales.[61] Analyses of official data also find that, "[c]ompared to non-gang incidents, gang incidents are more visible, more violent, more likely to involve a weapon, more likely to involve strangers, and more likely to involve fear of retaliation."[62] Since 1987, more than 90 percent of all gang-related homicides each year have involved a gun, a rate roughly 30 percent higher than corresponding figures for nongang homicides. Studies based on longitudinal self-report data reinforce cross-sectional findings of an association between admitted gang membership and self-reported crime and violence, revealing a peak in gang member involvement in such behaviors precisely during periods of active gang membership.[63] Contrary to social selection—that is, birds of a feather flocking together—explanations of the gang-crime/violence relationship, these studies offer powerful evidence of a gang "facilitative" effect.

Insight into the specific mechanisms underlying general statistical patterns is derived primarily from field studies, particularly those carried out in the observation tradition of the Chicago School of Urban Sociology. Despite differing time frames and clear racial and geographic differences among analyzed gangs, these studies regularly depict gangs as social contexts characterized by heightened concerns over respect and street-sanctioned means of achieving it.[64] Autobiographical and journalistic accounts featuring male and female gangbangers of varying races reiterate this theme.[65] Gangs appear to give a collective expression to the code of the streets, serving as "staging areas" for young males—and, increasingly, older males and young females—to demonstrate respected qualities and providing a ready sanctioning system for such attributes and behaviors.[66] They also offer their members protection and backup against those who try to achieve respect at their expense.

To earn respect on the streets, gangs and gang members must "send the unmistakable, if sometimes subtle, message that [they are] capable of violence, and possibly mayhem, when the situation requires it."[67] Much of this involves nonviolent posturing, in the form of appearances, mannerisms, and exaggerated accumulation of material goods and symbols of success (e.g., money, girls, etc.).[68] Having done time in prison also brings respect, because it is generally taken as a sign of a person's ability to survive in the roughest of social environments. As sporadic gang warfare makes clear, however, there is no substitute for displays of violence. Gangs and their members are under constant threat of violent victimization, even death, at the hands of rivals and other people wishing to enhance their own street position.[69] When attacked or otherwise disrespected (e.g., scratched out graffiti), they are expected, by themselves and others, to wage a successful defense or to exact revenge at a later point in time.[70] Failure to do so is tantamount to admitting weakness and inviting future attacks.

The emphasis on retaliatory violence in disadvantaged neighborhoods has been attributed to a "profound lack of faith in the police and the judicial system."[71] Residents of these areas, many of whom are people of color, know all too well the high costs associated with racial disparities in the criminal justice system, and they have often witnessed or been at the receiving end of questionable police tactics. Thus, these people have come to feel as though they cannot rely on legal means to handle their disputes and must take matters into their own hands, using violence if necessary.[72] For gangs and gang members faced with rivalries and clear expectations of violence as a means to protect personal and gang status, pressures to seek such "street justice" may be especially acute.[73]

Social Capital

Not all, or even most, youth living in the inner cities or other disadvantaged neighborhoods turn to gangs or violence. Variations seem to occur, in part, because of differential access to social capital, or the "the ability of actors to secure benefits by virtue of membership in social networks or other social structures."[74] Owing to individual talents and attributes, relatively favorable family circumstances, or a fortuitous meeting, some youth in these areas are able to maintain a strong adult presence in their lives and remain connected to conventional social institutions. As structural conditions have worsened,[75] however, more inner-city youth have become alienated from mainstream social networks (e.g., school, work, and church) and thus from the people who are in the best position to provide them with access to, or information about, openings in the legitimate opportunity structure. As Kelley notes,

> One way to understand conditions in the urban ghetto is by noting that children living in it often lack meaningful connections beyond their immediate kinship and neighborhood environments. This has two related consequences. First, the social capital generated by their families can only be parlayed into access to resources existing in their physical surroundings, including those made available by public assistance programs. Because those resources tend to be of poor quality, the advantages derived from social capital are few. That, in turn, has an effect upon adults' credibility when trying to control the behavior of children. Second, the truncation of social networks makes it unlikely that most impoverished children can maintain the kind of sustained contact with members of external social networks that would enable them to envision alternative paths out of the ghetto.[76]

The lack of meaningful ties to conventional opportunity structures paves the way for alternative culture systems that further limit access to mainstream social networks. As negative adult influences replace prosocial role models, youth become increasingly susceptible to gangs. Even if the most significant adults in their lives do not encourage gang participation and criminal behaviors, through their own involvement in these activities or other forms of approval, they are generally unable to offer sound advice or keep members of younger generations away from gang life.[77] Although participation in a gang tends to exacerbate young people's alienation from conventional adults and society, to these youth, gang networks appear to be the best way to form or solidify relationships through which important resources will flow.[78]

CONCLUSION

Many communities have been devastated by poverty, persistent joblessness, substandard schooling, community disinvestment, and bad policy. As families and other social institutions break down, youth are not taught what it means to be a good parent, worker, or college student. No one is there to show them a better life; their primary learning is how to get by on the streets. Although many turn to gangs in an effort to recapitalize their lives, gangbanging places these youth at increased risk of being processed through the justice system, where they receive a criminal record and must deal with all that it entails. By the time they reach adulthood, their options are limited. How can we expect people to prosper if all they can expect out of life is working at a dead-end job and if all they have grown up around is ghetto life? Men are locked up, dead, or unfit to be good parents; young women face the burden of raising children on their own and being the sole breadwinner. The community loses its potential leaders, and its political voice is compromised by the disproportionate number of adults who are in prison or otherwise subject to felon disenfranchisement. The result is that disadvantaged communities, often suffering from a multitude of problems, are powerless against policies that directly affect their lives and that may exacerbate already tough circumstances. Faced with such bleak prospects, it is not surprising that residents of these areas generally distrust the police and other outsiders and tend to take matters into their own hands. Their need to achieve or maintain street capital likely outweighs the potential loss of all other forms of capital, which are already in short supply.

The failure of tactics based on suppression and the placement of criminal justice professionals at the front lines of the so-called war on gangs highlights the need for a more comprehensive solution to the youth street gang problem.[79] Gangs and gangbanging are complex phenomena, involving a variety of factors and social processes. Although the suppression view of gangs "as simply another type of organized crime (or, more recently, terrorist units) requiring 'gang busting' (akin to 'union busting') may be appropriate for the small subset of gangs that conform most closely to images popularized by the media and some law enforcement officials," it "neglects the vast majority of gangs and the wide diversity among them."[80] Of greater concern is that the suppression model ignores the deprivations that give rise to the formation of gangs and encourage gang membership. Gang control programs that neglect such issues can provide, at best, only a false sense of security; at worst, they will intensify existing problems or create additional ones, as recently happened following the mass deportation of members of MS-13 back to El Salvador.[81]

Jim Short recently suggested that greater consideration be paid to gang intervention programs that make use of street workers to promote social capital and collective efficacy among gang members and their communities.[82] Lest past mistakes be repeated, however, street-worker programs should not dominate gang policy. Although such programs may be more suited to the task of building social capital among gang members than are singular suppression strategies, they must be based on theoretically informed research, carried out properly, and supplemented by other forms of capital building that recognize the sociocultural contexts in which they are implemented. If not, they are unlikely to succeed and may make things worse.[83]

Ultimately, what is needed is an approach that has as its starting point the location of gangs and gang activities within their social contexts and is sensitive to the realities faced by individual gang members. It must be based on criminological insights and theory rather than ideology and stereotyped images. "Gangs tend to be more violent than other local offenders; but most gang youth crime is nonserious and nonviolent.... That's not to deny the reality is bad. But our goal is to dissect the problem, not to pound the table."[84] Meeting this goal will require the development of a research and policy program that seeks to understand and address the difficulties that gang youth face in securing capital of all types—economic, social, human, political, and cultural. At the center of such a program must be the community, with the police and other agents of the criminal justice system playing secondary, albeit important, roles. Suppression should no longer be the first response; but rather the last alternative, to be employed only if all else has failed.

NOTES

1. The author thanks Jim Short, Buddy Howell, Andy Papachristos, and Pete Simi for their helpful comments on a previous draft of this manuscript.

2. Definitional issues continue to plague the study of gangs, but the terms "street gang" and "youth gang" typically exclude prison gangs, motorcycle gangs, skinheads, drug crews, taggers, play groups, and other such collectivities. Although there is much disagreement over the appropriateness of inclusion of criminal activity in the definition of gangs, "common to all definitions of street gangs is the fact that they are unsupervised youth groups that meet together with some regularity, over time, and that they are non-adult-sponsored and self-determining with respect to membership criteria, organizational structure, and acceptable behavior" (Short & Hughes, in press).

3. Curry & Decker, 2002; Miller, 2001.

4. Egley, Howell, & Major, 2004.

5. Battin et al., 1998; Chesney-Lind et al., 2005; Esbensen & Osgood, 1997; Fleisher, 1998; Hagedorn, 1988; Howell, Moore, & Egley, 2002; Levin & Pinkerson, 1994.

6. Major & Egley, 2002; Monti, 1994; Weisheit & Wells, 2001.

7. See Maxson, 1998.

8. See Bjerregaard, 2003; Klein, 1995; Webb & Katz, 2003.

9. Amoroso, 2005, para. 3.

10. Papachristos, 2005a, p. 645.

11. See Fleisher, 2002, 2006; McGloin, 2005; Papachristos, 2006.

12. It is important to consider whether individuals who are most central to the gang are those who are most criminally active. Evidence suggests that gang members who bring too much "heat" on the gang, from other gangs and/or from law enforcement, are relegated to the fringe by more central members (Hughes & Short, 2005). Thus, while a policy that targets the members who are most socially connected may counteract the group processes that contribute to elevated rates of crime and violence, it may also reduce a key source of constraint against those who are the most inclined to troublesome behaviors.

13. Spergel, 1995.

14. Klein, 1995; Short, 1997; Vigil & Yun, 2002; see Howell & Egley, 2005.

15. Vigil, 2002.

16. Hagedorn, 1988; Klein, 1995; Spergel & Curry, 1990, 1993.

17. Sampson, 1987; Wilson, 1987, 1996.

18. Hagedorn, 1988; Moore, 1991. Alliances and rivalries eventually led to the establishment of larger gang nations, such as Chicago's People and Folks and the Bloods and Crips of Los Angeles. On the streets, however, intergang alliances have been tenuous, with some gangs "flipping" from one nation to the other or fighting against, even killing, members of allied gangs (www.chicagomobs.org, 2006).

19. Hughes, 2005.

20. Field studies of drug-dealing gangs typically report wide discrepancies between the profits made by the few individuals in leadership positions and the more numerous "foot soldiers," who must endure the risks associated with slinging dope but generally earn no more doing this type of job than working for minimum wage (Padilla, 1993; Venkatesh, 1999).

21. Fleisher, 1998; Hagedorn, 1988.

22. Becker, 1964, p. 11.

23. Wilson, 1987, 1996.

24. Brotherton & Barrios, 2004; Snyder & Sickmund, 2006.

25. Devine, 1997.

26. Hughes, 2005; Coughlin & Venkatesh, 2003.

27. Hagedorn, 1994, 2002.

28. Today, far more African Americans and Hispanics are in prison than in college (Walker, Spohn, & DeLone, 2004).

29. Fleisher & Decker, 2001, p. 2; see also Hagedorn, 1988.

30. Hagedorn, 1988.

31. Howell, 1998; Howell et al., 2002.

32. Joe, 1994; Joe & Robinson, 1980; Vigil, 2002.

33. Thrasher, 1927.

34. Moore, 1988, pp. 5–6.

35. Cummings & Monti, 1993.

36. Wilson, 1987.

37. Geis, 2002, p. 259.

38. Mauer, 1998; Walker et al., 2004.

39. Fleisher & Decker, 2001.

40. Only two states, Maine and Vermont, allow prison inmates to vote. Most states also deny probationers and parolees the right to vote. "Each state has developed its own process of restoring voting rights to ex-offenders but most of these restoration processes are so cumbersome that few ex-offenders are able to take advantage of them" (The Sentencing Project, 2006, p. 1).

41. Uggen & Manza, 2002.

42. Petersilia, 2003.

43. Monti & Cummings, 1993.

44. Coughlin & Venkatesh, 2003; Hughes & Short, 2006; Stewart, 1998.

45. Coughlin & Venkatesh, 2003.

46. Hughes & Short, in press.

47. Katz & Jackson-Jacobs, 2004.

48. Hughes, 2005.

49. Short & Hughes, 2006.

50. The most well-known and best-documented cases of political activism occurred among the Almighty Latin King and Queen Nation in New York between 1995 and 1999 (see Brotherton & Barrios, 2004) and three black gangs in Chicago—the Blackstone Rangers, the Devil's Disciples, and the Vice Lords— during the 1960s and 1970s. None of these gangs evolved into a full-fledged social movement with lasting impacts, however, and all ultimately succumbed to "mounting external pressures, inadequate community support, and internal contradictions" (Hughes & Short, 2006, p. [47]). See also Spergel, 1995.

51. Cultural capital is defined by French sociologist Pierre Bourdieu (1986) as the symbols, attitudes, values, and knowledge necessary for acceptance in higher status society.

52. Moreover, some may choose not to leave their communities or try to "make it," even when given the chance, out of fear of failing or finding themselves returning to unwelcoming sentiments and suspicions that they think they are better than those who are less fortunate (see Portes, 1998). Family concerns also may be important, because some youth are expected to provide monetary support or care for their parents, siblings, and/or other blood relatives. Sometimes it is simply a matter of the youth feeling more comfortable in the only environment and lifestyle he or she has ever known.

53. Anderson, 1999, p. 33.

54. Hagedorn, 1988.

55. Anderson, 1999.

56. Monti, 1994.

57. Fischer, 1974, p. 1328; but see Coughlin & Venkatesh, 2003, pp. 56–57.

58. Federal Bureau of Investigation, 2005.

59. Elze, Stiffman, & Dorè, 1999.

60. Howell, 1998.

61. Fox & Zawitz, 2004. Because of definitional variations across police departments, these figures should be interpreted cautiously. "Member-based definitions, such as those used in Los Angeles, more broadly classify any homicide involving a gang member as gang-related. In contrast, more conservative motive-based definitions, such as those used in Chicago, classify a homicide as gang-related only if the crime itself was *motivated* by gang activity and, therefore, would be more commonly associated with group-level actions such as turf defense, drug dealing, or existing gang conflicts" (Papachristos & Kirk, 2006, p. 69; see also Maxson & Klein, 1990, 1996).

62. Hughes, 2005, pp. 99–100.

63. Esbensen & Huizinga, 1993; Thornberry, Krohn, Lizotte, & Chard-Wierschem, 1993; Thornberry, Krohn, Lizotte, Smith, & Tobin, 2003; see also Battin, Hill, Abott, Catalano, & Hawkins, 1998.

64. Cureton, 2002; Decker & van Winkle, 1996; Horowitz, 1983; Hughes & Short, 2005; Joe & Robinson, 1980; Sanders, 1994; Short & Strodtbeck, 1965; Vigil, 2002.

65. Dawley, 1979; Sanchez, 2000; Scott, 2004; Shakur, 1994; Sikes, 1998.

66. Anderson, 1999, pp. 76–78.

67. Anderson, 1999, p. 33.

68. Felson (2006) suggests that much of this signaling involves a type of "fakery" that allows each participant to "draw upon the nastiness of the whole" (p. 313) and "gain a free ride on the toughness of others, even when they are not present" (p. 314).

69. Decker & van Winkle, 1996.

70. Decker, 1996; Hughes & Short, 2005.

71. E.g., Anderson, 1999; Kubrin & Weitzer, 2003.

72. This has led to a self-fulfilling prophecy in which the distrust and disrespect of police and other parts of the criminal justice system supports traditional stereotypes and thereby increases the initial targeting and repression of seemingly violent populations (Bjerregaard, 2003).

73. Horowitz, 1983; Hughes & Short, 2005.

74. Portes, 1998, p. 6; see also Bourdieu, 1986.

75. Of particular importance are the long-standing reluctance among white people to live in minority neighborhoods and the relatively recent departure of middle-class African Americans from inner-city ghettos (Massey, 1990; Massey & Denton, 1994; Wilson, 1987).

76. Kelley, 1995, pp. 217–218.

77. Rivera & Short, 1967; Short, Rivera, & Marshall, 1964.

78. Fleisher, 2002, 2006; see also Sullivan, 1989.

79. See Spergel, 1995.

80. Hughes & Short, in press.

81. Papachristos (2005b, p. 53) argues that this policy "has amounted to unintentional state-sponsored gang migration," which has spread the gang problem rather than solve it.

82. Short, 2006.

83. Klein, 1969, 1971.
84. Felson, 2006, p. 308.

REFERENCES

Amoroso, K. (2005). *House passes bill to make gang crimes federal offenses.* The United States Conference of Mayors. Retrieved May 7, 2006, from www.usmayors.org/uscm/us_mayor_newspaper/documents/05_23_05/gangs.asp.

Anderson, E. (1999). *Code of the streets: Decency, violence, and the moral life of the inner city.* New York: W. W. Norton and Company.

Battin, S. R., Hill, K. G., Abott, R. D., Catalano, R. F., & Hawkins, J. D. (1998). The contribution of gang membership to delinquency beyond delinquent friends. *Criminology, 36,* 93–115.

Becker, G. (1964). *Human capital: A theoretical and empirical analysis.* New York: Columbia University Press.

Bjerregaard, B. (2003). Antigang legislation and its potential impact: The promises and pitfalls. *Criminal Justice Policy Review, 14,* 171–192.

Brotherton, D. C., & Barrios, L. (2004). *The Almighty Latin King and Queen Nation: Street politics and the transformation of a New York City gang.* New York: Columbia University Press.

Bourdieu, P. (1986). The forms of capital. In J. Richardson (Ed.), *Handbook of Theory and Research for the Sociology of Education* (pp. 241–258). New York: Greenwood Press.

Chesney-Lind, M., Pasko, L., Marker, N., Matsen, A. J., Lawyer, K., Johnson, E., Gushiken, T., & Freeman, S. (2005). *Gangs in Hawaii: Past and present findings* (Vol. 1). Honolulu, HI: Center for Youth Research.

Coughlin, B. C., & Venkatesh, S. A. (2003). The urban street gang after 1970. *Annual Review of Sociology, 29,* 41–64.

Cureton, S. R. (2002). Introducing Hoover: I'll ride for you, gangsta. In C. R. Huff (Ed.), *Gangs in America* (3rd ed., pp. 83–100). Thousand Oaks, CA: Sage Publications.

Cummings, S., & Monti, D. J. (1993). Public policy and gangs: Social science and the urban underclass. In S. Cummings & D. J. Monti (Eds.), *Gangs: The origins and impact of contemporary youth gangs in the United States* (pp. 305–320). New York: State University of New York Press.

Curry, G. D., & Decker, S. H. (2002). Defining and measuring the prevalence of gangs. In G. D. Curry and S. H. Decker (Eds.), *Confronting gangs: Crime and community* (2nd ed., pp. 1–31). Los Angeles, CA: Roxbury Publishing.

Dawley, D. (1979). *A nation of lords: The autobiography of the Vice Lords* (2nd ed.). Garden City, NY: Anchor Books.

Decker, S. H. (1996). Collective and normative features of gang violence. *Justice Quarterly, 13,* 243–64.

Decker, S. H., & Van Winkle, B. (1996). *Life in the gang: Family, friends, and violence.* Cambridge, UK: Cambridge University Press.

Devine, J. (1997). *Maximum security: The culture of violence in inner-city schools.* Chicago: University of Chicago Press.

Egley, A., Jr., Howell, J. C., & Major, A. K. (2004). Recent patterns of gang problems in the United States: Results from the 1996–2002 National Youth Gang Survey. In F. Esbensen, S. G. Tibbetts, & L. Gaines (Eds.), *American youth gangs at the millennium* (pp. 90–108). Long Grove, IL: Waveland Press.

Elze, D. E., Stiffman, A. R., & Dorè, P. (1999). The association between types of violence exposure and youths' mental health problems. *International Journal of Adolescent Medicine and Health, 11,* 221–255.

Esbensen, F. A., & Huizinga, D. H. (1993). Gangs, drugs, and delinquency in a survey of urban youth. *Criminology, 31,* 565–89.

Esbensen, F. A., & Osgood, D. W. (1997). *National evaluation of G.R.E.A.T.* Washington, D.C.: U.S. Department of Justice, Office of Justice Programs, National Institute of Justice. (NIJ Research in Brief, No. NCJ 167264)

Federal Bureau of Investigation. (2005). *Crime in the United States 2004.* Washington, D.C.: U.S. Department of Justice, Federal Bureau of Investigation.

Felson, M. (2006). *Crime and nature.* Thousand Oaks, CA: Sage Publications.

Fischer, C. (1974). Toward a subcultural theory of urbanism. *American Journal of Sociology, 80,* 1319–1340.

Fleisher, M. S. (1998). *Dead end kids: Gang girls and the boys they know.* Madison, WI: University of Wisconsin Press.

Fleisher, M. S. (2002). Doing field research on diverse gangs: Interpreting youth gangs as social networks. In C. R. Huff (Ed.), *Gangs in America* (3rd ed., pp. 119–217). Thousand Oaks, CA: Sage Publications.

Fleisher, M. S., & Decker, S. H. (2001). An overview of the challenge of prison gangs. *Corrections Management Quarterly, 5*(1), 1–9.

Fox, J. A., & Zawitz, M. W. (2004). *Homicide trends in the United States.* Washington, D.C.: U.S. Department of Justice, Office of Justice Programs, Bureau of Justice Statistics.

Geis, G. 2002. Ganging up on gangs: Anti-loitering and public nuisance laws. In C. R. Huff (Ed.), *Gangs in America* (3rd ed., pp. 257–270). Thousand Oaks, CA: Sage Publications.

Hagedorn, J. M. (1994). Homeboys, dope fiends, legits, and new jacks. *Criminology, 32,* 197–219.

Hagedorn, J. M. (2002). Gangs and the informal economy. In C. R. Huff (Ed.), *Gangs in America* (3rd ed., pp. 101–120). Thousand Oaks, CA: Sage Publications.

Hagedorn, J. M., with Macon, P. (1988). *People and folks: Gangs, crime, and the underclass in a rustbelt city.* Chicago: Lake View Press.

Horowitz, R. (1983). *Honor and the American dream: Culture and identity in a Chicano community.* New Brunswick, NJ: Rutgers University Press.

Howell, J. C. (1998). *Youth gangs: An overview.* Washington, D.C.: U.S. Department of Justice, Office of Justice Programs, Office of Juvenile Justice and Delinquency Prevention.

Howell, J. C., & Egley, A., Jr. (2005). Moving risk factors into developmental theories of gang membership. *Youth Violence and Juvenile Justice, 3,* 334–354.

Howell, J. C., Moore, J. P., & Egley, A., Jr. (2002). The changing boundaries of youth gangs. In C. R. Huff (Ed.), *Gangs in America* (3rd ed., pp. 3–18). Thousand Oaks, CA: Sage Publications.

Hughes, L. A. 2005. Studying youth gangs: Alternative methods and conclusions. *Journal of Contemporary Criminal Justice, 21,* 98–119.

Hughes, L. A., & Short, J. F., Jr. (2005). Disputes involving youth street gang members: Micro-social contexts. *Criminology, 43,* 43–76.

Hughes, L. A., & Short, J. F., Jr. (2006). Youth gangs and unions: Civil and criminal remedies. *Trends in Organized Crime, 9*(4), 43–59.

Joe, K. A. (1994). The new criminal conspiracy? Asian gangs and organized crime in San Francisco. *Journal of Research in Crime and Delinquency, 31,* 390–415.

Joe, D., & Robinson, N. (1980). Chinatown's immigrant gangs: The new young warrior class. *Criminology, 18*, 337–345.

Katz, J., & Jackson-Jacobs, C. (2004). The criminologists' gang. In C. Sumner (Ed.), *The Blackwell companion to criminology* (pp. 91–124). Malden, MA: Blackwell Publishing.

Kelley, M. P. F. (1995). Social and cultural capital in the urban ghetto: Implications for the economic sociology of immigration. In A. Portes (Ed.), *The economic sociology of immigration: Essays on networks, ethnicity, and entrepreneurship* (pp. 213–247). New York: Russell Sage Foundation.

Klein, M. W. (1969). Gang cohesiveness, delinquency, and a street-work program. *Journal of Research in Crime and Delinquency, 6*, 135–166.

Klein, M. W. (1971). *Street gangs and street workers*. Englewood Cliffs, NJ: Prentice Hall.

Klein, M. W. (1995). *The American street gang: Its nature, prevalence, and control.* New York: Oxford University Press.

Kubrin, C. E., & Weitzer, R. (2003). Retaliatory homicide: Concentrated disadvantage and neighborhood culture. *Social Problems, 50*, 157–80.

Levin, M., & Pinkerson, D. (1994). "Gang war: Bangin' in Little Rock." [VHS Tape]. New York: Home Box Office, Inc.

Major, A. K., & Egley, A., Jr. (2002). *2000 survey of youth gangs in Indian country.* Washington, D.C.: U.S. Department of Justice, Office of Justice Programs, Office of Juvenile Justice and Delinquency Prevention.

Massey, D. S. (1990). American apartheid: Segregation and the making of the underclass. *American Journal of Sociology, 96*, 329–357.

Massey, D. S., & Denton, N. A. (1994). *American apartheid: Segregation and the making of the underclass.* Cambridge, MA: Harvard University Press.

Mauer, M. (1998). *Race to incarcerate*. New York: The New Press.

Maxson, C. L. (1998). *Gang members on the move.* Washington, D.C.: U.S. Department of Justice, Office of Justice Programs, Office of Juvenile Justice and Delinquency Prevention.

Maxson, C. L., & Klein, M. W. (1990). Street gang violence: Twice as great, or half as great? In C. R. Huff (Ed.), *Gangs in America* (pp. 71–100). Newbury Park, CA: Sage Publications.

Maxson, C. L., & Klein, M. W. (1996). Defining gang homicide: An updated look at member and motive approaches. In C. R. Huff (Ed.), *Gangs in America* (2nd ed., pp. 3–20). Thousand Oaks, CA: Sage Publications.

McGloin, J. M. (2005). Police intervention considerations of a network analysis of street gangs. *Criminology and Public Policy, 4*, 607–635.

Miller, W. B. (2001). *The growth of youth gang problems in the United States: 1970–1998.* Washington, D.C.: U.S. Department of Justice, Office of Justice Programs, Office of Juvenile Justice and Delinquency Prevention.

Monti, D. J. (1994). *Wannabe: Gangs in suburbs and schools.* Oxford, MA: Blackwell.

Moore, J. W. (1988). Introduction. In J. M. Hagedorn, with P. Macon (Eds.), *People and folks: Gangs, crime, and the underclass in a rustbelt city* (pp. 3–17). Chicago: Lake View Press.

Moore, J. W. (1991). *Going down to the barrio: Homeboys and homegirls in change.* Philadelphia: Temple University Press.

Padilla, F. (1993). The working gang. In S. Cummings & D. J. Monti (Eds.), *Gangs: The origins and impact of contemporary youth gangs in the United States* (pp. 173–192). Albany, NY: State University of New York Press.

Papachristos, A. V. (2005a). Interpreting inkblots: Deciphering and doing something about modern street gangs. *Criminology & Public Policy, 4*, 643–652.

Papachristos, A. V. (2005b). Gang world. *Foreign Policy, 147*, 48–55.

Papachristos, A. V. (2006). Social network analysis and gang research: Theory and methods. In J. F. Short, Jr. & L. A. Hughes (Eds.), *Studying youth gangs* (pp. 99–116). Lanham, MD: AltaMira Press.

Papachristos, A. V., & Kirk, D. S. (2006). Neighborhood effects on street gang behavior. In J. F. Short, Jr. & L. A. Hughes (Eds.), *Studying youth gangs* (pp. 63–84). Lanham, MD: AltaMira Press.

Petersilia, J. (2003). *When prisoners come home: Parole and prisoner reentry.* New York: Oxford University Press.

Portes, A. (1998). Social capital: Its origins and applications in modern society. *Annual Review of Sociology, 24*, 1–24.

Rivera, R. J., & Short, J. F., Jr. (1967). Significant adults, caretakers, and structures of opportunity: An exploratory study. *Journal of Research in Crime and Delinquency, 4*, 76–97.

Sampson, R. J. (1987). Urban black violence: The effect of male joblessness and family disruption. *American Journal of Sociology, 93*, 348–382.

Sanchez, R. (2000). *My bloody life: The making of a Latin King.* Chicago: Chicago Review Press.

Sanders, W. B. (1994). *Gangbangs and drive-bys: Grounded culture and juvenile gang violence.* New York: Aldine de Gruyter.

Scott, M. (2004). *Lords of Lawndale: My life in a Chicago white street gang.* Bloomington, IN: Authorhouse.

Shakur, S. (1994). *Monster: The autobiography of an L.A. gang member.* New York: Penguin Books.

Short, J. F., Jr. (1997). *Poverty, ethnicity, and violent crime.* Boulder, CO: Westview.

Short, J. F., Jr. (2006). Promoting research integrity in community-based intervention research. Paper presented at the Festschrift Symposium to Honor the Work of Irving A. Spergel, January 20, Chicago, IL.

Short, J. F., Jr., & Hughes, L. A. (2006). Moving gang research forward. In J. F. Short & L. A. Hughes (Eds.), *Studying youth gangs,* (pp. 225–238). Lanham, MD: AltaMira Press.

Short, J. F., Jr., & Hughes, L. A. (in press). Youth violence. In L. Kurtz (Ed.), *Encyclopedia of violence, peace and conflict* (2nd ed.). Oxford: Elsevier.

Short, J. F., Jr., Rivera, R., & Marshall, H. (1964). Adult-adolescent relations and gang delinquency. *Pacific Sociological Review, 7*, 59–65.

Short, J. F., Jr., & Strodtbeck, F. L. (1965). *Group process and gang delinquency.* Chicago: University of Chicago Press.

Sikes, G. (1998). *8 ball chicks.* New York: Anchor Books.

Snyder, H. N., & Sickmund, M. (2006). *Juvenile offenders and victims: 2006 national report.* Washington, D.C.: U.S. Department of Justice, Office of Justice Programs, Office of Juvenile Justice and Delinquency Prevention.

Spergel, I. A. (1995). *The youth gang problem: A community approach.* New York: Oxford University Press.

Spergel, I. A., & Curry, G. D. (1990). Strategies and perceived agency effectiveness in dealing with the youth gang problem. In C. R. Huff (Ed.), *Gangs in America* (pp. 388–309). Newbury Park, CA: Sage Publications.

Spergel, I. A., & Curry, G. D. (1993). The national youth gang survey: A research and development process. In A. P. Goldstein & C. R. Huff (Eds.), *The gang intervention handbook* (pp. 359–400). Champaign, IL: Research Press.

Stewart, G. (1998). Black codes and broken windows: The legacy of racial hegemony in anti-gang civil injunctions. *The Yale Law Journal, 107*, 2249–2279.

Sullivan, M. L. (1989). *Getting paid: Youth crime and work in the inner city.* Ithaca, NY: Cornell University Press.

The Sentencing Project. (2006). *Felony disenfranchisement laws in the United States.* Washington, D.C.: The Sentencing Project.

Thornberry, T. P., Krohn, M. D., Lizotte, A. J., & Chard-Wierschem, D. (1993). The role of juvenile gangs in facilitating delinquent behavior. *Journal of Research in Crime and Delinquency, 30,* 55–87.

Thornberry, T. P., Krohn, M. D., Lizotte, A. J., Smith, C. A., & Tobin, K. (2003). *Gangs and delinquency in developmental perspective.* Cambridge: Cambridge University Press.

Thrasher, F. M. (1927, abridged 1963). *The gang: A study of 1,313 gangs in Chicago.* Chicago: University of Chicago Press.

Uggen, C., & Manza, J. (2002). Democratic contraction? Political consequences of felon disenfranchisement in the United States. *American Sociological Review, 67,* 777–803.

Venkatesh, S. A. (1999). The financial activities of a modern American street gang. *NIJ Research Forum, 1,* 1–11.

Vigil, J. D. (2002). *A rainbow of gangs: Street cultures in the mega-city.* Austin, TX: University of Texas Press.

Vigil, J. D., & Yun, S. C. (2002). A cross-cultural framework for understanding gangs: Multiple marginality and Los Angeles. In C. R. Huff (Ed.), *Gangs in America* (3rd ed., pp. 161–174). Thousand Oaks, CA: Sage Publications.

Walker, S., Spohn, C., & DeLone, M. (2004). *Color of justice: Race, ethnicity, and crime in America* (3rd ed.). Belmont, CA: Wadsworth.

Webb, V. J., & Katz, C. M. (2003). Policing gangs in an era of community policing. In S. H. Decker (Ed.), *Policing gangs and youth violence* (pp. 17–49). Belmont, CA: Wadsworth.

Weisheit, R. A., & Wells, L. E. (2001). The perception of gangs as a problem in nonmetropolitan areas. *Criminal Justice Review, 26,* 170–192.

Wilson, W. J. (1987). *The truly disadvantaged: The inner city, the underclass, and public policy.* Chicago: University of Chicago Press.

Wilson, W. J. (1996). *When work disappears: The world of the new urban poor.* New York: Vintage Books.

www.chicagomobs.org. (2006). *People and folks.* Retrieved February 25, 2006, from www.chicagomobs.org/peopleandfolks.htm.

CHAPTER 5

Juvenile Sex Offending

Camille Gibson

J uvenile sex offending occurs when a juvenile engages in sexual behavior without the other person's true consent (i.e., consent with full knowledge and an absolute freedom to engage or not)[1] or engages in sexual behavior that is aggressive, exploitive, manipulative, or threatening. A juvenile sex offender must be of the age of juvenile responsibility to be served by a juvenile justice system (e.g., in Texas this age is 10 to 16 years old). Thus, people below the minimum age limit are not be considered juvenile sex offenders and people above the limit are adult sex offenders. Notably, the upper age limit is usually 17 years, although it may be lower in some states, plus some states do not have a minimum age limit (e.g., Florida and Idaho). The victim may be of any age and the behaviors are numerous.

Sex offenses may be nonphysical sexual acts, such as making obscene phone calls, voyeurism, exhibitionism, and public masturbation, or sex acts involving physical contact, such as fondling, penetration of another's body orifice (for self-gratification), prostitution, coercing others into prostitution, forcible rape or sexual homicide, and the making or possession of child pornography.[2] What constitutes a sexual offense varies from state to state in terms of specifics. In Texas, for example, if two 14-year-olds agree to sexual intercourse, both could be charged with committing a felonious sexual offense. Generally, the law assumes that people under the age of maturity are incapable of consenting to sexual activity.

Some instances of sex offending are manifestations of a sexual disorder or paraphilia as classified by the *Diagnostic and Statistical Manual IV-Text Revision* (known as *DSM-IV-TR*) of the American Psychiatric Association. These acts include exhibitionism, fetishism (when it involves defacing the belongings of someone who does not consent, such as masturbating on a victim's shoe), frotteurism, pedophilia, sexual masochism during which a person is harmed, and voyeurism. The *DSM-IV-TR* also mentions paraphilia unspecified, which would include less common paraphilia such as zoophilia, necrophilia, autoerotic asphyxiation, and unsolicited scatologia (obscene phone calls). For the behaviors behind the paraphilia to be diagnosable disorders, the person must derive pleasure from the activities.

Usually, diagnoses of paraphilia are reserved for adults[3] and the behavior must exist for at least six months and interfere with life activities. Critics of the *DSM-IV-TR* question such criteria, stating that the six-month requirement is an arbitrary one.[4] It might also be argued that the age limit for these diagnoses (at least 16 years) and the five-year age difference between victim and offender requirements are also arbitrary. In the case of the latter, there may even be cultural implications.[5] Regardless, if not a diagnosable disorder, the paraphilic activity need only occur once for it to be an offense. Indeed, one of juvenile justice's most famous cases, *In re Gault*, began with a paraphilic act. The case involved a 15-year-old boy, Gerald Gault who was accused of an act of unsolicited telephone scatologia. However, whether Gault actually had a paraphilia is unclear.

A number of public misperceptions regarding sex offenders exist. Karen Terry notes that in 1950 Paul Tappan described the following myths, which persist today:[6]

> **Myth 1:** Sex offenders are oversexed, hence castration would cure them. Actually, sex offenders are more likely to be undersexed and the motivation for offending is often not sex but a sense of power and control.
> **Myth 2:** Most offenders are homicidal. Indeed, most cases of sex offending are minor offenses. In 1999, for example, there were nine cases of juvenile sexual homicide known to law enforcement which represented 12 percent of all such cases that year.[7]
> **Myth 3:** Most offenders recidivate. In actuality, studies reveal that as few as 5 percent of people who commit rape or sexual assault recidivate.[8] For juvenile males, most studies report sexual offense recidivism rates from 8 to 14 percent.[9] These recidivism rates are lower than rates for nonsexual offending, which are commonly reported to be as high as 58 percent.[10]
> **Myth 4:** Most offenders have an escalation in the seriousness of their behavior. Rather, most sex offenders limit themselves to a behavior with which they are comfortable.
> **Myth 5:** Future offending may be predicted. At best, mental health experts may assess the dangerousness of a sex offender, but they are unable to predict recidivism.
> **Myth 6:** Legislation will remove the problem. Indeed, legislation is of comfort to the public, but without the right legislation involving a recognition of the heterogeneity of sex offenders and the need to use appropriate responses, laws will do little to protect the public.

Other myths include the idea that most sex offending is done by strangers and that sex offenders are almost exclusively adults and male. Unmistakably, juvenile sex offenders do exist, and they tend to victimize relatives or friends over whom they have some control.[11] Retrospective accounts from adult sex offenders indicate that about a half of them begin sex offending as juveniles.[12] Although it was once commonly thought that juvenile sexual activity was largely mere innocent exploratory play, today, it is viewed more seriously because it is now understood that nondeviant sexual behavior often precedes juvenile sex offending.[13] Furthermore, for some juveniles, sex offending may be one of a range of delinquent activities.[14]

PREVALENCE

Data available on juvenile sex offending are problematic. Notably, sex offending is grossly underreported, especially for juvenile sex offending. Because most cases of juvenile sex offending involve a perpetrator who is a relative or family friend, the victim, and in some cases the victim's family, are often reluctant to report the incidents to the authorities. The younger the juvenile sex offender, the less likely it is that the offending will be taken seriously by the adults around him or her. Hence, official data from law enforcement are limited to cases reported. Given the guilt and stigmatization associated with sex offenses, self-report data are suspect because many sex offenders underreport their behaviors.[15] Even the often-referenced annual Child Maltreatment Reports from the U.S. Department of Health and Human Services[16] is weakened by the fact that it captures only cases known to and deemed credible by child protective services. Victimization surveys such as the National Crime Victimization Survey (NCVS) are also utilized; the NCVS, however, fails to capture the most vulnerable victims of juvenile sexual offending, youth under 12 years of age.

Nevertheless, from the data available, juveniles account for approximately 17 percent of all forcible rapes; 21 percent of other sex offenses;[17] 40 percent of sexual assaults against children under 6 years old; 39 percent of victimizations of children 6 to 11 years old; 27 percent of older juvenile victimizations; and 4 percent of adult sexual victimizations.[18] Although sexual aggression may be observed in very young children, it becomes more evident by ages 6 to 9 years.[19] This may be the result of the youngest victims' inability to articulate their victimization coherently. Significantly, sexual offenses are more likely to be reported to law enforcement when the offender is male, black, a stranger or nonintimate relative, and uses a firearm, and when there are multiple offenders. The most common age range of reported perpetrators is 12 to 14 years (accounting for 40 percent of rapes and sexual assaults) followed by 15- to 17-year-olds (accounting for 25 percent of rapes and sexual assaults).[20] Of all the cases of child maltreatment known to child protective services, nearly three-quarters of the perpetrators of sexual abuse are friends or neighbors.[21] Although reports of sex offending increased in the 1980s, reports of child sexual victimizations declined substantially in the 1990s. The reasons for these recent declines are not clear.[22]

RISK FACTORS

Risk factors are usually described in terms of individual characteristics and environmental factors. Individual indicators of risk include mental illness with a biological component such as a neurological problem, the presence of paraphilia, chemical changes in the brain, and increased testosterone levels. Other individual risk factors are attachment difficulties, low self-esteem, social incompetence, poor academic performance, learning difficulties, sexual ignorance, cognitive distortions, deviant sexual arousal, and a lack of empathy. Among juveniles who persist with sex offending into adulthood, low intelligence and poor school attainment appear to be risk factors.[23] Individual risk factors emphasized for juvenile sexual homicide offenders include low birth weight and birth complications, enuresis, alienation, rage, cruelty to animals as a child, paraphilia, and excitement from sexually violent fantasies.[24]

Environmental risk factors commonly include family dysfunction, lack of parental sensitivity, sexual and physical abuse, a substance-abusing mother, and exposure to hardcore pornography by age 6.[25] One study comparing 29 juvenile sex offenders and 32 nonsex offenders with conduct disorder concluded that the sex offenders were significantly more likely to have been from families with substantial deception, including family secrecy, lies, and myths.[26] On a less common environmental note, where animals are accessible, Fleming, Jory, and Burton found juvenile sex with nonhuman animals to be strongly related to juvenile sex offending against people.[27]

Notably, many of the risk factors for juvenile sex offending are also risk factors for nonsexual juvenile offending.[28] Thus, on the one hand, it appears that juvenile sex offending may simply be one of many maladaptive responses to the same sorts of stimuli. For example, Katz described offending in terms of thrill seeking.[29] Evidence suggests that indeed much juvenile offending, including juvenile sex offending, involves some pursuit of a thrill.[30] On the other hand, it appears that juvenile sex offenders experience more neglect, emotional abuse, physical abuse, and sexual abuse than nonsex offenders.[31] Even among juvenile sex offenders, evidence suggests that the intensity of the risk factors may vary in a predictive manner. One study of juvenile sex offenders by Smith, Wampler, Jones, and Reifman[32] found that among the most high-risk juvenile sex offenders there were reports of more social discomfort, lower self-esteem, more aggression, more extreme sexual fantasies, and less family cohesion.

Problematic in deciphering risk factors for juvenile sex versus nonsex offending is that many studies with these comparison examine incapacitated juveniles. Hence, their results are usually superficially more indicative of system practices than of offending etiology.[33] Nonetheless, the notion that the risk factors for both sex and nonsex offending might be more similar than not may be a valid one, because in most cases both types of offending cease by adulthood. This supports the notion put forth by the likes of Moffit that much juvenile offending is a developmental manifestation of youth.[34] Thus, it is often outgrown. Consider, for example, the circumstances of juvenile offending. Juveniles are more likely to sexually offend and to nonsexually offend in groups than adults.[35] One account of junior high school boys engaging in the group rape of a peer acquaintance may be found in the chapter on "trains" in the 1994 bestselling autobiographical book *Makes Me Wanna Holler* by acclaimed journalist Nathan McCall. McCall, who participated in the act, was 14 years old at the time. Notably, solo juvenile sex offenders tend to be older than those who offend in groups.[36]

For the most part, the literature discusses risk of juvenile sex offending in terms of recidivism. Yet, longitudinal studies of juvenile sex reoffending are few and often the samples involve fewer than 100 subjects.[37] It is commonly reported that juvenile sex offense recidivism is between 8 and 14 percent, while juvenile nonsex offense recidivism is between 16 and 54 percent.[38] When juvenile sex offenders do recidivate, it is more likely to be with a nonsexual offense.[39]

Juvenile risk of sexual reoffending is commonly assessed with some combination of instruments, namely the Juvenile Sex Offender Assessment Protocol II (J-SOAP-II), the Static 99 (which was developed for adult male sex offenders), the Rapid Risk Assessment for Sex Offenses Recidivism (RRASOR), the Matrix 2000, the Sex Offender Risk Appraisal Guide (SORAG), the Minnesota Sex Offender Screening Tool Revised (MnSOST-R), and the Juvenile Risk Assessment Scale (JRAS). A significant shortcoming of these risk assessment instruments is that most were normed on adult sex offenders and all were normed on males.

In terms of the risk of being victimized, a person's characteristics are significant in determining the dynamics of the sexual offense. People who are perceived to be vulnerable are at greater risk of juvenile sexual victimization. Juvenile sex offenders mostly choose younger victims. In cases in which the victim is an elderly female, however, the offense is often characterized by excessive beating and stabbing. This suggests an intent to both control and punish the victim.[40] Male victims, older victims, and victims who resist experience more aggression than others.[41] From a study of 126 juvenile sex offenders, Hunter and colleagues reported that the juvenile child molesters tended to act alone, have male victims, and victimize a relative. In cases of juvenile sexual homicide, they found that victim choice was largely a matter of access to acquaintances or strangers, and the victimization was accomplished with deception and planning.[42]

Hunter and colleagues offer the following description of a violent juvenile sexual offense:

In 1992, police arrested two brothers, ages 13 and 15, for the rape and attempted murder of a 36-year-old woman. The crime was particularly heinous because the youthful offenders emotionally and physically terrorized the victim. After the rape, the victim asked the brothers if they planned to kill her. When the 13-year-old said yes, the victim asked if she could look at her mother's photograph first. The youngest offender removed the unframed photo from her dresser and tore it into small pieces in front of the kneeling victim. Then, for no apparent reason, he began cutting and stabbing her. She started screaming, and when her neighbors responded to investigate, the subjects fled. As a result of the attack, the victim suffered partial paralysis on the left side of her body. The emotional scars may never heal.[43]

ETIOLOGY OF JUVENILE SEX OFFENDING

What constitutes a sex offense has varied in time and place through centuries and across cultures. For example, in ancient societies such as Egypt and Greece, involving young boys in sexual acts was fairly common. In Egypt, it was even considered beneficial to the boys.[44] Taking such liberties with children has not been a part of U.S. history. Until the early 1900s, deviant sexual behavior was largely regarded as a mental illness until social activists pushed for legislation to criminalize certain sex acts. One exception to deviant juvenile sexual behavior that has been illegal in America since the 1600s is bestiality.[45] This was usually referenced in statutes under buggery or unnatural sex acts and regarded as cruelty to animals. Hensley and colleagues describe a 1948 study by Kinsey, Wardell, Pomeroy, and Martin involving more than 5,000 males, which revealed that 40 to 50 percent of the adolescent males who grew up on farms had had sexual contact with an animal. Hensley and colleagues attribute the overall decline in cases of bestiality in the United States to a shift away from a predominantly farming economy.[46]

According to Terry, one particularly influential group in criminalizing sexual deviance was the Women's Christian Temperance Union (WCTU), which was particularly active from 1874 into the early 1900s. The WCTU and other segments of society were concerned about the sexual exploitation of young girls, the prostitution of both boys and girls, and widespread sexually transmitted diseases among youngsters. Thus, they lobbied against prostitution and for raising the age of consent to older than 10 years of age. By the 1920s, they had achieved the latter goal in that most of the country had ages of consent between 14 and 18 years old.[47]

Another wave of female-led activism in the 1960s led to the development of feminist ideas to attempt to explain the prevalence of males as sex offenders. A central theme was that male rape of females was facilitated by a cultural socialization that advocated male dominance,[48] sexual entitlement over women,[49] and a need for little intimacy and empathy.[50]

Most theories of sex offending, however, focus on the nature of family socialization as opposed to cultural socialization because sex-offending behaviors are not societal norms. They discuss individual characteristics, age, gender, and family circumstances in terms of some regressed development, cognitive distortion, improper learning, or biology. Frequently advocated in the literature is the idea that sexual deviance is learned or develops as an alternative way of relating to others because of social awkwardness. Supposedly, these problems begin in early childhood within a family or other primary social context that is lacking quality family caring. Therein, the juvenile is commonly miseducated sexually by sexual victimization or by witnessing or experiencing extreme physical abuse. If the abuse becomes associated with a sexual stimuli then sexual offending becomes more likely.

Deviant sexual fantasies are often discussed in the literature. However, with the exception of juvenile sexual homicide, the evidence of fantasies as connected to sex offending is unclear. Additionally, such fantasies often are not disclosed or disclosed in their entirety.[51] In response, polygraph testing has become common practice in therapeutic settings. It is difficult to ascertain whether the fantasies of sex offenders are more deviant or more frequent than that of nonsex offenders or even nonoffenders.[52]

Nevertheless, clinical efforts to understand juvenile sexual offending have led to the following commonly referenced typologies of juvenile sex offenders:

- O'Brien and Bera proposed a taxonomy with seven types: naïve experimenters, undersocialized child exploiters, sexual aggressives, sexual compulsives, disturbed impulsives, group influenced, and pseudosocialized.[53]
- Pithers, Gray, Busconi, and Houchens' typology of child sex offenders identified five types: sexually aggressive, nonsymptomatic, highly traumatized, abusive reactive, and rule breaker.[54]
- Prentsky, Harris, Frizzell, and Righthand identified six types: child molesters, rapists, sexually reactive children, fondlers, paraphilic offenders, and unclassifiable.[55]
- Worling offers four types: antisocial impulsive, unusual/isolated, overcontrolled/reserved, and confident/aggressive.[56]

THEORIES

Because juvenile sex offending involves a wide range of behaviors, not surprisingly the explanations are also wide ranging. Primarily, these explanations include elements of biology and psychology. The biological explanations may describe violent offenses as a result of experiences of physical abuse at a young age to a point at which the abuse produced certain chemical changes in the brain that make aggression more likely.[57] Although such changes might increase the likelihood of aggression in general, the aggression can become sexualized if the offender has learned to associate sexual stimuli with aggression.[58] For example, Myers offers an example of how such changes might have occurred in a 20-year-old sexual homicide offender. Myers speculates that the young man in his case study may have come to associate relations with a woman to violence from his experiences as a child, during which time he was cradled by his mother while his father punched her.[59] Others attribute violent sex offending to increased levels of testosterone. For the most part, however, when violence is involved, the behavior is described as primarily an act of domination and anger as opposed to sex.

Regarding psychological explanations for sex offending, Sigmund Freud was one of the first to theorize about deviant sexuality. Since then others

have built on his idea that sexual deviance may be the result of being fix-
ated in an earlier stage of development.[60] The fixation is usually the out-
come of experiences in the family context that hinder development,
locking the individual into a younger, often egocentric stage characterized
by diminished empathy.[61]

Among the most frequently used developmental constructs to explain
sex offending is attachment. Attachment theories, which as a group have
substantial empirical support, assert that parental insensitivity, especially
involving mothers, can lead to poor bonding or attachment experiences in
infancy and early childhood.[62] The result may be social incompetence that
could manifest in sex offending that indicates a preference for minors.
Alternately, the social incompetence could lead to feelings of frustrations
that manifest in sexual aggression toward people of any age. Not surprisingly, then, recent findings suggest that maternal substance abuse (which
can negatively affect maternal sensitivity) is a significant predictor of poor
treatment performance among juvenile sex offenders.[63] Attachment theorists include Bartholomew, Ward, Hudson, Marshall, and Siegert.[64]

Other theories of juvenile sex offending focus on cognition, learning,
and family dynamics. Cognitive explanations largely discuss the development of thinking errors that rationalize the offending behavior. Finkelhor
offered a cognitive explanation of sex offending with four propositions:
(1) a motivation exists to victimize a minor who is perceived as sexually
more enticing; (2) cognitive distortions become strong enough to overcome internal inhibitions; (3) external inhibitions are overcome with the
possibility of access to the child, absent a guardian to stop the motivated
offender; and (4) victim resistance is overcome often by selecting minors
perceived to be most vulnerable.[65]

Learning theories tend to describe the process of learning to sexually
offend as largely no different from other forms of learning involving modeling and behavior reinforcements.[66] Family dynamic theories focus on sex
offending within families by placing the responsibility for the offending on
the family unit as opposed to the perpetrator or the victim.[67] Many of the
theories of juvenile sex offending are integrative.

Children Who Sexually Offend

Children (defined as people who are prepubescent or usually younger than
12 years old) who sexually offend are usually referred to as "children with sexual behavior problems." Although most of these sexual behavior problems
cease by adulthood,[68] for a few children careful intervention is necessary. A
classification of sexual behavior problems in children by Berliner, Manaois, and
Monastersky illustrates this point. The classifications are as follows:[69]

- Precocious sexual behavior, for example, intercourse or oral genital contact between peers without force or coercion. This behavior may reflect
  a child's own victimization or some exposure to the behavior. The
  behavior may stop on its own or with some intervention.

- Inappropriate sexual behavior, such as ongoing or public masturbation, highly sexualized behavior, or sexual preoccupation. This may indicate early stages of deviant sexual arousal.
- Coercive sexual behavior, during which sex acts occur by threat or by force, or between people with significant disparity in size. These sexual behaviors are more about manifesting hostility than sexual gratification. Overall, these children are more prone to engage in nonsexual offending than repeated sex offending.

The general assumption about children who offend sexually is that they have been sexually miseducated, possibly by some form of victimization. Thus, their "offending" is simply a manifestation of learned behaviors. When victimized, these children may have been rewarded in some way, thus reinforcing the sexual behaviors. They may also have learned to use sexually deviant behavior to cope with an inability to form proper attachments, a problem which may have developed as a result of the child's own inappropriate behaviors, feelings of distrust of others, or having a sense of betrayal and stigmatization.[70] Often, sexualized behaviors in children do not alarm the adults who observe it, so they do not alert law enforcement or seek therapeutic intervention. Nevertheless, because sexually inappropriate behaviors in children may indeed harm victims or indicate the early beginnings of more serious sex offending, they warrant attention.

Juvenile Females Who Sexually Offend

Juvenile female sex offending has long been underreported. This might be attributed to both a societal belief that female sex offending is most rare, and to an endorsement of certain sexual behavior from females that would be most unacceptable from males.[71] These behaviors include female sexual aggressiveness toward a male, even a much younger male, and exhibitionism. Not surprisingly therefore, the literature on juvenile female sex offending is sparse and largely anecdotal. Of course, the result is that juvenile female sex offenders are at some disadvantage in the assessment and treatment of their condition. The extent to which juvenile females recidivate sexually is unknown.[72]

From cases known to law enforcement, juvenile females account for 1 percent of juvenile arrests for forcible rape and, excluding prostitution, 7 percent of juvenile arrests for sex offenses.[73] The National Center on Sexual Behavior of Youth offers the following facts from the literature on female juvenile sex offenders: The average offender is 14 years old; unlikely to have an exclusive attraction to one type of person; offend nonaggressively; rarely offend against adults; usually select a relative or acquaintance as victim whether male or female; and will otherwise be well-functioning people. Additionally, the National Center on Sexual Behavior of Youth reports that juvenile female offenders markedly differ from their male counterparts in that their accounts of their own childhood sexual victimization suggest victimization at younger ages and from numerous perpetrators. Their physical and sexual abuse is also reported as more severe and extensive. Regarding juvenile female prostitution, ongoing trauma among sexually abused adolescents precedes their entry into this activity.[74] Indeed, the retrospective accounts of adult female prostitutes reveal that 65 to 95 percent of them were sexually assaulted as children.[75] Clearly, more research on the occurrence, assessment, and treatment of juvenile female sex offending is necessary.

Legal Responses to Sex Offending

The current legal response to sex offending is largely punitive, wide in reach, and narrowly therapeutic. This legal posture has its roots in the 1970's notion that treatment for sex offenders is largely ineffective, a position that the therapeutic community no longer endorses.[76] For juvenile sex offenders, the legal response ranges from doing nothing to sentencing offenders to long periods of incarceration. In most states, only some juvenile sex offenders must register, often at the discretion of a judge, and they may also be subject to community notification laws.

Sex offender registries began as an investigative tool for law enforcement. They have become a civic tool with the intent of public protection and specific deterrence of potential sex offenders.[77] Some sex offender registries are available to anyone via the Internet with photographs and details of the person's sex-offending history. Arguably, the registries are not particularly effective because many studies indicate that most sex offenders, especially juvenile sex offenders, do not recidivate; plus the law does not protect the public from offenders yet to offend.[78]

Sexual violent predator (SVP) laws exist in some states to monitor and treat the most dangerous sex offenders. SVP laws require the civil commitment and mental health treatment of sexual offenders deemed prone to predatory violence after the offender has completed a criminal sentence and until such time when the person is deemed no longer predatory and sexually violent. These laws have been controversial given their imposition on the offenders' individual liberties, including those of juveniles who, unlike adults, do not have the benefit of full due process.

Often, the legal response to sex offending comes from a few cases sensationalized by the media, which, although often shocking to the public, constitute a minority of all sex offending—for example, the case of sex offender Wesley Alan Dodd. Dodd is an example of an infamous, calculating sex offender who began offending at age 13 with exhibitionism and soon thereafter progressed to the molestation of young boys and eventually sexual homicide. He was caught at age 28 after attempting to abduct a 6-year-old boy from a movie theater. In Dodd's home, investigators found a torture rack and a diary detailing his heinous acts and plans. He was executed in the state of Washington in 1993 for the 1989 killing of three boys, one of whom he also raped. They were William Neer (age 11), his brother Cole Neer (age 10), and Lee Iseli (age 4). In 1990, Washington became the first state to enact sex offender community notification laws.

On the federal level, the Jacob Wetterling Crimes Against Children and Sexually Violent Offenders Registration Act followed as an attachment to President Clinton's famed Violent Crime Control and Law Enforcement Act of 1994. Jacob Wetterling was an 11-year-old Minnesota boy who, in 1989, was abducted while bicycling. The Wetterling Act requires at least a 10-year registration for sex offenses against people of any age and for certain nonsexual offenses against children (e.g., false imprisonment of a minor) and the lifelong registration of some offenders.

Thereafter, the Megan's Law phenomenon began. The federal Megan's Law was adopted from a New Jersey law by that name. In 1994, a 7-year-old New Jersey girl was raped and murdered after having been invited by her twice-convicted sex offender neighbor, Jesse Timmendequas, to see his new puppy. New Jersey's Megan's Law was enacted that same year, and it required that sex offender registration information be made public. The New Jersey law was adopted federally in 1996, but the federal version left it to state entities to ascertain what type of information would be made public and how. States had the option of adopting the federal law if they wanted access to specific crime prevention federal funds, including funding to maintain a state offender registry. Of course, the law does not protect the public from potential sex offenders,[79] of whom some will be juveniles. Also, in many states, deregistration from the state register is possible after a period of time, usually 10 years with no new sex offenses.

Another significant law was enacted in 1996, the Pam Lychner Sexual Offender Tracking and Identification Act. It was an amendment to the Wetterling Act of 1994. Pam Lychner was a realtor who was attacked while meeting a potential client. The Lychner Act requires the lifelong registration for sex offenders who are convicted of multiple registration offenses or an aggravated sex offense. The Wetterling Act was further amended in 2000 by the Campus Sex Crimes Prevention Act, which requires that when a registered offender becomes employed or enrolled at an institution of higher education, he or she must report this status to law enforcement with jurisdiction over the institution.

Then, in July 2006, the federal Adam Walsh Child Protection and Safety Act became law. Adam Walsh, the 6-year-old son of John Walsh (who subsequently became the host of the television program *America's Most Wanted*), was abducted and decapitated in 1981 at the age of 6. The Adam Walsh Law requires the integration of state sex offender registries into the federal sex offender registry, which must also be made available to the public. It created mandatory minimum sentences for the most serious offenders against children and stiffer penalties for offenders who fail to comply with registration requirements. It eliminated statutes of limitations for felony sex offenses against children and provides funds for both the civil commitment of sex offenders and the training of law enforcement to stop child sexual victimizations facilitated via the Internet.

Other significant legal developments have occurred at the state level affecting juvenile sex offenders. Notably, in some states, such as Texas, whether a juvenile sex offender must register is left to the discretion of a judge. Also in Texas, all juveniles committed to a state residential facility must submit a deoxyribonucleic acid (DNA) sample for a DNA bank. Additionally, the state's juvenile sex offenders have to transfer to another school if their victim attends the same school and makes a request for that to happen. In other states, for example, New York and Florida, juveniles face mandatory transfers for certain sex offenses.

Another significant legal development involving juvenile sex offending is the application of the polygraph test. Although not admitted into court as evidence in cases of criminal prosecution, many courts will require the use of polygraphs to aid in the assessment of sex offenders. Both juveniles and adults, fearing legal and societal reprisal, tend to otherwise underreport the nature and frequency of their sex offending.[80] Data from the use of polygraphs with adult sex offenders reveal that they tend to overreport childhood victimization and underreport their sex offending as juveniles. The laws on polygraph use vary by state. In some cases, in which the offender faces possible additional liability from self-incrimination, polygraph use might be part of an immunity agreement.

Encouragingly, state laws have had a positive impact on the quality of therapeutic services that juvenile sex offenders receive. For example, in Texas, sex offender treatment may only be administered by a psychotherapist holding both a mental health license and a sex offender treatment provider license, both of which require continuing education to be maintained.

Treatment Programming

Given the facts established about juvenile sex offenders, it is largely accepted among sex offender treatment providers that an appropriate treatment approach in many cases will be a multisystemic one. Such treatment often means a collaborative effort involving the juvenile and his or her family, social services, the school, therapeutic personnel, and juvenile justice personnel. It is also understood that, unless there are significant consequences for noncompliance with treatment, many juvenile sex offenders will not comply.[81]

Therapeutic approaches to sex offending universally involve cognitive-behavioral therapy toward an acknowledgment of the juvenile's sex-offending cycle(s). These cycles involve moving from thoughts that lead to certain feeling that then manifest in inappropriate sexual behaviors. The cycle may be triggered by feelings, but between the feelings and the sexual behavior, the thoughts involve choices. Thus, therapy largely involves teaching sex offenders to become aware of their cycles and learning to make the right choices. For juveniles, this often involves sex education to correct any distorted thinking. To this end, triggers that the sex offenders might have mislabeled as causes are usually reframed as mere triggers.[82] Some juvenile sex offenders, therefore, may have multiple problems that establish the triggers. For example, learning difficulties or social rejection may trigger negative thoughts and feelings, which then trigger the juvenile's offense cycle.

Additionally, because a lack of parental (especially maternal) sensitivity is related to sex offending,[83] family treatment goals usually include educating parents to increase their awareness of all of their children and the family dynamics. This should result in improved supervision of the juvenile sex offender and the protection of any victims or potential child victims in the home.[84]

In rare cases, juveniles with severe paraphilic urges may receive hormonal treatments, such as cyproterone acetate, medroxyprogesterone, or gonadotrophin-releasing hormone analogs. These drugs alter testosterone levels to decrease libido, sexual fantasies, and deviant sexuality. The full effects of these drugs on juveniles are unknown and adverse effects potentially are severe. Thus, their administration is usually limited to 16-year-olds or older with careful medical monitoring.[85] Nonpharmacological ways of addressing paraphilic urges include systematic desensitization, satiation training, and covert sensitization.[86]

Successful programs (such as Florida's 12-month Specialized Treatment Program for Juvenile Sex Offenders) include a relapse prevention plan and, as necessary, anger management, communication, and social skills training.[87] Of course, any substance abuse issues need to be addressed. In cases in which a dual diagnosis involves sexually abusive behaviors and substance abuse, both are considered primary disorders because each condition will likely facilitate the existence of the other. Alcohol, for example, may be abused to numb guilt and reduce empathy, thus increasing the likelihood of a sexual offense.[88]

CONCLUSION

More research is needed to understand who sex offenders are and the circumstances surrounding juvenile sex offending. Because many risk factors for juvenile sex and nonsex offending overlap, more qualitative studies, followed by generalizable studies, are necessary to clarify the etiology of the two classes of behaviors.

Additionally, even though recidivism rates of juvenile sex offenders are low, the need remains for better assessments and treatment models designed specifically for juveniles. These models should improve the interventions with female juvenile sex offenders and the efforts to recognize early warning signs of those juveniles who are likely to persist with sex offending. Presently, despite the fact that it is clear that juveniles and adults differ substantially in sex offending and in their treatment needs, much of the programmatic approaches available to juvenile sex offenders are based on findings about adult male sex offenders. For example, it may be beneficial to remove an adult male child molester from his home if children are there. For a juvenile child molester, however, the family disruption that such a removal could cause might not be in the best interest of the juvenile or his or her family.[89]

Furthermore, certain potential therapeutic barriers must be addressed. Consider, for example, the legal and therapeutic discordance in Kentucky's 2004 state Supreme Court ruling in *Welch v. Commonwealth*. The case requires that Miranda warnings be given in therapeutic settings before juvenile sex offenders answer questions from therapists because such questioning amounts to a custodial interrogation. Data also suggest the need for proactive measures to improve parenting and family dynamics to eliminate familial risk factors.

All of the above suggestions will likely require a reeducation of the public on the heterogeneity of sex offenders in terms of levels of risk, age, and gender. This should help to dissuade politicians from pandering to moral panic by creating laws that sweep too broadly. In so doing, more progress may be made toward limiting sex offender registries and community notification for juveniles to only the most dangerous offenders. In all of this, however, it is still advised to heed the words of people like Sara Steen who cautioned against seeing juvenile sex offending as purely a disorder manifestation as opposed to an offense.[90]

NOTES

1. Finkelhor, 1979.
2. Terry, 2006.
3. Council on Sex Offender Treatment, 2004.
4. O'Donohue, Regev, & Hagstrom, 2000.
5. Martin & Pruett, 1998.
6. Terry, 2006.
7. Myers, 2002.
8. Bureau of Justice Statistics, hereafter BJS, 2003.
9. Vandiver, 2006.
10. National Center on Sexual Behavior of Youth, hereafter NCSBY, 2003.
11. NCSBY, 2004.
12. Saleh & Vincent, 2004.
13. Martin & Pruett, 1998.
14. Canter & Kirby, 1995.
15. Hindman & Peters, 2001.
16. U.S. Department of Health and Human Services, Administration on Children, Youth and Families, hereafter USDHHS, 2006.
17. Federal Bureau of Investigation, hereafter FBI, 2002.
18. Snyder & Sickmund, 2000.
19. Araji, 1997.
20. Hart & Rennison, 2003.
21. USDHHS, 2006.
22. Barbaree & Marshall, 2006.
23. Beckett, 1999.
24. Myers, 2002.
25. Righthand & Welch, 2001.
26. Baker, Tabacoff, Tornusciolo, & Eisenstadt, 2003.
27. Fleming, Jory, & Burton, 2002.
28. Epps, 1999; Terry, 2006; van Wijk et al., 2005.
29. Katz, 1988.
30. Brady & Donenberg, 2006.
31. Fleming, Jory, & Burton, 2002.
32. Smith, Wampler, Jones, & Reifman, 2005.

33. Garfinkle, 2003.
34. Moffit, 1993.
35. Garfinkle, 2003, discussing Zimring, 1998.
36. Bijleveld & Hendriks, 2003; Porter & Alison, 2006.
37. Fritz, 2003.
38. Fritz, 2003.
39. Prentsky, Harris, Frizzell, & Righthand, 2000.
40. Safarik, 2002.
41. Hunter, Hazelwood, & Slesinger, 2000.
42. Hunter et al., 2000.
43. Hunter et al., 2000.
44. Terry, 2006.
45. Hensley, Tallichet, & Singer, 2006.
46. Hensley et al., 2006.
47. Terry, 2006, referencing Odem, 1995.
48. Terry, 2006.
49. Hanson, Gizzarelli, & Scott, 1994.
50. Lisak & Ivan, 1995.
51. Hindman & Peters, 2001.
52. Terry, 2006.
53. O'Brien & Bera, 1986.
54. Pithers, Gray, Busconi, & Houchens, 1998.
55. Prentsky et al., 2000.
56. Worling, 2001.
57. Goleman, 1995, referring to remarks by Adrian Raine, 1995.
58. Myers, 2002.
59. Myers, 2002, p. 67.
60. Freeman-Longo, 1982, as cited in Ryan, 1997; Groth, 1979; Steele, 1986.
61. Ryan, 1997.
62. Bogaerts, Declercq, Vanheule, & Palmans, 2005.
63. Kelley, Lewis, & Sigal, 2004.
64. Bartholomew, 1990; Ward, Hudson, Marshall, & Siegert, 1995.
65. Finkelhor, 1984.
66. For example, Freeman-Longo, 1982, as cited in Ryan, 1997.
67. For example, Giaretto, et al. 1978, as referenced in Ryan, 1997.
68. NCSBY, 2005.
69. Berliner, Manaois, & Monastersky, 1986.
70. Erooga & Masson, 1999.
71. NCSBY, 2004.
72. NCSBY, 2004.
73. Snyder, 2000.
74. Farley, 2004.
75. Farley et al., 2003.
76. Heinz & Ryan, 1997.
77. Center for Sex Offender Management, 1999.
78. Garfinkle, 2003.
79. Garfinkle, 2003.
80. Hindman & Peters, 2001.
81. Erooga & Masson, 1999.
82. Terry, 2006.
83. Bogaerts et al., 2005.
84. Elliot & Smiljanich, 1994.

85. Gerardin & Thibaut, 2004.
86. Ertl & McNamara, 1997.
87. Kennedy & Hume, 1998.
88. Frey, 2006.
89. Grant, Thornton, & Chamarette, 2006.
90. Steen, 2001.

REFERENCES

American Psychiatric Association. (2000). *Diagnostic and statistical manual of mental disorders, (text revision)*. Arlington, VA: American Psychiatric Association.
Araji, S. (1997). *Sexually aggressive children: Coming to understand them*. Thousand Oaks, CA: Sage Publications.
Baker, A. J. L., Tabacoff, R., Tornusciolo, G., & Eisenstadt, M. (2003). Family secrecy: A comparative study of juvenile sex offenders and youth with conduct disorders. *Family Process, 42,* 105–116.
Barbaree, H. E., & Marshall, W. L. (2006). *The juvenile sex offender*. New York: Guilford Press.
Bartholomew, K. (1990). Avoidance of intimacy: An attachment perspective. *Journal of Social and Personal Relationships, 7,* 147–178.
Beckett, R. (1999). Evaluation of adolescent sexual abusers. In M. Erooga (Ed.), *Children and young people who sexually abuse others: Challenges and responses* (pp. 204–224). New York: Routledge.
Berliner, L., Manaois, O., & Monastersky, C. (1986). Child sexual behavior disturbance: An assessment and treatment model. Seattle, WA: Harborview Medical Center.
Bijleveld, C., & Hendriks, J. (2003). Juvenile sex offenders: Differences between group and solo offenders. *Psychology, Crime and Law, 9,* 237–245.
Bogaerts, S., Declercq, F., Vanheule, S., & Palmans, V. (2005). Interpersonal factors and personality disorders and discriminators between intra-familial and extra-familial child molesters. *International Journal of Offender Therapy and Comparative Criminology, 49,* 48–62.
Brady, S., & Donenberg, G. (2006). Mechanisms linking violence exposure to health risks behavior in adolescence: Motivation to cope and sensation seeking. *Journal of the American Academy of Child and Adolescent Psychiatry, 45,* 673–680.
Bureau of Justice Statistics. (2003). *Recidivism of sex offenders released from prison in 1994.* Washington D.C.: U.S. Department of Justice. Retrieved July 28, 2006, from www.ojp.usdoj.gov/bjs/abstract/rsorp94.htm.
Canter, D. V., & Kirby, S. (1995). Prior convictions of child molesters. *Science and Justice, 35,* 73–78.
Center for Sex Offender Management. (1999). *Sex offender registration: Policy overview and comprehensive practices.* Retrieved July 28, 2006, from www.csom.org/pubs/sexreg.pdf.
Council on Sex Offender Treatment. (2004). *Rules and regulations relating to Council on Sex Offender Treatment.* Austin, TX: Council on Sex Offender Treatment.
Elliott, D. M., & Smiljanich, K. (1994). Sex offending among juveniles: Development and response. *Journal of Pediatric and Health Care, 8,* 101–105.
Epps, K. J. (1999). Causal explanations: Filling the theoretical reservoir. In M. C. Calder (Ed.), *Working with young people who sexually abuse: New pieces of the jigsaw puzzle* (pp. 8–26). Dorset: Russell House.

Erooga, M., & Masson, H. (Eds.). (1999). *Children and young people who sexually abuse others: Challenges and responses.* New York: Routledge.

Ertl, M. A., & McNamara, J.R. (1997). Treatment of juvenile sex offenders: A review of the literature. *Child and Adolescent Social Work Journal, 14,* 199–221.

Farley, M. (2004, October). Prostitution is sexual violence. *Psychiatric Times, 21,* 7–8, 10.

Farley, M., Cotton, A., Lynne, J., Zumbeck, S., Spiwak, F., Reyes, M.E., Alvarez, D., & Sezgin, U. (2003). Prostitution and trafficking in nine countries: An update on violence and posttraumatic stress disorder. In M. Farley (Ed.), *Prostitution, trafficking, and traumatic stress* (pp 33–74). Binghamton, NY: Haworth.

Federal Bureau of Investigation. (2002). *Crime in the United States 2002: Persons arrested.* Uniform Crime Reports. Retrieved July 28, 2006, from www.fbi. gov/ucr/cius_02/html/web/arrested/04-table38.html.

Finkelhor, D. (1979). What's wrong with sex between adults and children? Ethics and the problem of sexual abuse. *American Journal of Orthopsychiatry, 49,* 692–697.

Finkelhor, D. (1984). *Child sexual abuse: New theory and research.* New York: Free Press.

Fleming, W. M. Jory, B., & Burton, D. L. (2002). Characteristics of juvenile offenders admitting to sexual activity with nonhuman animals. *Society and Animals, 10,* 31–45.

Freeman-Longo, R. E. (1982). Sexual learning and experience among adolescent sexual offenders. *International Journal of Offender Therapy and Comparative Criminology, 26,* 235–241.

Frey, C. (2006). *Double jeopardy: A counselor's guide to treating juvenile male sex offenders/substance abuser.* Alexandria, VA: American Correctional Association.

Fritz, G. K. (2003, February). The juvenile sex offender forever a menace? *The Brown University Child and Adolescent Behavior Letter, 19,* 8.

Garfinkle, E. (2003). Coming of age in America: The misapplication of sex-offender registration and community notification laws to juveniles. *California Law Review, 91,* 163–208.

Gerardin, P., & Thibaut, F. (2004). Epidemiology and treatment of juvenile sexual offending. *Pediatric Drugs, 6,* 79–91.

Giaretto, H., Giaretto, A., & Sgroi, S. M. (1978). Coordinated community treatment of incest. In A. Burgess, N. Groth, L. Holstrom, & S. Sgroi (Eds.), *Sexual assault of children and adolescents* (pp. 231–240). San Francisco: Lexington Books.

Goleman, D. (1995, October 3). Early violence leaves its mark on the brain. *New York Times,* p. C1.

Grant, J., Thornton, J., & Chamarette, C. (2006, May). Residential placement of intra-familial adolescent sex offenders. *Trends and Issues in Crime and Criminal Justice, 315,* 1–6.

Groth, A. N. (1979). *Men who rape.* New York: Plenum Press.

Hanson, R. K., Gizzarelli, R., & Scott, H. (1994). The attitudes of incest offenders: Sexual entitlement and acceptance of sex with children. *Criminal Justice and Behavior, 21,* 187–202.

Hart, T. C., & Rennison, C. (2003). *Reporting crime to the police, 1992–2000: Bureau of Justice Statistics Special Report.* Washington, D.C.: U.S. Department of Justice.

Heinz, J., & Ryan, G. (1997). The legal system's response to juvenile sexual offenders. In G. Ryan & S. Lane (Eds.), *Juvenile sexual offending* (pp. 201–210). San Francisco: Jossey-Bass.

Hensley, C., Tallichet, S. E., & Singer, S. D. (2006). Exploring the possible link between childhood and adolescent bestiality and interpersonal violence. *Journal of Interpersonal Violence, 21*, 910–923.

Hindman, J., & Peters, J. M. (2001). Polygraph testing leads to better understanding adult and juvenile sex offenders. *Federal Probation, 65*, 8–15.

Hunter, J. A., Hazelwood, R. R., & Slesinger, D. (2000, March). Juvenile sexual homicide. *The FBI Law Enforcement Bulletin*, 1–7.

Katz, J. (1988). *Seductions of crime.* New York: Basic Books.

Kelley, S. M., Lewis, K., & Sigal, J. (2004). The impact of risk factors on the treatment of adolescent sex offenders. *Journal of Addictions and Offender Counseling, 24*, 67–81.

Kennedy, W. A., & Hume, M. P. (1998, January). Juvenile sex offender program reduces recidivism. *The Brown University Child and Adolescent Behavior Letter, 14*, 1–6.

Kinsey, A., Wardell, C., Pomeroy, B., & Martin, C. E. (1948). *Sexual behavior in the human male.* Philadelphia: W. B. Saunders.

Lisak, D., & Ivan, C. (1995). Deficits in intimacy and empathy in sexually aggressive men. *Journal of Interpersonal Violence, 10*, 296–308.

Martin, E. F., & Pruett, M. K. (1998). The juvenile sex offender and the juvenile justice system. *American Criminal Law Review, 35*, 279–332.

McCall, N. (1994). *Makes Me Wanna Holler.* New York: Vintage Books, Random House.

Moffit, T. E. (1993). Adolescent-limited and life-course-persistent antisocial behavior: A development taxonomy. *Psychological Review, 100*, 674–701.

Myers, W. C. (2002). *Juvenile sexual homicide.* London: Academic Press.

National Center for Sexual Behavior of Youth. (2003, July). *NCSBY fact sheet: Adolescent sex offenders: Common misconceptions vs. current evidence, 3*, 1–4. Retrieved July 26, 2006, from www.ncsby.org/pages/publications/ASO%20Common%20Misconception%20vs%20Current%20Evidence.pdf.

National Center for Sexual Behavior of Youth. (2004, January). *NCSBY Fact Sheet: What research shows about female adolescent sex offenders.* Oklahoma: Center on Child Abuse and Neglect, University of Oklahoma.

National Center for Sexual Behavior of Youth. (2005, Spring). Adolescent sex offenders: Questions answered. *ATSA Forum, (n.n.).* Retrieved July 23, 2005, from http://newsmanager.commpartners.com/atsa/issues/2005-01-12/5.html.

O'Brien, M. J., & Bera, W. (1986). Adolescent sexual offenders: A descriptive typology. *Preventing Sexual Abuse, 3*, 1–4.

Odem, M. E. (1995). *Delinquent daughters: Protecting and policing adolescent female sexuality in the United States.* Chapel Hill, NC: University of North Carolina Press.

O'Donohue, W., Regev, L. G., & Hagstrom, A. (2000). Problems with the DSM-IV diagnosis of pedophilia. *Sexual Abuse: A Journal of Research and Treatment, 12*, 95–105.

Pithers, W. D., Gray, A., Busconi, A., & Houchens, P. (1998). Children with sexual behavior problems: Identification of five distinct child types and related treatment considerations. *Child Maltreatment, 3*, 384–406.

Porter, L. E., & Alison, L. J. (2006). Examining group rape: A descriptive analysis of offender and victim behavior. *European Journal of Criminology, 3*, 357–381.

Prentsky, R., Harris, B., Frizzell, K., & Righthand, S. (2000). An actuarial procedure for assessing risk with juvenile sex offenders, *Sexual Abuse, 12*, 71–89.

Righthand, S., & Welch, C. (2001). *Juveniles who have sexually offended: A review of the professional literature.* Washington, D.C.: Office of Juvenile Justice and Delinquency Prevention.

Ryan, G. (1997). Theories of etiology. In G. Ryan & S. Lane (Eds.), *Juvenile sexual offending* (pp. 19–35). San Francisco, CA: Jossey-Bass.

Safarik, M. E. (2002). The elderly female victim. In Wade C. Myers (Ed.), *Juvenile sexual homicide* (pp. 147–161). London: Academic Press.

Saleh, F. M., & Vincent, G. M. (2004). Juveniles who commit sex crimes. *Adolescent Psychiatry: The Annals of the American Society of Adolescent Psychiatry, 28,* 183–208.

Smith, S., Wampler, R., Jones, J., & Reifman, A. (2005). Differences in self-report measures by adolescent sex offender risk group. *International Journal of Offender Therapy and Comparative Criminology, 49,* 82–106.

Snyder, H. (2000). Juvenile arrests 2000. *OJJDP Juvenile Justice Bulletin.* Washington, D.C.: U.S. Department of Justice.

Snyder, H., & Sickmund, M. (2000). *Juvenile sex offenders and victims: 1999 national report.* Washington, D.C.: Office of Juvenile Justice and Delinquency Prevention.

Steele, B. F. (1986). Lasting effects of childhood sexual abuse. *Child Abuse and Neglect: The International Journal, 10,* 283–291.

Steen, S. (2001). Contested portrayals: Medical and legal social control of juvenile sex offenders. *The Sociological Quarterly, 42,* 325–350.

Tappan, P. W. (1950). *The habitual sex offender: Report and recommendations of the Commission on Habitual Sex Offender.* Trenton, NJ: Commission on Habitual Sex Offenders.

Terry, K. J. (2006). *Sexual offenses and offenders: Theory, practice and policy.* Belmont, CA: Wadsworth.

Vandiver, D. (2006). A prospective analysis of juvenile male sex offenders: Characteristics and recidivism rates as adults. *Journal of Interpersonal Violence, 21,* 673–688.

van Wijk, A., Loeber, R., Vermeiren, R., Pardini, D., Bullens, R., & Doreleijers, T. (2005). Violent juvenile sex offenders compared with violent juvenile nonsex offenders: Explorative findings from the Pittsburgh Youth Study. *Sexual Abuse: A Journal of Research and Treatment, 17,* 333–352.

Ward, T., Hudson, S., Marshall, W., & Siegert, R. (1995). Attachment style and intimacy deficits in sexual offenders: A theoretical framework. *Sexual Abuse: A Journal of Research and Treatment, 7,* 317–335.

Worling, J. R. (2001). Personality-based typology of adolescent male sexual offenders: Differences in recidivism rates, victim-selection characteristics, and personal victimization histories. *Sexual Abuse: A Journal of Research and Treatment, 13,* 149–166.

Zimring, F. E. (1998). *American youth violence.* New York: Oxford University Press.

CASES CITED

In re Gault, 387 US 1 (1967).
Welch v. Commonwealth (2004). 149 S.W.3d 407 (Ky. 2004).

CHAPTER 6

Bad Boys in Bars: Hogging and Humiliation

Jeannine A. Gailey and Ariane Prohaska

A couple of years ago a local alternative news magazine in Cleveland, Ohio, ran an article titled, "Big Game Hunters: They're Men Who Chase Chubbies for Sport and Pleasure. They Call it Hogging."[1] The title was superimposed over a picture of a man wearing a pig mask and holding a bouquet of flowers. Having never heard of hogging, we gave it a gander. We quickly realized that the sport was "picking up" women who these men perceived to be overweight or unattractive; they called it hogging because overweight women in their eyes are hogs. We wondered why would men do such a thing. As we learned from the article and later research,[2] picking up women deemed unattractive or overweight was usually the result of a bet among friends or of the need for the guy to achieve sexual gratification, often because he was "hard up" or needed a "slumpbuster." We were horrified. Because we had never heard of such a thing, part of the shock was the language they used to discuss their actions. They claimed that what they were doing was harmless and that the women they perceived as overweight or unattractive somehow deserved to be mistreated.

In this chapter, we discuss some of the reasons young men hog, the way they overcome stigmatization, and the justifications they provide to neutralize their behaviors. First, hogging is just one way in which groups of young men can achieve and maintain masculinity in their peer groups. Second, to achieve masculinity and recognition from one's peers, they must carefully negotiate the situation so that they are not stigmatized or ridiculed. This is usually accomplished by humiliating the women either in person or behind their back as they gossip with their friends. Third, much about the way men account for their actions can be understood in the context of Sykes and Matza's Techniques of Neutralization.[3] Before we begin, however, it is important to understand some features of and things about hogging and the "typical" hogger.

Hogging is a practice during which men prey on women they deem overweight or unattractive to satisfy their competitive or sexual urges.[4] It usually takes place when a group of men decide to make the evening "more interesting" by betting on who can "pick up" the most overweight or unattractive woman, or it occurs around bar closing when men decide they will "settle" for an overweight woman to satisfy their sexual urges. Previous research[5] and our interview with Sarah Fenske (the author of the *Scene Magazine* article) indicate that men who hog are usually in their late teens or early twenties. They are also likely to be involved in fraternities or the military, but hogging may occur among any group of men. In these types of groups, men may humiliate or degrade women to prove their manhood to other group members and for a good laugh. For example, the men we interviewed said they often hog out of boredom to make the evening more fun and interesting. One of our respondents discussed how this takes place when the evening is boring, stating, "Your friends are there, so you make a bet to try to go talk to the ugliest girl, knowing that it's just going to be a laugh for you and your friends." Hogging is funny, a joke, something that men do to pass time. In sum, from what we know, hoggers are typically young, early twenties or late teens, and tend to be in college, especially fraternities or sports, or are in the military or attend military school. We now turn to a discussion of how hogging enables men to achieve masculinity in their peer groups.

HOMOSOCIAL INTERACTIONS AND MASCULINITY

Most sociologists agree that gender is something that one accomplishes or does by upholding the normative expectations of one's gender role.[6] Therefore, when discussing masculinity or femininity, it is important to understand the cultural standards for gendered behavior. Kimmel argues that there are multiple masculinities, with the dominant, hegemonic masculinity being the one most rewarded in contemporary society.[7] Hegemonic masculinity is rooted in such values as control, dominance, competition, and aggression while simultaneously devaluing emotional attachment. Men reward each other with power and prestige if they adhere to the masculine ideal. Men achieve the masculine ideal in different ways, such as participating in sports, drinking heavily, or pursuing women for sexual purposes. According to Connell, men are judged by how closely they adhere to these ideals.[8] It is important that other men believe that they are "real men." Masculinity, then, is a "homosocial enactment"[9] because men participate in activities that adhere to the hegemonic ideal so that other men will recognize their masculinity. Homosociality refers to social bonds between people of the same sex and more broadly to same-sex-focused social relations.[10] Research on men and masculinity indicates a strong relationship between homosociality and masculinity: men's lives tend to be highly organized around relationships with other men.[11]

Most men, however, are unable to live up to these normative expectations.[12] Hegemonic masculinity is most easily achieved by white, upper- and middle-class, heterosexual men; in other words, men in power who control access to scarce resources in society.[13] Men who do not fit into this category may participate in "hypermasculine" behaviors to compensate for not achieving the masculine ideal.[14] Hypermasculinity often involves violence toward other men, women, and themselves.

Related to hypermasculinity, the term "hostile masculinity"[15] encompasses the belief that sexual aggression toward women is the result of men's extreme adherence to the traditional male gender expectations. Hostile masculinity consists of two components: (1) control and domination toward women; and (2) insecurity, defensiveness, and distrust of women. If men cannot have the finer things in life, such as cars, money, or power, they find other ways to express their manhood. Men who participate in this behavior are looking for another way to live up to normative masculine standards and demonstrate that they are "men."

According to the hegemonic masculine ideal, sex is not about intimacy, but rather is about conquest.[16] One way men achieve status in their peer groups is by engaging in sexual acts with numerous women. An important part of facilitating as many sexual encounters as possible is being able to wear down a woman's resistance, and alcohol is often the easiest way to do this.[17] Because hogging usually occurs in bars or at parties that serve alcohol, it is likely that this form of sexual predation is similar to other sexual acts pursued by men to achieve proof of manhood. Flood's research in Australia indicated that male-male peer relationships tend to structure and give meaning to heterosexual encounters.[18] Therefore, placing bets on who can take home the heaviest or ugliest woman seems to be one way men could achieve masculinity in their peer groups.

Our previous research and that of Flood (forthcoming) indicate that this behavior in fact does occur.[19] In our study on hogging and masculinity, we found that interviewees who were familiar with hogging discussed it (40 times throughout the 13 interviews) as a way to gain status within the male peer group whether through winning the bet, entertaining others, or by receiving sexual gratification.[20] One interviewee noted,

> ... but [if] they want a quick, you know, quick sex fix, [they] might go up towards your, you know, heavier set or your uh, most people might consider your more ugly women to satisfy their sexual needs instead of going after someone that would be more attractive to you because they know they can get a one-night stand out of this girl instead of, you know, trying to chase someone you know might already have a half dozen suitors....

When the goal is sex, hoggers perceive overweight women as easy to "pick up." Thus, they see themselves as able to gain status in the group more easily by approaching overweight women. The conversations with their friends that follow the encounter affirm their masculinity.

We also tested Malamuth and colleagues' notion of hostile masculinity[21] to determine whether control and domination, insecurity, defensiveness, or distrust of women played a part in hogging. We found that hogging is a way to mask insecurities about being rejected by "attractive" women.[22] One *Scene Magazine* interviewee reported, "You're not embarrassed getting shot down by them. You're not embarrassed when they leave."[23] Therefore, hogging is an easy way to maintain emotional distance from women (rather than being hurt by women to whom they may be attracted). Furthermore, control and domination were achieved by the way men talked to the women.

In addition to interviews, we conducted a content analysis (a method in which the researcher looks for themes in written text) on the *Scene Magazine* article and 13 accounts of hogging found on CollegeStories.com. CollegeStories.com is a Web site on which students from across the country write about their college experiences, which consist mostly of tales of drinking and sex. The content analysis revealed that men assert their masculinity through inexpressiveness and independence (mentioned 29 times) and adventurousness and aggression (mentioned 11 times), but gaining status in the group was the most frequently coded form of masculinity (mentioned 34 times). Once hogging takes place, the participants must be sure that they have achieved status in their group and won't be labeled or ridiculed for being with a woman who is considered unattractive by cultural standards. One CollegeStories.com writer noted,

> So one night two of my buddies made a bet and it was either how many girls they could get with total in one night that were either nasty or fat or which one could do the biggest one, they had to pick ... and one kid had, I swear to god this girl weighed like 250 pounds and, um, he took her home and he won the bet.[24]

This quote reveals the entertainment that hogging created, as well as the status gained in the group for the winner of the bet. In the following section, we discuss how men avoid stigma by humiliating and mistreating the women they call hogs.

STIGMA AVOIDANCE THROUGH HUMILIATION AND MISTREATMENT

Offenses against women stem from the dominant gender system. Socialization and patterns of routine interaction encourage men to victimize women and, in turn, impose the victim role on women. Rape, domestic violence, and the mistreatment of women in general are part of a bigger problem in the United States, that is, culturally accepted misogyny.[25] As Schur states, "the two tendencies to stigmatize women and to absolve men of responsibility for victimizing women—are closely related."[26] Both reproduce the dominance of male privilege and power in society.[27] Schur notes on many occasions that the mere fact a woman has violated a gender norm is enough to "justify" treating the woman as a deviant. For women, "becoming an attractive object is a role obligation."[28] Therefore, overweight women are more likely to be stigmatized than overweight men are. For women, obesity isn't just a physical state, but rather serves as evidence of a character defect.[29] Women who are obese are seen as lazy, out of control, deviant, unattractive, and nonsexual.[30] Therefore, men who engage in sexual relationships with women perceived as overweight or unattractive often try to avoid stigmatization by claiming that they were hogging. Their claim of hogging is easier to accept by their male peers if they also degrade or in some way humiliate the woman.

Society's tolerance of the mistreatment of women can be interpreted in terms of the links between the supposed offenses and patterns of approved behavior. If male behavior patterns incorporate elements of compliance to persisting gender norms, it is unlikely that they will be labeled deviant. Hogging, therefore, is unlikely to be labeled deviant by many people in our culture. Conversely, having intercourse with or being attracted to a woman who does not meet conventional standards of beauty is considered deviant, because the woman is violating gender roles by not living up to her obligation as an attractive object.[31] Therefore, even though hogging isn't likely to be labeled deviant, sexual relations with overweight or unattractive women is, which implies that the men who participate in this behavior must find some way to avoid stigmatization.

In previous research,[32] we found evidence that stigma avoidance occurs when men have sexual relations with women they consider overweight or unattractive. Both the men we interviewed and the men in the content analysis we performed stated that they would make fun of each other if someone had been sexually involved with an overweight or unattractive woman. Some of the men indicated that, if they had been with a woman who was overweight, they would try to keep it a secret; others stated that they did not care who knew, but their friends would question their behavior and make fun of them. One respondent indicated that the behavior could be ignored if his friend had a "good excuse." He stated, "but I mean if they have a legitimate reason for it, we just let it go." According to our data, as long as the men are drunk or "hard up," they can justify their behavior to their friends and do not have to worry about being stigmatized. In the *Scene Magazine* article, one of the men stated about a friend, "if he can keep his friends from finding out, he'll keep seeing hogs on the side. He likes them. They don't expect anything. They're just cool."[33] An interviewee indicated something similar: he revealed that his friends who hog probably really like the women, but they are afraid to admit it. He said, "he's embarrassed, because he knows she's ugly and so he can't face his friends. 'Yeah I know she's ugly but she's easy,' but I think honestly that they actually do like her...." Being the brunt of a joke is a definite concern because it decreases their status. One account of hogging described on the CollegeStories.com was from a man who convinced a college freshman to leave through the window because he knew his friends would ridicule him for being with her if they saw her. He described the scene as follows:

> I could hear some of my frat brothers talking trash and laughing about last night in the living room upstairs. There was no way she would ever be able

to walk past these guys without my life being ruined. I convinced her that if she went upstairs she would be known as a house slut and that I didn't want her to have that reputation so soon into her first year at school (pretty good, huh?). I explained to her that the only alternative was to leave through the window.

Another man reported receiving eight drunken voice-mails from friends who were laughing and yelling "FAT" after he had left the bar and spent the night with an overweight woman.

The joy of hogging isn't only about winning bets or receiving sexual gratification, it's also about recounting the story to friends. One of the men interviewed by Fenske stated,

> Indeed, much of the fun seems to come in the telling, in recounting the tale that can top all others. Part of hogging's appeal is knowing he can tell his buddies later. "He loves it," explains his roommate, "and he loves telling the story."[34]

Stigma avoidance comes in the form of humiliation too. The *Scene Magazine* article provides a good example of how men humiliate and degrade women they view as hogs:

> I just talk to them like they're complete disgusting pigs. You gotta break 'em down with insults. Comment on their fat—"You're a dirty little pig." They call me a dick, an asshole, but after a few beers, they're into it.[35]

One of the men we interviewed described a particular type of humiliation that he and his fraternity brothers engage in when they are hogging for sport, called a rodeo. The following quote is his description of a rodeo:

> A rodeo is when your buddy meets a girl and takes her back to his room to have sex and two or three guys are waiting in the closet, and [as] they're getting into it and right before she either appears as if she's going to get off or right before she's really getting into it, three guys jump out. One with a camera, one with a stopwatch, and one just there to yell, and they time how long the guy can hang on to the girl. That's what a rodeo is.[36]

This quote illustrates how men who hog humiliate and dehumanize women they view as overweight or unattractive. Unfortunately, rodeos aren't unique to this fraternity in Northeast Ohio. Flood writes about a similar event in Australia. Flood's participants reported getting a hotel room and drawing names. The man whose name isn't drawn has to bring back the heaviest woman he can find. The other men wait and hide. While having sex, he ties her to the bed on her hands and knees. His friends come out of hiding and turn on the lights. He jumps on her back and tries to restrain her as she attempts to free herself.[37] Flood's data indicate other instances of abuse as well, such as hitting golf balls between the legs of a woman who was drunk and passed out. The *Scene Magazine* article reveals a similar behavior:

They'd each donate $100. Then they'd go barhopping. If one of the guys found a willing hog, everyone would hurry back to the dorm to surreptitiously watch the guy usher his prize into the room—and neglect to lock the door behind him. At the end of the year, the guy who'd rodeoed the biggest girl collected the pot, all $1,400 of it.[38]

Few men who participate in hogging have sympathy for the women or, at least, they do not report feeling sympathy. Most hoggers think the woman is "lucky" because she received sexual attention. They are assuming, of course, that heavy women do not receive male attention or sexual gratification and that they desire it. Yet, it's not just the storytelling or the discourse that is degrading, the behavior is as well: rodeos, name calling, and taking advantage of women who are so intoxicated that they don't care, don't remember, or have lost consciousness is appalling. Although there is little dispute that these behaviors are abusive, sometimes they cross over into rape and sexual assault (i.e., the woman is passed out). In the following section, we discuss how men who hog neutralize their behavior to avoid stigma and guilt.

NEUTRALIZATIONS AND JUSTIFICATIONS

Sykes and Matza conceptualized five ways people attempt to neutralize deviant behaviors: denial of responsibility (it's okay because the person had no control over the occurrence); denial of victim (the person harmed deserves it); denial of injury (no one was harmed); condemnation of condemners (those who criticize have done the same or worse); and appeal to higher loyalty (attachment to the group is more important than others).[39] Deviant actors construct justifications to avoid adverse social censure for deviance that precedes the behavior and that also may follow it (making it acceptable to self and others).

In previous research,[40] we conducted interviews and performed a content analysis on the *Scene Magazine* article and of stories posted on CollegeStories.com. We coded the interviews and content analysis material in the same manner, coding for all five of the neutralization techniques. The interviews revealed that around two-thirds (n = 9) of the men used at least one neutralization technique and eight used multiple techniques. Of the 13 men interviewed, nine knew about hogging, two admitted to doing it, and seven denied their own personal participation but discussed occasions during which their friends hogged or when they participated in the bets. For the content analysis, each account had at least one neutralization technique and several included multiple instances. The techniques that these data revealed, in order of frequency, where as follows: denial of victim (49 times), denial of responsibility (43 times), appeal to higher loyalty (21 times), denial of injury (16 times), and condemning condemners (10 times).

Denial of victim was most often associated with the belief that women who are overweight or unattractive are not "normal" and therefore deserve to be mistreated. The men not only expressed that women who deviate from the thin ideal of society deserve this treatment, but also indicated that these women are not really women at all, and therefore there is no victim.[41] The following statement from the *Scene Magazine* article exemplifies this mentality: "They understand their place, they know they're pigs. They don't get it like a normal girl could. They're desperate."[42] A young man who wrote about one of his sexual experiences on CollegeStories.com expressed a similar idea, "Feeling utterly rejected, I went downstairs to try to find some leftover, desperate chick who was hanging out late [at] night."[43]

Denial of responsibility, the second most frequently found category, was employed when the men said they were too drunk to "know any better" or because they hadn't had sex in a long time and had reached a point of desperation. For example, one the college students who wrote an account for CollegeStories.com said that his friend asked whether he had sex with a woman who was overweight, and he replied, "I just slurred back 'amanthgottado, watamanthgottado' (translation: a man's gotta do, what a man's gotta do)." A completely different account from a college student on CollegeStories.com echoed the previous quote, noting that, "One night I ended up sleeping with this chick that was a little too gifted in girth for my tastes. She is cool and all, and we are friends, she just isn't someone that I would normally go for. But sometimes you gotta do what you gotta do." As we mentioned at the beginning of the chapter, hogging usually involves a bar and drinking, and many of the men justified their behavior by saying that they were drunk. We asked one of our participants if hogging was usually blamed on being drunk, he replied, "Yeah, if she's not attractive then it's them [the man] being drunk."[44]

Appeal to higher loyalty, denial of injury, and condemnation of condemners were all employed either in the interviews or accounts we analyzed, but to a much lesser extent. All but two of the men we interviewed thought that hogging was normal and funny. This was surprising to us. In fact, we've found that many people find it humorous. During several occasions in which we've discussed hogging in undergraduate classes that we teach, both male and female students laugh. A greater percentage of the women are appalled, but many laugh and argue that there is nothing wrong with it. We disagree. In the following section, we offer concluding thoughts and discuss some possibilities for diminishing the behavior.

CONCLUSION

The goals of this chapter were to discuss the reasons men hog, how men avoid stigma, and how they, in turn, neutralize their behaviors. Our research indicates that men are able to maintain normative gender expectations and achieve masculinity by hogging. Because hogging often involves betting, men are able to compete and, if they win, gain status in the group. But even when hogging doesn't involve betting, masculinity can still be achieved because they have succeeded in a sexual conquest. It is a delicate situation, however, because women who are perceived as unattractive or overweight are often considered deviant for violating the gendered expectation of beauty and thinness. Therefore, men who have sexual relations with deviant women are also likely to be labeled deviant by their peers if their peers believe they are attracted to or genuinely like the women. To avoid the stigma and label, we argue, men use humiliation and mistreatment to "prove" to their peers that they really don't like the women and that they were simply hogging. They then use techniques of neutralization to describe their actions and justify them (i.e., claiming they were drunk, needed to "get laid," and so on). One shortcoming thus far in our research is that we have been unable to tease out the differences between men who hog for sport and those who hog for pleasure. One of the men we interviewed said,

> If they're just trying to get laid then they would prefer a girl that's prettier and a little bit thicker or a little bit fatter than a girl that's just fat and ugly. But if it's a bet they try to find the biggest nastiest girl they can.

It is clear that these are two different dynamics and that not all men who hog for pleasure also hog for sport and vice versa. It is something that we hope future research will be able to disentangle. The next logical question is what, if anything, should be done to address this troubling behavior? Hogging for the most part involves behaviors that are not illegal, so we can't argue for stiffer penalties or fines. Instead, we suggest that knowledge is power. Many women, in fact, most women, have never heard of hogging. It's something that men keep quiet. We think that informing as many people as possible is one way to help decrease occurrences. If women are aware that men may try to hit on them or pick them up in a bar only to humiliate them, then perhaps women will be able to make informed choices in these situations. Informal social control may prevent or at least decrease occurrences; therefore, calling attention to these troubling behaviors is important. Consciousness raising may also be an effective tool.

On a broader level, rigid gender expectations, along with inflexible beauty ideals, limit the experiences of both men and women. It is clear that hogging exists partly because of the beauty ideal of American society. As long as overweight women are considered deviant, some men will continue to participate in this behavior. Additionally, as long as standards of masculinity are rigid and unachievable for most men, negative sexual consequences will exist for all women.

NOTES

1. Fenske, 2003.
2. Gailey & Prohaska, 2006; Prohaska & Gailey, in press.
3. Sykes & Matza, 1957.
4. Gailey & Prohaska, 2006.
5. Gailey & Prohaska, 2006; Prohaska & Gailey, in press.
6. West & Zimmerman, 1987.
7. Kimmel, 1994.

8. Connell, 1987.
9. Kimmel, 1994, p. 129.
10. Bird, 1996, p. 121.
11. Flood, in press; Kimmel, 1994.
12. Connell, 1987; Kaufmann, 1994; Kimmel, 1994.
13. Connell, 1987.
14. Kimmel, 1994.
15. Malamuth, Sockloski, Koss, & Tanaka, 1991.
16. Kimmel, 1998.
17. Kimmel, 1998.
18. Flood, in press.
19. Prohaska & Gailey, in press; Flood, in press.
20. Prohaska & Gailey, in press.
21. Malamuth et al., 1991.
22. Prohaska & Gailey, in press.
23. Fenske, 2003, p. 15.
24. Gailey & Prohaska, 2006, p. 39.
25. Martin & Hummer, 1989; Sanday, 1990.
26. Schur, 1984, p. 133.
27. Gailey & Prohaska, 2006.
28. Schur, 1984, p. 66.
29. Schur, 1984.
30. Austin, 1999; Schur, 1984, 1988.
31. Schur, 1984.
32. Gailey & Prohaska, 2006.
33. Fenkse, 2003, p. 16.
34. Fenske, 2003, p. 17.
35. Fenske, 2003, p. 15.
36. Gailey & Prohaska, 2006, p. 46.
37. Flood, in press, p. 11.
38. Fenske, 2003, p. 17.
39. Sykes & Matza, 1957.
40. Gailey & Prohaska, 2006.
41. Gailey & Prohaska, 2006.
42. Fenske, 2003, p. 17.
43. Gailey & Prohaska, 2006, p. 40.
44. Gailey & Prohaska, 2006, p. 41.

REFERENCES

Austin, S. B. (1999). Fat, loathing and public health: The complicity of science in culture of disordered eating. *Culture, Medicine and Psychiatry, 23,* 245–268.

Bird, S. R. (1996). Welcome to the men's club: Homosociality and the maintenance of hegemonic masculinity. *Gender & Society, 10,* 120–132.

Connell, R W. (1987). *Gender and power.* Stanford, CA: Stanford University Press.

Fenske, S. (2003). Big game hunters: They're men who chase chubbies for sport and pleasure. They call it hogging. *Scene Magazine, 34,* 15–18.

Flood, M. (in press). Men, sex, and homosocialty: How bonds between men shape their sexual relations with women. *Men and Masculinities.*

Gailey, J. A., & Prohaska, A. (2006). "Knocking off a fat girl": An exploration of hogging, male sexuality and neutralizations. *Deviant Behavior, 27,* 31–49.

Kaufmann, M. (1994). Men, feminism, and men's contradictory experiences of power. In H. Brod & M. Kaufman (Eds.), *Theorizing masculinities* (pp. 142–164). Thousand Oaks, CA: Sage Publications.

Kimmel, M. S. (1994). Masculinity as homophobia: Fear, shame, and silence in the construction of gender identity. In H. Brod & M. Kaufman (Eds.), *Theorizing masculinities* (pp. 119–141). Thousand Oaks, CA: Sage Publications.

Kimmel, M. S. (1998). Clarence, William, Iron Mike, Tailhook, Senator Packwood, The Spur Posse, Magic ... and US. In M. E. Odem & J. Clay-Warner (Eds.), *Confronting rape and sexual assault* (pp. 263–276). Wilmington, DE: Scholarly Resources, Inc.

Malamuth, N. M., Sockloski, R. J., Koss, M. P., & Tanaka, J. S. (1991). Characteristics of aggressors against women: Testing a model using national college students. *Journal of Consulting and Clinical Psychology, 59*, 670–681.

Martin, P. Y., & Hummer, R. A. (1989). Fraternities and rape on campus. *Gender and Society, 3*, 457–473.

Prohaska, A., & Gailey, J. A. (in press). Fat women as "easy targets": Achieving masculinity through hogging. In S. Solovay and E. Rothblum (Eds.), *Fat studies reader*. New York: Frances Goldin Literary Agency.

Sanday, P. R. (1990). *Fraternity gang rape: Sex, brotherhood, and privilege on campus*. New York: New York University Press.

Schur, E. M. (1984). *Labeling women deviant: Gender, stigma, and social control*. Philadelphia: Temple University Press.

Schur, E. M. (1988). *The Americanization of sex*. Philadelphia: Temple University Press.

Sykes, G. M., & Matza, D. (1957). Techniques of neutralization: A theory of delinquency. *American Sociological Review, 22*, 667–670.

West, C., & Zimmerman, D. H. (1987). Doing gender. *Gender and Society, 1*, 125–151.

CHAPTER 7

Delinquency, Alcohol, and Drugs

Frances P. Reddington

In the study of delinquency, much attention is paid to adolescent use of alcohol and drugs and their impact on juvenile crime and violence. This is a topic frequently discussed and debated in the literature, in the media, in state capitals, and around family dinner tables.

ADOLESCENTS IN THE UNITED STATES AND ALCOHOL USE

According to the American Medical Association, when prohibition was lifted in the United States, many states set 21 as their legal drinking age. In the early 1970s, however, many states began to experiment with the legal drinking age limit by lowering the age to 20 or 19, while some states lowered the age down to 18. Research at the time suggested that car crashes and injuries among this age group increased tremendously. Some states pretty quickly returned their legal drinking age to 21. However, in 1984, the federal government enacted the Uniform Drinking Age Act, which basically meant that states that did not conform to 21 as the legal drinking age would receive reduced federal funding for transportation.[1] Presently, all states appear to be in compliance. According to an article "Alcohol Problems and Solutions,"[2] the United States has the highest legal drinking age in the world.

Many sources will tell you that alcohol is the number one drug of choice of American teens. And all states' statutes will tell you that alcohol possession and consumption is illegal for minors. A report from the Federal Interagency Forum on Child and Family Statistics suggests that adolescent underage heavy drinking has remained stable since the mid-1990s after a pretty steady decline starting in 1980. Survey results indicate that 11, 21, and 28 percent of 8th, 10th, and 12th graders, respectively, reported that they had consumed five or more drinks in a row at least one time during the previous two weeks. The ethnic pattern for heavy drinking also remained stable, with white and Latino youth indicating higher levels of heavy drinking than black youth.[3]

Perhaps one of the most widely used surveys of adolescent behavior concerning alcohol use is the National Household Survey of Drug Abuse, conducted by the Substance Abuse and Mental Health Services Administration (SAMHSA). Major findings from the 2004 survey suggest that between the years 2002–04, the rate of underage drinking remained stable. About 28 percent of youth from ages 12 to 20 admitted drinking alcohol in the month before the survey. That is about 10.8 million youth. One out of five of these youth responded that they were binge drinkers and just over 6 percent reported that they were heavy drinkers. When broken down by race, rates of alcohol use were divided as followed: 32.6 percent of white youth, 26.6 percent of Latino youth, 24.4 percent of American Indian or Eskimo youth, 19.1 percent of black youth, 16.4 percent of Asian youth, and 26.4 percent of youth who reported they were of two or more races.

The Monitoring the Future Study examined a pattern of how adolescents perceive the availability of alcohol. Ninety-two percent of 12th graders state that alcohol is "fairly" or "very" easy for them to get. More than 80 percent of 10th graders report the same thing, as did more than 60 percent of 8th graders.[4]

According to the National Institute on Alcohol Abuse and Alcoholism, the use of alcohol increases tremendously between middle school and high school. In addition, the use of alcohol by an adolescent increases the risk of alcohol dependency, the chance of a serious auto accident, and is associated with high-risk behaviors.

ADOLESCENTS IN THE UNITED STATES AND DRUG USE

The use of illegal drugs by American adolescents is of major concern. Numerous studies try to assess the prevalence, frequency, onset, and amount of use of illegal drugs by juveniles. According to the 2003 National Survey on Drug Use and Health, 11.2 percent of youth in the United States between the ages of 12 and 17 reported that they used illegal drugs. Thirty percent of these youth reported that they had used an illegal drug in their lifetime, and 21.8 percent reported that they had used an illegal drug within the past year. Almost 8 percent of the responding youth said that they were currently using marijuana, which was cited as the most used illegal drug within this age group. Lifetime use of other drugs fell sharply below the use of marijuana. For example, 13 percent of youth reported using psychotherapeutic drugs for nonmedical reasons, while 10.7 percent of youth reported using inhalants. Lifetime cocaine use was reported by 2.6 percent of respondents, while Ecstasy use was reported by 2.4 percent. All other surveyed substances' lifetime use fell to below 2 percent.[5]

The National Institute on Drug Abuse and the University of Michigan found in their 2004 Monitoring the Future Study of 8th, 10th, and 12th graders that 51.1 percent of 12th graders reported using an illegal drug, as did 21.5 percent of 8th graders and 39.8 percent of 10th graders. The Centers for Disease Control and Prevention in 2003 found that while 40.2 percent of high schoolers surveyed stated that they had used marijuana in their lifetime, the number represented a 7 percent decrease from 1999 and a little over 4 percent decrease from 2001.[6]

What do all these figures mean? First, the use of illegal drugs by juveniles in this country has shown a significant downturn in the recent past. Overall usage, however, remains significantly high. An extensive body of research had been completed to see what effects illegal drug use has on adolescents. Research suggests that adolescents who use drugs might develop an antisocial attitude, health-related problems, and, of course, delinquent behavior. Research strongly suggests that the earlier illegal drug use is initiated, the higher the risk of developing more serious drug problems.[7]

ADOLESCENT ARRESTS FOR ALCOHOL VIOLATIONS

Trying to determine arrest rates for alcohol abuse is not easy. On the national scale, we can examine arrests for Driving Under the Influence, Liquor Law Violations, and Drunkenness. Of these categories, by far, the most arrests are seen for Liquor Law Violations. Liquor Law Violations include "being in a public place while intoxicated through the use of alcohol or drugs. In some states it includes public intoxication, drunkenness and other liquor law violations, but not driving under the influence."[8] The good news is that between 1999 and 2003 (the last complete year for which statistics are available) the number of arrests for Liquor Law Violations decreased 22 percent. There was a 6 percent decrease between 2002 and 2003 in the number of Liquor Law Violations. One area of concern in the latest figures available is that, of the total number of Liquor Law Violations arrests in 2003, 35 percent (more than one-third) of the arrests were of girls.[9]

When it comes to driving under the influence, there has been a 9 percent decrease in the number of arrests since 1999, and a 4 percent decrease from 2002 to 2003. Twenty percent of the total arrests in 2002 for driving under the influence were girls. The offense of drunkenness reflects a 19 percent arrest rate decrease for the period between 1994 and 2003, with a 6 percent decrease from 2002 to 2003. Twenty-three percent of the arrests for drunkenness in 2003 were females and 13 percent of the arrests were of children under the age of 15.[10]

What do these decreasing arrest rates tell us? Two ideas come to mind. First, the obvious answer would be that juveniles are committing fewer alcohol-related crimes and thus the arrest rates are going down as a reflection of declining activity. Second, although the activity level remains the same or is decreasing slightly, the police may be less likely than they have been in the past to arrest for this type of crime. There are several possible explanations for this: (1) budgets may be requiring that police investigate and arrest for more serious crimes; (2) because general arrest statistics reflect only the most serious crime committed, the alcohol crimes are greatly underrepresented in official statistics (evidence in juvenile justice literature suggests that this may be a contributing factor); and (3) more diversion programs may exist for police to refer alcohol-involved youth, thus avoiding the official arrest statistic. Whatever the reason, the pattern of arrest demonstrates a viable decline.

ADOLESCENT ARRESTS FOR DRUG ABUSE VIOLATIONS

Although the number of juvenile arrests in the United States has been decreasing, Drug Abuse Violation arrests among juveniles have not shown the same pattern. Drug law violations include "unlawful sale, purchase, distribution, manufacture, cultivation, transport, possession or use of a controlled or prohibited substance or drug or drug paraphernalia or attempt to commit these acts."[11] Arrests for Drug Abuse Violations began to rise sharply in the 1990s and have just begun to show some gradual decline. There was a 19 percent increase in Drug Abuse Violations between 1994 and 2003. Between 1999 and 2000, there was a slight drop of 3 percent, but between 2002 and 2003 arrests again increased 4 percent.[12]

Two facts regarding the arrests of juveniles for Drug Abuse Violations are worth mentioning specifically. The first is the fact that 17 percent of juveniles arrested for Drug Abuse Violations in 2003 were under the age of 15. Second, although arrests of girls showed tremendous percentage increases higher than boys for Weapons Law Violations and Simple and Aggravated Assaults, rate increases in arrests for Drug Abuse Violations for both genders was just over 50 percent from 1980 through 2003. If you look at the more recent rate from 1990 to 2003, the percentage increase for girls versus boys in Drug Abuse Violations arrests is 184 percent for girls compared with 81 percent for boys.[13]

Concerns about this issue have led to research being conducted regarding girls and their illegal drug use. Female juveniles favor marijuana as their drug of choice. In a study released in 2006, it is suggested that girls are now more likely to start using marijuana than boys. In addition, teenage girls also report higher illegal use of prescription drugs than do boys. Causes for this higher use offered in the literature range from depression, stress, higher susceptibility to peer pressure than boys, low self-esteem, and anxiety. In addition, many experts suggest that the effects of drug abuse are more "profound" on young women than they are on boys— both psychologically and physically.[14] Obviously, if girls bring different issues to the table, societal and juvenile justice responses will have to adapt. This need will be discussed later in this chapter.

THE DRUGS/ALCOHOL AND DELINQUENCY CONNECTION

Much research has been completed attempting to discern the drugs/ alcohol and delinquency connection. A wealth of research addresses this topic, yet perhaps one of the most comprehensive studies released comes from the National Center on Addiction and Substance Abuse (CASA). According to one of their recent reports,[15] 80 percent of youth arrested have one or more of the following characteristics:

- Test positive for drug use
- Have taken drugs or drunk alcohol before committing their crime
- Admit substance abuse
- Commit a drug- or alcohol-related crime

Half of the children arrested tested positive for drugs. Of those tested, more than 90 percent tested positive for marijuana, more than 14 percent for cocaine, close to 9 percent for amphetamines, almost 8 percent for methamphetamines, and just under 3 percent for opiates. Although alcohol is not generally tested for, almost 40 percent of the youths arrested admitted that they had used alcohol before committing their crime. Thus, the most common drugs used by juvenile arrestees are alcohol and marijuana. In addition, the study suggests that the youth who are arrested for a drug- or alcohol-related offense demonstrate other characteristics as well to suggest substance abuse. When comparing the youth arrested just once in a year to the nonarrested youth, the following statistics are startling. Arrested youth are—

- More that 2 times most likely to have used alcohol
- More than 3½ more likely to have used marijuana
- More than 4 times more likely to have used prescription drugs for recreation
- More than 7 times more likely to have used Ecstasy
- More than 9 times more likely to have used cocaine
- More than 20 times more likely to have used heroin

The study suggests that the alcohol, drugs, and delinquency connection runs through all categories of crimes. The majority of youth arrested for either violent crimes or property crimes were involved in the use of some substance at the time of the crime. In addition, the study suggests that only 3.6 percent of juveniles arrested ever receive any type of drug or alcohol treatment and that substance-abusing offenders are more likely to be repeat offenders. The CASA study offered some strong conclusions: "Instead of helping, we are writing off these young Americans—releasing them without needed services, punishing them without providing help to get back on track, locking them up in conditions of overcrowding and violence, leaving these children behind."[16]

Let us next examine how the juvenile court responds to those young people that come into their system.

JUVENILE DRUG USE, GANGS, AND VIOLENCE

Wondering whether a growth in the number of youth gangs and more aggressive media coverage of youth gangs (which created public fear) was based on the reality of gang activity, the Office of Juvenile Justice and Delinquency Prevention researched youth gang activity and published the results of a study by Howell and Decker in 1999. One of the major research areas of the project was the relationship among gangs, drug trafficking, and violence. Gangs did not seem to tie themselves to drug activities until the 1960s. Gang involvement in drug trafficking seemed to blossom in the mid-1980s during the cocaine era. The increased demand for cocaine, as well as financial need, may have been the impetus behind this movement.

This report regarding youth gangs and drugs concluded that little empirical evidence supported the notion that the majority of youth gangs specifically create networks to traffic drugs. Interstate drug trafficking and extensive networking is the pattern of adult gangs. However, "youth gang members actively engage in drug use, drug trafficking, and violent crime."[17] Youth who belong to gangs are more likely to traffic drugs and be involved in violence than youth who do not belong to gangs. Gang members are more likely to promote individual drug use.

JUVENILE COURT AND ITS RESPONSE

The number of arrests of juveniles for Drug Abuse Violations is going to affect the juvenile court and its functioning. From 1990 until 1999, the number of drug offense cases referred to U.S. juvenile courts increased 169 percent. The drug offense cases in 1999 accounted for 11 percent of all delinquency cases referred to juvenile court. In 1990, that number was just 5 percent.[18] These numbers present challenges to the juvenile court.

One of the first major decisions in the juvenile justice system is the decision of whether to detain the juvenile in a securely locked facility. Most juveniles do not have bail as an option in juvenile court. Generally speaking, if a juvenile is detained in juvenile court, the reason is for the safety of the child or the community, the likelihood that the child will flee, or the assumption that the child will commit a crime if released. Only about 20 percent of all juvenile offenders are detained.[19] Between 1991 and 2000, the percentage of substance abusers detained increased more than any other offense category. In 2000, for example, 11.3 percent of detained youth were detained on Drug Abuse Violations.[20]

The next major decision in the juvenile justice system is to decide whether the case should be waived up to the adult criminal court system.

The juvenile court has always had the option to use the transfer process if a child could not be rehabilitated within the juvenile system. Once the juvenile court was created, the majority of cases were handled in juvenile court and transfer was not a common process. This began to change in the late 1980s and early 1990s when the United States experienced a "get tough on juvenile offenders" movement. Drug-offending youth was one of the groups seemingly targeted for tough treatment.

During the early 1990s, a higher percentage of drug law violation cases were waived to adult court than any other offense group. The juvenile system appeared to believe that drug law violators would be better served in the adult system. Throughout the 1990s, however, the percentage of drug abuse violations being transferred has dropped. Overall, only about 1 percent (or less) of all juvenile cases are transferred out of juvenile court annually. In 2000, Drug Abuse Violation cases made up 14.1 percent of all the cases that were transferred to the criminal courts.[21]

When a juvenile case is heard in juvenile court, the judge must enter a disposition for the juvenile. A disposition is somewhat equivalent to adult sentencing. The most common disposition seen in juvenile court is juvenile probation. Likewise, the most common disposition for those juveniles adjudicated delinquent on drug charges is probation, followed by placement outside the home as the second most seen disposition.[22] Between 1991 and 2000, drug abuse violators placed on probation increased 276 percent. In 2000, out-of-home placement was ordered in 20 percent of drug abuse cases, a 76 percent increase since 1991.[23]

These statistics suggest that the juvenile justice system now keeps more drug abuse violators in the juvenile justice system. Although most of these juveniles are kept in the community placed on probation, one out of five are disposed in residential placements. The increase of youth into these dispositions begs the question whether the juvenile justice system is now more equipped to deal with the drug-involved youth while on probation or in residential treatment, because they are using these dispositions more often. A review of basic fundamental skills training of juvenile probation officers suggests that the recommended basic curriculum focuses on job skills knowledge of the system and lacks in-depth coverage of adolescent drug and alcohol issues.[24] Drug and alcohol issues most likely would include specialized training, which would be taken after one has been employed for some time and already has been working with substance-abusing youth.

Two additional issues emerging from the literature include concerns about racial and gender disparity in juvenile court treatment. Between 1991 and 2000, Drug Law Violation cases referred to juvenile court for female offenders increased a whopping 311.4 percent—a much higher percentage increase than the 181.2 percent increase seen for males.[25] Perhaps the biggest concern about these numbers and the juvenile justice system response centers on the idea that traditionally male treatment programs are simply being "painted pink" and presented to female offenders.[26] This approach would not prove successful. It has already been suggested that juvenile females present different reasons for drug involvement and suffer different consequences because of this involvement. The system must address these differences to create successful gender-based drug treatment programs.

Some sobering statistics exist about juvenile justice treatment of minority drug-offending youth. Black teens are 1.8 times more likely to be arrested for a drug offense, while white juveniles are 4.2 times more likely to be arrested for driving under the influence and 4.3 times more likely to be arrested for drunkenness. Black teen drug offenders are more likely to be detained, formally processed, transferred, and placed out of their homes for drug offenses than are white youth.[27] Clearly, some diversity issues still have not been rectified within the juvenile justice system.

CASA estimated in its report that the cost of managing substance-abusing juvenile offenders in the juvenile justice system costs a staggering $14.4 billion annually. CASA estimates that if you were to add in the costs of other public and private entities the costs might double. CASA also notes that a mere 1 percent of this $14.4 billion goes toward treatment. With costs of this magnitude, the substance-abusing juvenile offender requires new responses from the juvenile justice system.

The Juvenile Drug Court

One of the innovations that the juvenile court has tried in its response to adolescent drug abuse is the juvenile drug court. Juvenile drug courts were first established in 1995. By 2001, when the U.S. Department of Justice issued a report on Juvenile Drug Court Programs, it was estimated that more than 140 juvenile drug courts were in operation and more than 125 were planning to become operational in the near future.[28]

In June 2006, the U.S. Department of Justice released a special report on drug courts. Their major conclusion about juvenile drug courts was summed up in the introduction to the report:

> Compared to adults, juveniles can be difficult to diagnose and treat. Many young people referred to drug court have no established pattern of abuse or physical addiction. Others have reached serious levels of criminal and drug involvement. Neither general treatment research nor drug court evaluations have produced definitive information on juveniles. Most juvenile drug court teams are still exploring whether their mission should be prevention or intervention.[29]

The Paradox of the Juvenile Court Response and Society's Confusion about Youth

As stated in the preceding section, one of the juvenile court responses to the initial increase in juvenile law violators was to transfer them into the adult system. This response was part of a changing societal view about offending juveniles and the subsequent response to their misbehavior by the juvenile justice system and, thus, by society. The late 1980s and 1990s followed a get-tough approach to juvenile crime. On the heels of a moral panic over juvenile misbehavior and a conservative agenda toward offenders in the mid-1980s, an actual increase in juvenile crime in the early 1990s led to a more punitive approach to juvenile offenders.

All states made it easier to transfer youth into the adult criminal justice system. Age requirements were lowered, crime criteria were broadened, and the authority to transfer was extended beyond the juvenile court judge. Debates on how to treat juvenile offenders raged in newspapers and magazines, in numerous documentaries, and even in the Supreme Court of the United States. On the one hand, the argument heard was "if you are old enough to do the crime you are old enough to do the time." As previously mentioned, this get-tough approach was heavily applied to juvenile offenders charged with Drug Law Violations.

The concept of adolescent development, immaturity, and decreased criminal responsibility based on chronological age was replaced with the concept that the punishment needed to fit the act—not the offender. And, apparently, drug violations were considered among the most serious crimes adolescents could commit. That, or the juvenile justice system simply had no idea how to treat the issue and they passed it on to an equally ill-equipped adult system. This concept that juvenile offenders needed punishment, and not treatment, has continued throughout the early 2000s.

Now here is the paradox. On the one hand, society began examining the ages at which it grants adult privileges and wondering whether it needed to set those ages back because teens are not mature or responsible enough to handle such adult responsibilities. On the other hand, legislators, the media, and the American public also demanded that the juvenile justice system hold children criminally responsible at younger and younger ages. For example, it was during this time period (the mid-1980s) that the federal government enticed states to increase the legal drinking age back to 21. Currently, a ranging debate is going on in Massachusetts about raising the legal driving age to 17½ years. The motivation for the age change is to curb accidents among young drivers who are not mature enough to take the responsibility of driving seriously and who also make bad choices and decisions as they drive. These youth do not seem to fully understand the risks or long-term consequences of their choices.

SOCIETY'S RESPONSES: THE D.A.R.E. PROGRAM

Perhaps the most well known of society's responses to the concern of youth and drug and alcohol use is the creation of D.A.R.E.—the Drug Abuse and Resistance Education programs created in 1983 in Los Angeles by then–Police Chief Darryl Gates. The program is school-based and was designed to prevent students' future use of alcohol, tobacco, and illicit drugs. The program uses uniformed police officers in the classroom who teach from a highly structured set of lessons that were developed by the Los Angeles Police Department (LAPD) and the LA school district. The program is designed for older elementary school-age children and is usually most active in the 5th or 6th grades, although there are components

for younger and older students as well as for families. The LAPD really
bought into the concept of D.A.R.E. and allowed 10 officers to teach the
curriculum to more than 8,000 students the first year of the program. By
the mid-1990s, D.A.R.E. had grown to an international program serving
thousands of children.[30]

Although perhaps the most widely known adolescent drug program in
the country, reports researching the effectiveness of D.A.R.E. have presented a less successful story. The primarily cited purposes of the D.A.R.E.
program are to achieve the following:

- Teach students to recognize pressures to use drugs from peers and from
  the media
- Teach students the skills to resist peer inducements to use drugs
- Enhance students' self-esteem
- Teach positive alternatives to substance use
- Increase students' interpersonal, communication, and decision–making
  skills[31]

Research indicates that D.A.R.E. is not effective in reducing drug use
by the students who have gone through the program. *USA Today* reported
on a 1994 Department of Justice Study that "The D.A.R.E. program's
limited effect on adolescent drug use contrasts with the programs popular-
ity and prevalence. An important implication is that D.A.R.E. could be
taking the place of other more beneficial drug education programs that
kids could be receiving."[32]

If you were to check the D.A.R.E Web site today, the first thing
that you notice is that the top line reads "The New D.A.R.E. Program—
Substance Abuse and Violence Prevention: Inside the 21st Century School
House."[33] The Web site continues to explain that D.A.R.E. is going high
tech and will be more interactive and move to a decision-based model of
instruction. To quote the Web site:

> Gleaming with the latest in prevention science and teaching techniques,
> D.A.R.E. is reinventing itself as part of a major national research study that
> promises to help teachers and administrators cope with ever-evolving federal
> prevention program requirements and the thorny issues of school violence,
> budget cuts, and terrorism. Gone is the old style approach to prevention in
> which an officer stands behind a podium and lectures students in straight
> rows. New D.A.R.E. officers are trained as "coaches" to support kids who
> are using research-based refusal strategies in high-stakes peer pressure envi-
> ronments. New D.A.R.E. students of 2004 are getting to see for them-
> selves—via stunning brain imagery—tangible proof of how substances
> diminish mental activity, emotions, coordination and movement. Mock
> courtroom exercises are bringing home the social and legal consequences of
> drug use and violence.[34]

The same Web site directs the viewer to a section that discusses an evaluation of the new program. Now geared at 7th through 9th graders, the
program focuses on "taking charge of your life." The University of Akron

is studying the success of the program and, to date, finds the program to be effective.

TARGETING THE RIGHT ISSUE

A recent report from the Pacific Institute for Research and Evaluation (PIRE) suggests that although alcohol use by minors is the more significant problem over drug use by adolescents, the alcohol issue remains largely ignored. The study suggests that underage drinking costs Americans nearly $62 billion a year, if you analyze the costs of acts of violence and traffic accidents. The study suggests that alcohol kills four times the number of young people as drugs do, yet spending by the federal government is 25 times higher for drug abuse issues over underage drinking issues. The study states the following:

> The lack of enforcement of legal drinking laws continues to contribute to the problem of underage drinking... Minors obtain alcohol in three principal ways: through illegal purchases, at parties, and from the family liquor cabinet or refrigerator. Research shows interventions can successfully reduce underage consumption, including regular police checks on sellers and servers of alcohol, improving age-checking technology, zero alcohol tolerance for drivers under 21, driving curfews, and "social host" policies that hold adults liable when minors drink at home parties.[35]

Some concern is expressed here that we are targeting the wrong issue although that seems unlikely in the face of such overwhelming statistical evidence. The study suggests in the above quotation that part of the problem is that law enforcement is not taking the issues seriously. The belief is still held that alcohol is not a drug and is not particularly harmful to minors. In the different state statutes, Minor in Possession remains a status offense on some books and not a delinquent act. With today's resources, law enforcement, by necessity, will have to address more serious delinquent offenders and may pull back their work with status offenders and less serious delinquent offenders.

In addition, there may be some political pull. It is estimated that youth will spend up to $22 million a year on alcohol. It is also suggested that the alcohol business spends its advertising dollar, or rather $4.8 billion of them, wisely. Research suggests that youth who are more aware of beer ads are also more likely to indicate positive views about drinking. Children are more familiar with the Budweiser frogs than with Smokey the Bear.[36] Research by The Center of Alcohol Marketing and Youth says that children were exposed to almost one-third again as many alcohol ads in 2004 than they were in 2001.[37]

Also of major significance are the following allegations: the alcohol industry donates heartily to both the Democratic and Republican parties— more than an estimated $11.7 million in 2000. When the American Medical Association released its 2003 study entitled "Reducing Underage Drinking—A Collective Responsibility," the National Beer Wholesalers

Association tagged the report as a misuse of federal funds. In addition, the government's $1 billion dollar initiative "Youth Anti-Drug Media Campaign" was heavily lobbied to exclude information about alcohol by the same association.[38]

LEGALIZATION OF DRUGS?

According to the U.S. Department of Justice in a report entitled "Speaking Out Against Drug Legalization" there are 10 significant reasons why drugs should not be legalized in the United States. They are as follows:[39]

- We have made significant progress in fighting drug use and drug trafficking in America. Now is not the time to abandon our efforts.
- A balanced approach of prevention, enforcement, and treatment is the key in the fight against drugs.
- Illegal drugs are illegal because they are harmful.
- Smoked marijuana is not scientifically approved medicine. Marinol, the legal version of medical marijuana, is approved by science.
- Drug control spending is a minor portion of the U.S. budget. Compared with the social costs of drug abuse and addiction, government spending on drug control is minimal.
- Legalization of drugs will lead to increased use and increased levels of addiction. Legalization has been tried before and failed miserably.
- Crime, violence, and drug use go hand in hand.
- Alcohol has created significant health, social, and crime problems in this country, and legalized drugs would only make the situation worse.
- Europe's more liberal drug policies are not the right model for America.
- Most nonviolent drug users get treatment, not jail time.

Of course, those who lobby for the decriminalization of drugs have different takes on these arguments. In 1999, according to the Cable News Network, then–New Mexico Governor Gary Johnson advocated for the legalization of marijuana and heroin. He believed they should be legalized because of the expense of the war on drugs. He is reported to have stated,

> "Control it, regulate it, tax it. If you legalize it, we might actually have a healthier society. ...Marijuana is never going to have the devastating effects on us that alcohol and tobacco have on us. If marijuana is legalized, alcohol abuse goes down because people will have a substance choice.[40]

These sentiments echo many of the sentiments heard in the argument to legalize certain illegal drugs.

But would legalization of drugs really accomplish these cited goals? Probably not, according to Robert L. Maginnis of the Family Research Council. He says that the myth that legalization will decrease the crime rate is just that—a myth. According to Maginnis, most criminals commit crime while on drugs and are not pure drug law violators. Thus, if drugs were legal, crime might increase because drugs contribute to the act, but are not the act itself. It is highly unlikely that this debate will end any time in the near future.

CONCLUSION

The use of alcohol and drugs by minors in American society has presented numerous challenges to society in general and to society's institutions, such as the juvenile courts, in particular. There appears to be no argument that alcohol use by teenagers is greater than drug use is. What does appear to be in question is whether this use is as dangerous and causes as many risks and whether people believe this. The current U.S. debate about the legal drinking age and whether it is too high centers mostly on the threats that youth pose when they drink and get behind the wheel of a car, putting us all at risk. Less concern is expressed about the harm that a reduced drinking age might expose youth to in terms of other issues. Such risks include an increased chance of alcohol dependency and less inhibition about exhibiting high-risk behaviors. As discussed, if these risks are true, then why is underage drinking so largely ignored? In addition, the economic costs are high as are the human costs. Some people suggest that the clout of the alcohol manufacturers and lobbyists works to keep the issue quiet. Another suggestion offered is that law enforcement does not approach underage drinking with the same concern with which they approach the use of drugs by minors.

Drug use by adolescents is decreasing in the United States, although the number remains high. During the peak years of concern about adolescent drug use, the juvenile court saw a tremendous increase in the number of juvenile Drug Law Violations coming to juvenile court. In the early 1990s, one of the responses by the juvenile court was to transfer those youth to the adult court system. Of particular concern were the increased percentage rates of girls and young offenders being referred to juvenile court for Drug Abuse Violations. Along with this concern came the concern that girls use drugs for different reasons than male offenders, and, thus, treatment must be different as well. Currently, most juveniles arrested and formally handled in juvenile court are put on probation and stay in the community. According to the CASA reports, the juvenile legal system currently spends $14.4 billion annually on substance abuse offenders. According to the same report, however, only 3.6 percent of youth in the system receive any type of effective drug or alcohol treatment.

What will the future hold for dealing with this major societal problem? The most widely recognized, used, and funded program, D.A.R.E., has given itself a much needed face-lift and reworked its drug abuse resistance education program into a "substance abuse and violence prevention program fit for 21st century schools." While preliminary data indicate that the program is proving more effective than the original program, the jury remains out. It is just too early to tell. It is also too early to tell how effective juvenile drug courts will be with juvenile substance abusers. Evaluations of these courts will have to be ongoing and thorough.

Decriminalization of drugs is not likely to happen any time soon. And if it ever does happen, it is highly unlikely that recreational drug use will be made legal for minors. So what will happen? Would adolescent drug use of legalized drugs become a gray area like Minor in Possession is and only carry minor penalties? Would that lead to the treatment that many of these children need? Most likely not, because drug-abusing children would be even more likely to fall through the cracks of society's institutions.

This is a tough call. We can't ignore the problems drugs and alcohol present to our children and thus our society. We have to be glad that the numbers are showing declines, but we have to try to understand why that is and remain vigilant in our fight to find and use approaches that truly work.

NOTES

1. American Medical Association, hereafter AMA, 2004.
2. Hanson, 2005.
3. Federal Interagency Forum on Child and Family Statistics, hereafter FIFCFS, 2006.
4. Johnston, O'Malley, Bachman, & Schulenberg, 2005.
5. Office of National Drug Control Policy, hereafter ONDCP, 2006, August.
6. ONDCP, 2006, August.
7. ONDCP, 2006, August.
8. National Center on Addiction and Substance Abuse, hereafter CASA, 2004.
9. Snyder, 2005.
10. Snyder, 2003.
11. CASA, 2004.
12. Snyder, 2005.
13. Snyder, 2005.
14. ONDCP, 2006, February.
15. CASA, 2004.
16. CASA, 2004, p. iii.
17. Howell & Decker, 1999, p. 8.
18. Stahl, 2003.
19. Stahl, 2003.
20. CASA, 2004.
21. CASA, 2004.
22. Stahl, 2003.
23. CASA, 2004.
24. Reddington & Kreisel, 2000, 2003.
25. CASA, 2004.
26. Krisberg, 2006.
27. CASA, 2004.
28. Cooper, 2001.
29. Schmitt, 2006, p. iii.
30. Ringwalt et al., 1994.
31. Bureau of Justice Assistance, 1991, in Ringwalt et al., 1994.

32. Drug Reform Coordination Network, n.d.
33. D.A.R.E., 1996.
34. D.A.R.E., 1996.
35. Pacific Institute for Research and Evaluation, 2006.
36. AMA, 2003.
37. The Center of Alcohol Marketing and Youth, 2006.
38. AMA, 2003.
39. U.S. Department of Justice, 2003.
40. Cable News Network, 1999.

REFERENCES

American Medical Association. (2003, September). *Reducing underage drinking—A collective responsibility, Fact sheet.* Retrieved August 27, 2006, from www.ama-assn.org/ama1/pub/upload/mm/388/iom_fact_sheet.pdf.

American Medical Association. (2004, December). *Minimum legal drinking age.* Retrieved May 18, 2006, from www.ama-assn.org/ama/pub/category/13246.html.

Cable News Network. (1999). *Legalizing drugs.* Retrieved July 25, 2006, from www.cnn.com/US.9910/06/legalizing.drugs.01.

The Center of Alcohol Marketing and Youth. (2006). *Children, youth saw over 30% more alcohol ads on television in 2004 than in 2001.* Retrieved July 27, 2006, from www.camy.org/factsheets/index.php?FactsheetID=25.

Cooper, C. (2001). *Juvenile drug court programs.* Juvenile Accountability Incentive Block Grants Program. Washington, D.C.: Office of Juvenile Justice and Delinquency Prevention.

D.A.R.E. (1996). *New D.A.R.E: Substance abuse and violence prevention, inside the 21st century school house.* Retrieved July 24, 2006, from www.dare.com/home/newdareprogram.asp.

Drug Reform Coordination Network (DRC.net). (n.d.). *A different look at D.A.R.E.* Retrieved July 24, 2006, from www.drcnet.org/DARE/section5.html.

Federal Interagency Forum on Child and Family Statistics. (2006). *America's children in brief: National indicators of well being.* Washington, D.C.: Federal Interagency Forum on Child and Family Statistics.

Hanson, D. J. (2005). *Alcohol problems and solutions.* Retrieved Jan. 10, 2007, from http://www2.potsdam.edu/hansondj/LegalDrinkingAge.html#world drinkingages.

Howell J., & Decker, S. (1999). *The youth gangs, drugs, and violence connection.* Washington, D.C.: Office of Juvenile Justice and Delinquency Prevention.

Johnston, L., O'Malley P., Bachman, J., & Schulenberg, J. (2005). *Monitoring the future: National results on adolescent drug use: Overview of key findings, 2005.* Washington, D.C.: National Institute on Drug Abuse.

Krisberg, B. (2006, July 19). Florida justice study harsher to underage girls, study finds. *Orlando Sentinel,* D1.

Maginnis, R. L. (2004, June). *Legalization of drugs: The myths and the facts.* Family Research Council. Retrieved July 25, 2006, from www.sarnia.com/groups/antidrug/arguments/myths.html.

National Center on Addiction and Substance Abuse (CASA). (2004). *Criminal neglect: Substance abuse, juvenile justice and the children left behind.* New York: National Center on Addiction and Substance Abuse at Columbia University.

National Institute on Alcohol Abuse and Alcoholism. (n.d.). *The facts about youth and alcohol.* Washington, D.C.: National Institute on Alcohol Abuse and Alcoholism.

Office of National Drug Control Policy (ONDCP). (2006, February 9). *Girls and drugs. A new analysis: Recent trends, risk factors and consequences.* Washington, D.C.: Executive Office of the President.

Office of National Drug Control Policy (ONDCP). (2006, August). *Juveniles and drugs.* Retrieved August 9, 2006, from www.whitehousedrugpolicy.gov/drugfact/juveniles/.

Pacific Institute for Research and Evaluation (PIRE). (2006, July). *New study shows a "tidal wave" of underage drinking costs: But prevention spending is a fraction compared to drugs.* News Release, July, 2006.

Reddington, F., & Kreisel, B. (2000, December). Training juvenile probation officers: National trends and practice. *Federal Probation, 64,* 2, 28–32.

Reddington, F., & Kreisel, B. (2003, June). Basic fundamental skills training for juvenile probation officers—Results of a nationwide survey of curriculum content. *Federal Probation. 67*(1), 41–45.

Ringwalt, C., Green J., Ennett S., Iachan R., Clayton R., & Leukefeld, C. (1994). *Past and future directions of the D.A.R.E. program: An evaluation review.* Washington, D.C.: National Institute of Justice, Office of Justice Programs.

Schmitt, G. (2006). *Drug courts: The second decade.* Washington, D.C.: National Institute of Justice, Office of Justice Programs.

Snyder H. (2005). *Juvenile arrests 2003.* Washington, D.C.: Office of Juvenile Justice and Delinquency Prevention.

Stahl, A. (2003). *Drug offense cases in juvenile courts, 1990–1999.* Washington, D.C.: Office of Juvenile Justice and Delinquency Prevention.

Substance Abuse and Mental Health Services Administration (SAMHSA). (2005). *2004 national survey on drug use & health: Overview.* Retrieved July 27, 2006, from http://oas.samhsa.gov/nsduh/2k4nsduh/2k4overview/2k4 overview.htm#toc.

U.S. Department of Justice (2003). *Speaking out against drug legalization.* Washington, D.C.: Drug Enforcement Administration.

CHAPTER 8

Where There's Smoke: Juvenile Firesetting through Stages of Child Development

Alan I. Feldberg, John H. Lemmon, and Thomas Austin

Fire has been a powerful but mysterious force throughout all of human history. All civilizations have attempted to understand and control this essential element. For example, in Greek mythology, Prometheus's gift of fire gave to man something that had heretofore had been reserved for the gods. This was the power to start and use fire safely. His eternal punishment signified that the gods believed man could never be trusted to handle this potent force. Fire has the potential to sustain and advance life, but it also has the power to destroy it. The gods may have been right.

In 2005, fires in the United States accounted for property losses of more than $10 billion, claimed the lives of 3,675 civilian victims, and 17,925 civilian injuries.[1] According to data compiled by the U.S. Fire Administration in 2001, arson is the leading cause of fire in the United States, accounting for more than 267,000 fires annually with property losses estimated at $1.4 billion annually. Arson is also the second leading cause of fire deaths, resulting in 475 fatalities and 2,000 injuries. In 2004, arson accounted for 36,500 structure fires (i.e., buildings), causing 320 deaths and totaling $714 million in property losses.[2]

Arson appears to be a serious problem among children. Almost one-half of all people arrested for arson are juveniles, as reported by the Bureau of Justice Statistics.[3] According to the National Fire Association, children account for more than one-half of the arsons committed over the last nine years.[4] According to recent juvenile arrest statistics, arson was the criminal offense with the highest representation of child offenders in the arrest population.[5] Children are also the most likely victims of juvenile firesetting, accounting for 85 percent of the lives lost.[6]

In addition to the direct impact of fire, several authors have investigated the meaning of firesetting in the development of violence and other forms of criminality. MacDonald studied the differences between more violent and less violent adult inpatient psychiatric patients. He reported that firesetting was one of a triad of predictors that was associated with aggressive adult behaviors, the other two being animal cruelty and enuresis.[7] Current theorists, including Merz-Perez and Heide,[8] primarily focused on the role of animal cruelty as a precursor to violent juvenile crime but also considered firesetting as a risk factor as well. Douglas and Olshaker[9] included juvenile firesetting as an aspect in the profiles of some of America's most violent criminals. To the extent that juvenile firesetting is a precursor to serious criminal behaviors, juvenile firesetters require considerable monitoring and intervention. Firesetting is considered a developmental step toward more serious criminality.[10]

The following section outlines some of the developments in the areas of theory and research that illustrate the movement from general to comparative models of causation and includes key research studies that have examined these models.

ADVANCEMENTS IN THEORY AND RESEARCH

Why do children set fire? The answers to this question have been difficult to ascertain. Historically, Sigmund Freud speculated on unconscious motivations of firesetting related to conflicts over unacceptable homosexual urges. Freud was particularly intrigued by the behavior of some male arsonists who urinated on fires to extinguish them. Based on these observations, Freud formulated his ideas about a dynamic connection between firesetting and urethra satisfaction.

Freud's speculation on the unconscious psychological motivations for firesetting was in vogue into the 1960s. Expanding on Freud's theory building, Lewis and Yarnell[11] studied records of prisoners who had either arson histories or arson tendencies and reported that arsonists were repressed individuals who frequently masturbated at the scene of their fires. Bachelard[12] also theorized about the symbolism of fire, not just in terms of psychopathology, but also in terms of the psyche in general, family functioning, and life-span development from birth to death.

More contemporary researchers have challenged the veracity of early psychoanalytic theory building, including the results of Lewis and Yarnell's research.[13] Other limitations of Freud's psychoanalytic model include problems in verifying unconscious motivations, an overemphasis on a singular cause for all firesetting, and his failure to provide a practical blueprint for treatment. As a result, more contemporary theorists such as Heath, Gayton, and Hardesty[14] have concluded that psychoanalytic thinkers have become less focused on underlying and unconscious factors and more focused on ego functioning and object relations. Modern attempts to understand juvenile firesetting have bypassed Freud's unconscious model in favor of a more conscious and goal-directed psychology.

In contrast to general theories of firesetting that emphasize a singular cause, current theory development features a comparative approach that features multiple causations. In Fineman's review of the juvenile firesetting literature, he questions the assumption that children who set fires have similar backgrounds, motives, drives, and reinforcement histories. Fineman argued that there are four motivational typologies of juvenile firesetting. The majority of firesetters are motivated by curiosity. He indicated that curious firesetters usually set only one fire, which generally frightens them and prompts them to call for help. He suggested that good education programs would generally be effective in eliminating this type of firesetting. Fineman also identified children motivated by crises as well as those who use fire for delinquent purposes. Fineman finally speculated a fourth typology, which he described as pathological firesetting. He believed that pathological firesetters had varied motivations that required extensive psychotherapy.[15] Elaborations on these pathological motivation types are certainly in order to advance our understanding of firesetting behaviors.

Other theorists have also suggested that the motivation for firesetting can be classified into specific typologies. Canter and Fritzon have suggested a four-part typology classified along two dichotomously arranged dimensions that include (1) firesetting directed at people versus objects and (2) firesetting motivated by expressive (emotional) needs versus instrumental (goal-directed) incentives (e.g., expressive-person firesetting motivated by anxiety compared with instrumental-person firesetting motivated by revenge).[16]

Santtila and his colleagues found some evidence to support Canter and Fritzon's typology. Using a sample of 230 juvenile firesetters in England, they were able to classify 35 percent of the fires as instrumental-person (motivated by revenge), 59 percent as instrumental-object (motivated by pragmatic reasons such as covering up a crime), 29 percent as expressive-object (motivated by fire fascination), and 14 percent as expressive-person (motivated by a cry for help). They also identified specific risk factors associated with each typology (e.g., the expressive-person typology was associated with a history of institutionalization for child maltreatment and a diagnosis of depression; the instrumental-object typology was associated with a history of prior convictions for thefts, vandalisms, and burglaries). One implication of the Santtila study is that different motivations to set fires follow different development pathways.[17]

The idea of relating risk factors to motivational types was proposed by Kolko and Kazdin in the 1980s with their presentation of a three-part ecological model of fireplay and firesetting.[18] Their model was a conceptual blueprint of firesetting derived from reviews of the existing literature and included the following: (1) a learning element suggesting that juvenile firesetting was related to early exposure to firesetting activities; (2) an individual risk-factors element that could include such factors as a limited awareness of fire hazards, emotional deficits including discomfort with human interactions, difficulties in handling face-to-face conflicts, social immaturity, or isolation; and (3) a parent/family risk-factors element that could include poor parental supervision, parent-child attachment disorders, parental pathologies such as histories of alcohol abuse, mental health problems, criminal behaviors, and stressful family life events like divorce or the death of a parent. One implication of Kolko and Kazdin's ecological model is that specific motivational types might be associated with the different risk factors. Furthermore, motivational types may be dynamic, meaning that they vary from early childhood through adolescence, while others may be static, meaning that they remain constant throughout each stage of child development.

Kolko later reported four psychological profiles among juvenile firesetters. These included curious firesetters who set fires out of fascination, pathological firesetters who set fires as a symptom of their psychopathology, expressive firesetters who set fires as a cry for help, and delinquent firesetters who set fires as a function of their antisocial behaviors.[19] In contrast, Putnam and Kirkpatrick argued that there are only two motivational types: (1) expressive (e.g., arson as an expression of psychopathology or unresolved trauma) and (2) instrumental, where firesetting is employed to achieve an established goal (e.g., arson for profit, to conceal a crime, and so forth).[20] The authors also outlined a number of causal explanations.

Researchers have identified specific firesetting risk factors. Their findings suggest that firesetters exhibit higher levels of antisocial behavior, conduct disorder, impulsivity, and lower levels of sociability, and that their families exhibit more dysfunctional parental systems and pathological family dynamics.[21] Little is known, however, about the impact of these risk factors on the development of different motivational typologies. Additionally, Putnam and Kirkpatrick emphasize the need for a validated classification system that distinguishes high- and low-risk youth firesetters.

In addition, little is known about the factors that transition a child from fireplay to more serious firesetting. From a developmental perspective, Kolko and Kazdin discuss using a risk assessment theory explanation, stating that firesetting behavior evolves as the child matures, that it is produced by individual and environmental risk factors, and that firesetting motivations change as children mature.[22] Unfortunately, a paucity of literature elaborates on how firesetting behaviors emerge or change over time.

Currently, there is no consensus in the literature of juvenile firesetter typologies, definition of terms, and explanations about how these typologies might develop over time. We now our turn attention to a conceptual framework that lays the groundwork for a developmental theory of motivational typologies.

TOWARD A DEVELOPMENTAL EXPLANATION OF JUVENILE FIRESETTING MOTIVATION

Examination of developmental changes over the life span has been part of considerable psychological theory building, beginning with Freud's theories of psychosexual development and extending through Eric Erikson's stages of identity, Piaget's exposition of cognitive development, and Kohlberg's concepts of the development of moral reasoning. Each of these theorists indicated qualitative changes in psychological functioning over the course of human development. Additionally, the community mental health movement has examined and addressed pertinent risk factors to mitigate negative developmental trajectories.[23] Thus, developmental theory has had a considerable impact on treatment approaches as well as preventative efforts with children in many areas of delinquency but not in juvenile firesetting. Many of these psychological concepts have advanced contemporary criminological theories, particularly work in the field of human ecology.

The idea of an ecological approach emphasizing the importance of individual and environmental risk factors affecting child development was initially spelled out by child development experts.[24] The ecological model underscores the life-span theories of youth offending, including Loeber and Farrington's work in the field of developmental criminology. To adequately conceptualize juvenile firesetting typologies, it might be worthwhile to consider life-span models of general youth offending that consider changes in motivations and behaviors over time.[25]

For example, Loeber's stacking model of problem behaviors suggests that serious youth offending is a function of the interaction of biological, family, and community risk factors that place troubled children on a trajectory to a life of chronic and serious criminality.[26] As an illustration, a child is born with neurological impairment caused by low birth weight as a result of poor prenatal care. The poor prenatal care is symptomatic of the mother's attachment conflicts with her unborn child. After the birth, the mother experiences more difficulty attaching to her damaged child, thus inhibiting positive reciprocal social and emotional interaction. Moving into early childhood, the child continues to receive inadequate parental nurturing and supervision, which further exacerbates his cognitive and social impairment. The child's ability to tolerate his growing frustrations becomes overwhelmed. As a result, the child becomes mistrusting, lacking in self-control, incompetent, irritable, and cynical. By the time he enters school, he has established a set of stable, negative beliefs that promote further rejection by teachers and peers who might have helped him. He acts out aggressively and finds membership in a peer group composed of similar children. Within this isolating peer group, he continues to model and refine his antisocial attitudes and behaviors. At this point, the child is on a trajectory toward a delinquent career.

Loeber's research further differentiated three developmental pathways, resulting in specific typologies of antisocial behavior, including status offenses, property offenses, and violent crimes.[27] The authority avoidance pathway begins with oppositional behavior leading eventually to status offenses (e.g., truancy, violations of curfew, and running away from home). The covert pathway begins with minor problematic behaviors particularly lying and minor theft. This leads to more serious property crimes, including vandalism and arson. The covert pathway eventually transitions to felony-level crimes, such as burglaries. The overt pathway begins with minor aggression, such as bullying, which leads to physical fighting and finally transitions to violent crimes, such as aggravated assaults and homicides. Loeber and his colleagues also reported that some children move along multiple pathways (e.g., covert to overt pathways). These youths tended to be the most serious and persistent offenders. It would be worthwhile to apply a similar developmental analysis specifically targeting juvenile firesetters.

In the following section, we present a seven-part juvenile firesetting typology. Consistent with the ecological model, we will present clinical case studies that illustrate the developmental pathways of different types of firesetters. Our clinical evidence indicates that some of these pathways are static (remain constant) while others are dynamic (changes or varies) over the developmental stage from early childhood through adolescence.

CASE STUDIES ON THE SEVEN MOTIVATIONAL TYPES OF JUVENILE FIRESETTERS

In the present essay, a seven-part typology of juvenile firesetting motivations is espoused. Although there may be other motivations for firesetting, for the most part, they are idiosyncratic. Most juvenile firesetting is well explained by the following typology. In general, the motivation scheme includes three types of firesetting motivation that are considered nonpathological and four subtypes of firesetting that are considered pathological. The terms *nonpathological* and *pathological* are applied in respect to the child having an unhealthy psychological connection to fire, not to other, more general, psychological issues. For example, a child may have serious psychopathology, such as bipolar illness, and be a nonpathological firesetter. Finally, as the discussion unfolds below, the authors want to clarify that motivational profiling relates to the psyche of the child, not necessarily to the intensity, size, or impact of the child's fire. The central element of pathological firesetting is the child's relationship to fire, which serves to inhibit unpleasant feelings or excite a desired state of feeling.

In general, the typology of the firesetting motivation should direct treatment and intervention strategies. Pathological firesetters should receive more robust clinical interventions that focus on firesetting itself. Nonpathological firesetters generally require less robust treatment efforts that focus specifically on firesetting issues. Treating general psychological issues of nonpathological firesetters (such as depression, Attention Deficit Hyperactivity Disorder, and trauma responses) can predictably reduce the incidence of future firesetting. However, the treatment of pathological firesetting demands a clinical treatment approach that undermines the child's psychological relationship with fire and replaces this relationship with healthier ways to regulate psychological processes.

The following three motivations are considered nonpathological. These include curious/accidental firesetting, crisis firesetting, and delinquent firesetting. Each will be discussed below.

Nonpathological Firesetting

Curious and accidental firesetting are usually grouped together and, in fact, they may be closely related to one another. Curiosity-set fires are set to satisfy some interest about fire and fire dynamics. There is an experimental "I wonder what will happen if…" quality to the motivation of the juvenile. By implication, this type of firesetter does not already know the answer to his or her curiosity and does not understand basic fire dynamics. An example from our clinical population was a client who, as a young child, had seen his parent use a lighter and became curious about whether he could make it work. He picked it up and lit the lighter. The three-year-old became curious about what would happen if he touched the flame to a piece of paper. As the flames burned, the child was shocked at how the flame rose toward his hand and how hot it became.

An accidental fire resulted when the child dropped the paper (because it burned his hand) on a couch, which eventually led to a chain reaction that consumed his parent's home. From a motivational standpoint, one would surmise that the child who set this type of fire was naïve about fire, how it burns, and its potential impact.

From a logical standpoint, as children acquire fire knowledge, curiosity and accidental fires are less likely to be their motivations. While Fineman pointed out that curious firesetters would generally be frightened by their fire in a manner that deters future firesetting, in a minority of cases, curiosity firesetting can be the gateway to other problematic firesetting.[28] In cases such as these, firesetting motivation can change over time to other forms of nonpathological (i.e., delinquent) or pathological firesetting (e.g., fire fascination or thrill seeking).

Frequently, children who set curiosity-motivated fires may have two general psychological characteristics that relate to their fire activity. First, they are frequently more curious than the average child about aspects of their environments, such as mechanical devices (e.g., telephones, computers, and so forth). Second, these children have a strong tendency to satisfy their curiosity through doing, rather than thinking. Their cognitive styles usually involve external actions on their environments rather than being ideationally predisposed.

The second motivational typology is the crisis or "cry-for-help" firesetter. Crisis firesetting can be established as the motivation when two conditions are met. First, the child must be living through a discernable crisis that he or she perceives as inescapable. Second, the child must use the fire as an attempt to avoid or resolve the crisis. An example from our clinical population was a child who was being sexually abused by a caretaker and was too frightened and ashamed to tell authorities. The child set a fire to a back porch, went to his neighbor's home, called 911, waited while emergency personnel extinguished the fire, and when asked if he was responsible for the fire, readily acknowledged that he had set the fire. He was removed from the abusive home environment and, because of this, his safety was restored.

For the cry-for-help firesetter, there is no denial of complicity in setting the fire. In fact, the child will evidence some relief that his or her own crisis is being solved as the result of his or her actions. According to Canter and Fritzon's scheme, crisis firesetting is expressive and person focused.[29] In this type of firesetting, the common metaphor, "where there is smoke, there is fire" actually makes a lot of sense, meaning the fire is symptomatic of a serious and unresolved crisis.

The third motivational subtype is delinquent firesetting. In these cases, fire has an instrumental function that demonstrates defiance toward authority and societal norms. This function is used no differently than rocks might be used to break windows or spray cans might be used to produce graffiti. Additionally, fire can be used to disguise another crime. Canter and Fritzon categorized this type of firesetter as instrumental and object focused. In one of our cases, two youths stole a jeep from a neighbor, went joyriding, got into an accident, and then attempted to burn the jeep with gasoline to destroy any evidence that would link them to the theft.

In our experience, the delinquent firesetter is gratified by the excitement and victorious sense of defiance over society's rules rather than with the fire itself. Frequently, delinquent firesetting is done by a group of youths associated within a negative peer culture. They maintain a sense of loyalty to one another when setting their fires. When confronted by the authorities, however, delinquent firesetters frequently are disloyal to their peers. They are prone to blame their coconspirators while absolving themselves of any wrong doing.

Pathological Firesetting

Pathological firesetting occurs when children have significant psychological relationships with fire. A number of considerations reflect this pathological relationship with fire. In a minority of cases, genuinely psychotic children may have delusions and hallucinations in which fire is a prominent feature, or even worse, they may experience command hallucinations "telling them" to set fires.

For the most part, however, pathological firesetting is driven by two dynamics: obsession and regulation of emotion. Obsession is a thinking function whereas regulation is an emotional function. In terms of obsession, some children are intensely preoccupied with fire and may think, dream, and fantasize about fire continually. This may be reflected in a preoccupation with movies, television programs, and video games that feature vivid images of fires and explosions.

Children who use fire to regulate their emotions psychologically use fire to inhibit feelings that create emotional discomfort or to generate feelings that invoke pleasure. For some pathological firesetters, fire can be used to excite as well as to inhibit feelings. Among these types of firesetters, fire is a means to regulate emotional experiences. Four subtypes of pathological firesetting include revengeful, maladaptive coping, thrill seeking, and fire fascination. In each of these subtypes, the psychology of fire obsession and the regulation of emotions can be observed and explained.

Revengeful firesetting occurs when fire is used to "get back" at another person for perceived or real injuries or insults. The revengeful firesetter uses fire in a manner meant to inhibit the feelings of anger that have accumulated over time. Frequently, these children express feelings of relief following their firesetting. In addition to anger, revengeful firesetters are frequently ineffective in controlling their environments. The act of firesetting provides them a sense of control, justice, and relief from anger. At times, the trigger within the child's psyche for his or her anger can be highly exaggerated. The child can perceive an injustice and nurture his or her anger for a considerable length of time. Additionally, our culture can reinforce a child's revengeful ideations. For example, the mass media reinforces the notion that fire can be righteous equalizer by depicting evildoers being destroyed by fires and explosions.

In one of our cases, a teenager believed that he was unfairly blamed for starting a fight on his school bus and was denied the privilege of riding the bus for 30 days. Approximately one-and-a-half years later, this teen set fire to the home of his accusers. While in treatment, he talked about his enduring obsessions and conflicts about whether to set the fire. When he finally set it, he felt relief because his need for revenge was met. This case illustrates the pathology of a revenge firesetter driven by his obsessions and needs to regulate his emotions.

The next pathological firesetting subtype is maladaptive coping. In setting a fire, the child uses maladaptive coping when he or she relies on the fire to diminish feelings that create discomfort. Typically, these feelings may include variations of depression, anxiety, or tension. Often these children evidence poor self-esteem in part because they feel rejected by both family and peers. The child who sets fires as a maladaptive coping mechanism may stare into the fire and go into a trance-like state during which time anxiety and tension dissipate. Some maladaptive children may employ an active imagination that accompanies the fire. They may fantasize themselves as strong or invincible in ways that compensate for an underlying sense of powerlessness.

In one of our cases, an older teen set fires in a public park. While the fire was burning, he fantasized about being able to sexually seduce females whom he otherwise felt would never accept him. Because the maladaptive coping firesetter uses fire to reduce unpleasant emotions, he is similar to revengeful firesetters in that both use fire as a way to inhibit unpleasant feelings. Maladaptive coping firesetters, however, are unique in their obsession with setting fires. In our clinical experience, these are the children who set the greatest number of fires, sometimes numbering in the hundreds.

The next subtype of firesetter is excitatory in nature and motivated by thrill seeking. Thrill seekers set fires to experience drama and pleasure. They usually derive enormous gratification from a grandiose notion that they can avoid detection. The thrill seeker usually enjoys the "cat and mouse" game of outsmarting the authorities. Over the course of time, the thrill seeker's fires frequently become progressively more damaging and larger. The fire that once created a thrill is no longer intense enough and a bigger fire is necessary to obtain the same level of satisfaction. An example of one such thrill seeker was John Orr, a prominent fire investigator from California who effectively used his professional expertise to disguise a prolific career as an arsonist.

A clinical example from our caseload featured a teenager who set fires in different neighborhoods of his community alerting the authorities through a 911 emergency call after each fire. Typically, this youth would set three separate fires a day. His fires progressed to become increasingly serious and eventually led to a significant injury of a firefighter. As he set more fires, he developed a sense of invulnerability to ever being caught. Over time, his fires became bigger and he became more arrogant about being apprehended. In fact, he used his arrogance to protest his innocence on several occasions when he was under investigation before finally admitting his complicity after the fourth investigation. The thrill seeker may not be as obsessed with firesetting as this boy was by his perceived prowess in avoiding detection.

The last subtype of pathological firesetting is fire fascination. The fire-fascinated youth, like the thrill seeker, has an excitatory relationship to fire. This type of firesetter is obsessed with one or more aspects of the fire to which he or she is attracted. This attraction may include the colors and motions of flame or the mysteriousness of fire as an element that is not quite solid, liquid, or gaseous. One of our fire-fascinated youths spoke of the almost magical manner in which burning a piece of paper made it shrivel up and then disappear. Fires of this nature are started to "fuel" the psyche's desire for stimulation and fascination. Fire-fascinated youth are stimulated by fire and, even long after they understand the basic dynamics of fire, they continue to set them out of a sense of fascination, excitement, and fun. As in the case of the thrill seeker, the fire-fascinated offender progresses to more serious firesetting. The fire-fascinated youth wishes to create bigger fires to satisfy his or her need for stimulation and excitement.

TWO PATHWAYS IN THE DEVELOPMENT OF PATHOLOGICAL FIRESETTING

In this section, we will explore how the psychology of pathological firesetting can dynamically change or remain static over the child's developmental course. The general consensus is that children are not born as pathological firesetters. Firesetting is an acquired behavior. Consistent with the ecological model, the combination of genetic propensities and environmental factors places children on a trajectory toward serious firesetting behaviors.[30]

In this chapter, we focus on two differing pathways that frequently have been observed in our clinical work. The first represents a relatively static pathway involving fire fascination. The second is a more dynamic pathway, involving maladaptive coping and delinquency. Clinical material is presented to illustrate each pathway.

The Static Fire Fascination Pathway

The development of the fire-fascinated firesetter begins early and usually has a psychologically static (or stable) pattern, at least through adolescence.

The cornerstone of this type of firesetting involves profound attachment disorders that begin in infancy and continue throughout childhood. Neglect occurs early and pervasively. Even when parents are physically present, they are psychologically absent and insensitive to the needs of the child. The lack of attunement between the child and their attachment figures profoundly affects the child's basic internalization (almost like imprinting) of a relationship style. Most likely, one of the deficits resulting from this attachment style includes a lack of visual contact between parent and child that normally is one of the features of healthy attachment. Lack of a sufficient attachment pattern with a parental figure frequently sets the stage for fire fascination.

First experiences with fire are notable. The child is exposed to fire at an early age, often thanks to the smoking habits of the adults in their presence. Cigarette lighters or matches are frequently available so that the child has access to these ignition devices. In addition, the parents fail to teach the child the dangers of "playing with fire." Initial firesetting occurs by the time the child is 4 to 6 years old, if not earlier.

The attachment problems are compounded by the parent's responses to the child's firesetting. Effective correction is absent when the child first begins to "play" or "experiment" with fire. Consequently, the child does not make the connection between fire and danger and does not become involved as a participant in understanding and using fire safety. In addition to the lack of parental supervision, there is a glaring lack of consistency in correcting the child that range from no reaction to erratic and overly harsh punishment, such as burning the child's hand.

In the absence of an adequate attachment to parents, the child develops a faulty attachment to fire as a substitute. The child creates a visual relationship to fire, almost as though this visual process replaces the visual tracking healthier children have to human attachment figures. The child becomes fascinated with one or more visual properties of fire. He or she enjoys his or her ability to control the appearance of fire, a control he or she could not establish in his or her relationship to a person.

As the child develops, the early deficit in relation to the primary attachment figure continues to impede the formation of mutually gratifying and trusting relationships with others, both adults and peers. The firesetter may emulate interactions with others by using a veneer of social skills, but he or she remains distant and puzzled by the relations that others have. Such children become superficial, isolated, and nontrusting of others. When they become "stressed out" or frustrated, they do not have the internal map that helps them to seek out and avail themselves of others to provide solace, even if they could turn to others in their environment.

In elementary school, these children are isolated from others. In middle school, they become more aware of not fitting in to their social environment. They also become aware that there are similar attachment-deficit children in their environment. These children begin to emulate those who are socially engaged, and they create a pseudo-bond to one another. Defensively, they may develop a façade that they are tough and don't need or care about others. They become more conscious of their lack of connections and their increasing sense of alienation and they further disengage by refusing to meet the goals and expectations of others. At this point, school performance, even when there is considerable intellectual capacity, rapidly deteriorates. If and when their peers become aware of the child's attraction to fire, they may be further ostracized when they are referred to as "pyromaniacs."

Because these children do not have the internal relationship maps, they continue to be alienated and rejected by others, thus exacerbating their attraction to fire. Fire becomes their "friend," and the firesetter has control over this friend. If a small fire provides excitement and a capturing of the symbolic yet elusive attachment figure, a bigger fire does so even more. Fires are set with a sense of excitement, control, and power. Because of the progressive nature of this type of firesetter, at some point, they set a fire large enough to draw the attention of legal authorities.

A Clinical Example

"Matt" was raised by a single parent, barely having any contact with his biological father. His mother was diagnosed with bipolar disorder. She smoked cigarettes and marijuana and was careless with her lighters. As a teenager, Matt took pride in himself for being fearless. As a child, he never learned the concept of danger. By the time he understood the danger of fire, he was so enamored by it that he continued to light fires and had a preoccupation with video games and movies that contained fire themes. As described above, Matt's mother erratically responded to his early behavior problems. On many occasions, she failed to discipline her son. On the occasions during which she did respond, however, she was so heavy-handed that she was charged with physically abusing him.

Matt was an intelligent youngster who was interested in how things worked. At an early age, he began to play with his mother's lighters. At the age of 5, he once found himself in his mother's bedroom with her lighter. While she was taking a shower, he lit one of her lighters and set a piece of her clothing on fire. He held the clothing in his hand and, when the flames made contact with his hand, he dropped the clothing on his mother's bed. The mattress caught on fire and quickly began to burn out of control. Matt's mother became aware of the fire and fortunately was able to get her son and herself out from the apartment safely. Unfortunately, their apartment and four other units were destroyed.

Matt was enrolled in fire safety education following this event. However, this intervention, while usually successful for children, failed for Matt. He continued to have a fascination for the blue color of flame and was attracted to the way this color emerged from fire and moved around in the flames. His firesetting temporarily receded but then resumed. Matt became overly involved in video games that depicted fire. As he got older, cognitively he understood the dangers of fire, but this understanding did not interfere with his desire to continue setting fires. He continued to set a variety of fires into his middle teenage years before his coming to our program.

Matt's relationship style was characterized by its superficiality and manipulative quality. He exuded a tough exterior that spoke loudly to others as it proclaimed "I don't need anybody." He became affiliated with a gang that supported his superficial style. He did not open up to others about himself or the stresses of his life.

Matt had a variety of very intense feelings about his mother, her mood swings, and her sexual liaisons with others. He avoided communicating his distress to others primarily because he had no anticipation that anyone would be psychologically available. Additionally, he had no map "inside his head" that communicating his feelings would lessen his distress. Consistent with this style, Matt had been to see counselors in the past but had never allowed himself to be part of a therapeutic relationship.

Matt is an example of a static, fire-fascinated teen. His fascination began early and has been unabated by attempts at intervention. He has set fires at every stage of his development from preschool, through elementary and middle school, and into high school. He secretly maintains a relationship to fire that he can control and, in some ways, he is more invested in this relationship than he is to people.

A Dynamic Pathway: Maladaptive Coping to Delinquency

Two themes differentiate this dynamic pathway from the static, fire-fascinated pathway described above. First, maladaptive coping firesetters typically do not have an early formation of fire relationships or firesetting history. Their relationship with fire begins in later childhood or early adolescence. More important, whereas fire-fascinated children maintain a constant fixation with fire from early childhood, maladaptive coping is a stress-reduction mechanism that later evolves into other types of motivations such as revenge or delinquency.

Although the maladaptive coping firesetters may experience neglect in their family background, it does not occur as early, as persistently, or as damagingly as with fire-fascinated children. Attachment processes may not be optimal, but they may (at one time) have been adequate. In the case of maladaptive coping, these children begin life with basic safety and nurturing needs being met by their parents and family. As a result, they do not show evidence of having any particular interest in fire during early childhood.

Maladaptive coping children seem to have sufficient resources to develop adequately into their grade-school years. Frequently, however, these children experience an increase in stress sometime in later childhood or early adolescence. This surge of stress is related to events over which they have no control. The increase in stress overwhelms their capacity to cope. An example might be the psychological incapacitation of a parent because of drug abuse or alcoholism, or the loss of a parent as the result of divorce, illness, or death. As the stress increases, these children may attempt a variety of nonfire-related ways to diminish their overwhelming stress. Several examples include substance abuse, sexual promiscuity, acceptance into a negative peer coalition, or self-mutilation. They begin to falter in school and in their communities. They may have had previous success in school but their grades plummet and they seek escape from what stresses them.

At some point, fire is introduced to them and they discover that fire can be an effective tool for stress reduction. The relationship with fire begins to build based on this functional use of fire as a tool to reduce stress. Once the utility of the fire is discovered, these youths begin to frequently light fires. They typically will continue to employ other forms of maladaptive coping while simultaneously setting their fires.

Although these children have formed adequate parent-child relationships that sustained them early on, their attachment maps are not sufficiently developed to access other caring or competent adults who might provide meaningful support for them. As the stress increases, these children cannot avail themselves of other potentially helpful adults (e.g., teachers, ministers) even when efforts are made to help them. As their parents become increasingly overwhelmed with their own problems, they become psychologically unavailable to their children. The children become distressed and psychologically "lost," and begin to grasp at anything that offers temporary relief from their problems.

Maladaptive coping children eventually develop a relationship with fire that is based on stress reduction. Often times, these children look at fire and "space out." Basically, they use fire to psychologically dissociate themselves from the stress in their lives. Their experience with fire is almost trance-like and hypnotic. To this point, however, the fires are contained and relatively safe. Typically, they engage in persistent firesetting. They may set several hundred fires without creating a destructive one or causing a legal problem for themselves.

Gradually, maladaptive coping firesetters develop a sense of comfort and competency in setting fires. At some point, they "cross over" and begin to use fire for different psychological purposes other than stress reduction. For example, the youth who first set fire to calm down now sets fire to his school to destroy the building out of revenge or to destroy evidence of a delinquent act. It is for these subsequent fires that the youth is arrested and referred to the juvenile justice system.

A Clinical Example

"Ryan" is a 16-year-old youth. His early home life has been fairly stable and he had memories of his family functioning well. During this time, he also functioned well both behaviorally and academically. Ryan recalls that his father drank when he was a child, but his drinking did not seem to be a problem. As Ryan got older, however, his father's progressive alcoholism led to more dysfunction. His father became less rationale and attentive to the needs of his family. For example, his father would begin to vacuum the home late at night while yelling curses and complaints out loud. Both activities would disrupt the sleep of family members. The father's memory functions began to deteriorate as well. Ryan reported asking his father to take him places such as a doctor's appointment. The next day, his father would have no recall of his commitment to Ryan. As expected, his father's alcoholism created strife in the overall functioning of the family.

Ultimately, Ryan's own functioning began to deteriorate. Although he had been a good student, his grades dropped and he began to skip school. He started to associate with a delinquent peer group. Ryan began to smoke marijuana and drink alcohol. He and his peers began to get together to use drugs and would go into the forest to start campfires. With this exposure, Ryan discovered that fire alleviated his stress. He then began to set small fires on his own. For months, these fires remained small and contained.

Eventually, Ryan and his peers became increasingly disenfranchised with school. They hatched a plot to set fire to the school "to make it go away." Although brighter than average, Ryan gave no thought to the potential impact the fire would have in terms of risk to others or the effect on the community. To start the fire, they brought in water bottles filled with gasoline, spread the gasoline in a hallway, ignited it, and left the scene. Ryan was not motivated to set this fire to destress himself but rather to destroy the building to avoid going to school. Shortly thereafter, the boys were apprehended and held accountable for their crime.

CONCLUSION AND IMPLICATIONS

According to Greek mythology, humankind was incapable of understanding and using fire wisely. Science debunks this myth. Although fires can be mishandled, only a small percentage of people intentionally set them for destructive or lethal purposes. Most people handle fire without creating problems. Science provides a method to understand the motivational factors and pathways that lead to destructive firesetting. Science can also help us to help those who set destructive fires, benefiting them, their families, and their communities.

This chapter presents seven motivational typologies of juvenile firesetting. Our clinical experience tells us that these typologies fall into two broad categories, pathological and nonpathological. The pathological firesetter has developed a psychological relationship with fire and uses it for revenge, maladaptive coping, thrill seeking, or to stimulate a sense of fire fascination. The nonpathological firesetter sets fire out of curiosity, by accident, or for instrumental purposes that can include a cry for help or delinquency.

These typologies follow certain patterns that we call pathways. Some pathways remain static and involve a constant motivational typology over time. Dynamic pathways, in contrast, involve an evolution of different typologies over the period from early childhood through adolescence. The delineation of common pathways of developing firesetting problems has implications for theory building, research, prevention, and the treatment of juvenile firesetters.

Our model identifies seven motivational typologies along with two significant pathways of firesetting behavior, which are consistent with the ecological approach. The model we articulated applies the ideas of the life-span theorists, particularly Loeber and Farrington's Theory of Developmental Criminology, to a specific population of youth offenders, namely, juvenile firesetters. The ecological approach has aided our efforts thus far but certainly has not been exhausted in terms of its usefulness in understanding juvenile firesetters. The ecological approach has the potential to elucidate the individual and environmental risk factors that underscore the etiology of firesetting. Research is needed to examine the effects of such risk factors as attachment problems, stress/anxiety, child maltreatment, depression, and sociopathy, along with demographic characteristics, to offer a fuller understanding of how these factors relate to various firesetting typologies.

A heightened understanding of these processes will also provide clear nodal points for intervention to further decrease the likelihood of progression from less problematic to more problematic juvenile firesetters. This holistic approach can guide an array of community organization and prevention services along with legal, casework, and clinical interventions.

Several other research-related issues need to be addressed as well. Empirical examination of the seven motivation subtypes is warranted to validate the conceptual model presented in this chapter. One approach would involve comparing equivalent groups of pathological and nonpathological firesetters on such outcomes as age at onset, the number of fires set, the amount of fire damage, or the number of fire victims. Another research question should consider whether some motivational subtypes (i.e., fire fascination) may be more prevalent among juvenile firesetters than others (i.e., revenge). Research is also needed to identify risk factors associated with specific typologies and to determine how these risk factors affect firesetting pathways over time. For instance, parental neglect may be a robust predictor of fire fascination in early childhood, whereas antisocial peer group affiliation may be the strongest predictor of adolescent firesetting. Answering questions of this nature will inform the best practice models of prevention and treatment.

A number of clinical implications emerged from our model as well. Thus far, knowledge of juvenile firesetting has developed primarily through inductive processes. A natural consequence of the inductive process is that knowledge easily becomes fragmented because ideas that seem inherently logical to the practitioners are not empirically validated. Different professionals in different environments are constantly creating their own conceptual blueprints based on personal experiences. It is time to advance the science of juvenile firesetting by subjecting motivational typologies to empirical validation on a variety of children who engage in fire play and firesetting behaviors.

In this chapter, we have argued that motivational typology is a key component of treatment planning. According to our model, different treatment strategies should be applied to children based on their firesetting typology. For curious and accidental firesetters, we recommend fire safety education for the child and their family as the primarily intervention. Additionally, the psychological aftermath of firesetting may include guilt and anxiety that would require psychotherapy, in part to prevent the repetition of further firesetting activities. For children who set fire as a cry for help, interventions should focus on de-escalation of crises and teaching competencies in problem-solving. Fire safety education may be useful for this type of firesetter. For delinquent firesetters, treatment should focus on correcting problems with authority, helping them to accept positive structure, and replacing their criminal excitement with prosocial pride.

For pathological firesetters, treatment intervention should be more intensive and may have to include the provision of external structure to preclude further firesetting until the pathology is addressed. Because many of these children suffer from attachment problems and trauma, their capacity for increased relatedness needs to be fostered along with a healing of their past traumas. Cognitive-behavioral interventions can be employed to correct the pathological reliance on fire for excitation or inhibition of psychological processes. Finally, pathological firesetters require treatment interventions that focus on increasing their capacities to regulate their emotions in more adaptive ways.

Some examples have been provided suggesting correlates between types of firesetters and types of personality functioning. This material has been based on our clinical experiences. It would be timely to use standardized psychometric measures to confirm and modify this work.

As the science of juvenile firesetting progresses, a more comprehensive risk assessment process needs to be developed that provides for the motivational profile, personality factors, and peer and family relationships. An assessment process of this nature would provide richer data enhancing our understanding of juvenile firesetters while informing our clinical practice models.

Currently, the field of juvenile firesetting has not received the professional attention it deserves. This is due, in part, to the lack of a conceptual understanding of what motivates children who set fires and how to treat them. This chapter presents a model ready for empirical validation and clinical application. Further study in the areas of theory construction, research, and clinical practice is in order to fully develop this field of inquiry.

NOTES

1. National Fire Protection Association, hereafter NFPA, 2006a.
2. U.S. Fire Administration, hereafter USFA, 2005.
3. U.S. Department of Justice, hereafter USDOJ, 1999.
4. NFPA, 2006b.
5. Snyder, 1998; USDOJ, 1999.
6. Putnam & Kirkpatrick, 2005; see also USFA, 2004.
7. MacDonald, 1963.
8. Merz-Perez & Heide, 2004.
9. Douglas & Olshaker, 1995.
10. See discussion in Douglas & Olshaker, 1995; Loeber & Farrington, 2001.
11. Lewis & Yarnell, 1951.
12. Bachelard, 1964.
13. See discussion in Williams, 2005.
14. Heath, Gayton, & Hardesty, 1976.

15. Fineman, 1980.
16. Canter & Fritzon, 1998; see also the discussion in Santtila, Hakkanen, Alison, & White, 2003.
17. Santtila et al., 2003.
18. See discussion in Kolko & Kazdin, 1986.
19. Kolko, 2002.
20. Putnam & Kirkpatrick, 2005.
21. Kolko & Kazdin, 1990; Santtila et al., 2003.
22. Kolko & Kazdin, 1986.
23. See discussion in Caplan, 1964.
24. See Bronfenbrenner, 1977, 1979.
25. See discussions in Catalano & Hawkins, 1996; Gottfredson & Hirschi, 1990; Hawkins, Catalano, & Miller, 1992; Loeber, 1988, 1990, 1996; Loeber & Farrington, 2001; Moffit, 1997; Patterson, Capaldi, & Banks, 1991; Thornberry, Lizotte, Krohn, Farnsworth, & Jang, 1994.
26. Loeber, 1988, 1990, 1996.
27. Loeber, et al. 1993; see discussion in Loeber & Farrington, 2001.
28. Fineman, 1980.
29. Canter & Fritzon, 1998.
30. See discussion in Loeber & Farrington, 2001.

REFERENCES

Bachelard, G. (1964). *The psychoanalysis of fire.* Boston: Beacon Press.
Bronfenbrenner, U. (1977). Toward an experimental ecology of human development. *American Psychologist, 32,* 513–531.
Bronfenbrenner, U. (1979). *The ecology of human development: Experiments by nature and design.* Cambridge, MA: Harvard University Press.
Canter, D., & Fritzon, K. (1998). Differentiating arsonists: A model of firesetting actions and characteristics. *Legal and Criminological Psychology, 3,* 73–96.
Caplan, G. (1964). *Principles of preventive psychiatry.* New York: Basic Books.
Catalano, R. F., & Hawkins, J. D. (1996). The social developmental model: A theory of anti-social behavior. In J. D. Hawkins (Ed.), *Delinquency and crime: Current theories* (pp.149–197). New York: Cambridge University Press.
Douglas, J. E., & Olshaker, M. (1995). *Mindhunter: Inside the FBI's elite serial crime unit.* New York: Simon & Schuster.
Erikson, E. (1950). *Childhood and society.* New York: Norton.
Fineman, K. (1980). Firesetting in childhood and adolescence. *Psychiatric Clinics of North America, 3,* 483–500.
Freud, S. (1964). *The standard edition of the complete psychological works of Sigmund Freud, Volume XXII (1932–36).* London: The Hogarth Press.
Gottfredson, M. R., & Hirschi, T. (1990). *A general theory of crime.* Stanford, CA: Stanford University Press.
Hawkins, J. D., Catalano, R. T., & Miller, J. Y. (1992). Risk and protective factors for alcohol and other drug problems in adolescence and early adulthood: Implications for substance abuse prevention. *Psychological Bulletin, 112,* 64–105.
Heath, G. A., Gayton, W. F., & Hardesty, V. A. (1976). Childhood firesetting. *Canadian Psychiatric Association Journal, 21,* 229–237.
Kolko, D. (Ed.). (2002). *Handbook on firesetting in children and youth.* Boston: Academic Press.

Kolko, D., & Kazdin, A. E. (1986). A conceptualization of firesetting in children and adolescents. *Journal of Abnormal Child Psychology, 14,* 49–61.

Kolko, D., & Kazdin, A. E. (1990). Matchplay and firesetting in children: Relationship to parent. marital, and family dysfunction. *Journal of Clinical Child Psychology, 19,* 229–238.

Lewis, N. D. C., & Yarnell, H. (1951). Pathological firesetting (pyromania). *Nervous and mental disease monograph, 82.* Nicholasville, KY: Coolidge Foundation.

Loeber, R. (1988). Natural histories of juvenile conduct problems, delinquency, and associated substance use: Evidence for developmental progressions. In B. B. Lahey & A. E. Kazdin (Eds.), *Advances in Clinical Psychology* (Vol. 11, pp. 73–124). New York: Plenum.

Loeber, R. (1990). Development and risk factors of juvenile antisocial behavior and delinquency. *Clinical Psychology Review, 10,* 1–41.

Loeber, R. (1996). Developmental continuity, change, and pathways in male juvenile problem behaviors and delinquency. In J. D. Hawkins (Ed.), *Delinquency and crime: Current theories* (pp. 1–27). New York: Cambridge University Press.

Loeber, R., & Farrington, D.P. (2001). The significance of child delinquency. In R. Loeber & D. P. Farrington (Eds.), *Child delinquents: Development, intervention, and service needs* (pp. 1–22). Thousand Oaks, CA: Sage Publications.

Loeber, R., Wung, P., Keenan, K., Giroux, B., Stouthamer-Loeber, M., Van Kammen, W. B., & Maughen, B. (1993). Developmental pathways in disruptive child behavior. *Development and Psychology, 5,* 101–132.

MacDonald, J. M. (1963). The threat to kill. *American Journal of Psychiatry, 8,* 125–130.

Merz-Perez, L., & Heide, K. (2004). *Animal cruelty: Pathway to violence against people.* Walnut Creek, CA: AltaMira Press.

Moffitt, T. E. (1997). Adolescence-limited and life-course-persistent offending: A complementary pair of developmental theories. In T.P. Thornberry (Ed.), *Advances in criminological theory* (Vol. 7), *Developmental theories of crime and delinquency* (pp.11–54). New Brunswick, NJ: Transaction Publishers.

National Fire Protection Association. (2006a). *NFPA: Fire loss in the United States during 2005–Abridged report.* Retrieved August 2, 2006, from www.nfpa.org.

National Fire Protection Association. (2006b). *NFPA rews release: Arson reaches historic low in 2003.* Retrieved March 8, 2006, from www.nfpa.org.

Patterson, G. R., Capaldi, D. M., & Banks, L. (1991). An early starter model of predicting delinquency. In D. J. Pepler & K. H. Rubin (Eds.), *The development and treatment of childhood aggression* (pp.139–164). Hillsdale, NJ: Lawrence Erlbaum.

Putnam, C. T., & Kirkpatrick, J. T. (2005). Juvenile firesetting: A research overview. *Juvenile Justice Bulletin.* Washington, D.C.: Office of Juvenile Justice and Delinquency Prevention.

Santtila, P., Hakkanen, H., Alison, L., & Whyte, C. (2003). Juvenile firesetters: Crime scene actions and offender characteristics. *Legal and Criminological Psychology, 8,* 1–20.

Snyder, H. N. (1998). *Juvenile Arrests 1997.* Washington, D.C.: U.S. Department of Justice.

Thornberry, T. P., Lizotte, A. J., Krohn, M. D., Farnsworth, M., & Jang, S. J. (1994). Delinquent peers, beliefs, and delinquent behavior: A longitudinal test of interactional theory. *Criminology, 32,* 47–83.

U.S. Department of Justice. (1999). *Juvenile Arson, 1997* (OJJDP Fact Sheet #91). Washington, D.C.: U.S. Department of Justice.

U.S. Fire Administration. (2001). *Arson in the United States.* Retrieved August 1, 2006, www.usfa.fema.gov.

U.S. Fire Administration. (2004). *Juvenile arson: Youth firesetting facts* (Fact sheet). Washington, D.C.: Federal Emergency Management Administration. Retrieved January 8, 2006, from www.usfa.fema.gov/fire service/arson/arson-aaw3.shtm.

U.S. Fire Administration. (2005). *USFA arson fire statistics.* Retrieved August 1, 2006, from www.usfa.fema.gov.

Williams, D. L. (2005). *Understanding the arsonist: From assessment to confession.* Tucson, AZ: Lawyers & Judges Publishing.

CHAPTER 9

Weapons of Minors' Destruction: Youthful Offenders and Guns

H. R. "Rudy" Hardy Jr.

In 1991, a 12-year-old student from northern New Jersey fired three rounds from a 0.380 semiautomatic handgun in a schoolyard during recess. The shots missed their target, but injured three other students. Upon questioning, the 12-year-old revealed that he had purchased the firearm on the street three days earlier for $300. During the investigation that followed, an agent from the Bureau of Alcohol, Tobacco, Firearms, and Explosives (ATF) asked the boy if, supplied with $300 and given 30 minutes, could he leave school and return with a handgun similar to the one that he had possessed earlier. The boy replied, "What do I do with the extra 15 minutes?" At that moment, the agent investigating the case realized the severity of the firearms trafficking problem in that area.[1] In this example, the juvenile used a relatively small caliber, but sophisticated firearm, but the public's perception is that youths have access to and use high-capacity and sophisticated firearms. This perception is apparent in news media reports.

Researchers, too, have noted the increasing frequency of youths not only in gangs, but also in schools reporting carrying and using handguns. Surveying high school students about what caliber guns they owned, Sheley and Wright from Tulane University were surprised when one respondent pulled a gun out of his clothes to provide an accurate answer.[2]

THE GUN PROBLEM

Gun violence has led law enforcement agencies and communities to attempt to find solutions to this problem. Although gun control legislation is inherently difficult to garner support for, The Gun-Free Schools Act passed in 1994 mandated that students carrying weapons into schools face automatic expulsion. According to a report from the Department of Education for the school year 1998–99, more than 3,900 students were expelled for bringing a firearm to school. Of those, 57 percent were high school students, 33 percent were junior high schools students, and 10 percent were elementary school students.[3] The results are not too surprising if you factor in that many problem students, those who may be at highest risk to obtain and carry a weapon, may already have dropped out of school by 10th or 11th grade. Also during this study period, 60 percent of 6th- to 12th-grade students said they could "get a gun if they wanted." And, a 2003 questionnaire[4] found that 6 percent of high school students reported carrying a gun in the 30 days before the survey.

Access to and Sources of Guns

The apparent ease with which juveniles access firearms is particularly troubling. Through the analysis of gun violence problems, it has become obvious that limiting the sources of both illegal and legal guns reduces the number of illegal guns in the neighborhoods. A firearm in the hands of a juvenile increases the seriousness of confrontations that could best be resolved in a different way. Youths involved in gangs, drug trafficking, or illegal drug activities are likely to possess or use firearms. Addressing this problem requires the involvement of multiple agencies and the community, as well as substantial investments in analysis, coordination, and implementation.[5]

In 2000, 28,663 people died from gunfire in the United States. Of these deaths, 16,586 (58 percent) resulted from suicide, 10,801 (38 percent) resulted from homicide, and 1,276 (4 percent) were reported as unintentional self-harm or deaths cased by undetermined intent. Firearm fatalities are the seventh leading cause of death in the United States.[6] These numbers were taken from death certificate reports. In addition, for every fatal shooting, there are roughly three nonfatal shootings.[7]

The impact of gun violence is even more serious among juveniles and youth. The firearm homicide rate for children under 15 years of age is 16 times higher in the United States than in 25 other industrialized countries combined. Of those youth ages 15 to 24, the U.S. firearm homicide rate is 5 times higher than in Canada and 30 times higher than in Japan, and the firearm homicide rate for the 15- to 24-year-old age group increased 158 percent during the 10-year period from 1984 to 1993.[8] A teenager in the United States today is more likely to die of a gunshot wound than from all the "natural causes of death combined"[9] and the chances are more likely for African American males. According to Kennedy,[10] there are almost six nonfatal woundings per homicide among teens, a rate twice that of older adults.

In a 1996 National Youth Gang Survey, youth gang members were reported to have been involved in 2,364 homicides in large cities and 561 homicides in suburban counties.[11] In a 1997 study of juvenile gang members, 50 percent admitted to using a gun in a crime.[12] There can be no doubt that the effects of firearms violence are a significant national crime problem. The psychological toll on a community is great. Armed drug dealers terrorize parts of our cities, and many citizens live in constant fear. Regardless of the "who, what, when, where, why, and how," some people feel that the type of firearm—that is, its make, model, and caliber—has a huge impact on the homicide rate. It has been hypothesized that the proliferation and use of semiautomatic handguns and large caliber handguns are directly associated with the homicide rate.

DEFINITIONS AND TYPES OF FIREARMS

A crime gun is any firearm that is illegally possessed, used in crime, or suspected to have been used in crime. An abandoned firearm may also be categorized as a crime gun if it is suspected that it was used in a crime or illegally possessed.[13] A Federal Firearms Licensee (FFL) is any person, partnership, or business entity holding a valid license issued by the ATF.[14]

To provide a general understanding of firearms and ammunition, the following concepts and definitions were extracted from ATF[15] and Giannelli[16] and will be used throughout this article. Firearms can be categorized into three basic types: handguns, rifles, and shotguns.

A handgun is a weapon designed to fire a small projectile from one or more barrels. It is held in one hand and has a short stock designed to be gripped by that one hand. There are three classifications of handguns: revolvers, pistols, and derringers. A revolver is a handgun that contains its ammunition in a revolving cylinder that typically holds five to nine cartridges each within a separate chamber. Before a revolver fires, the cylinder rotates and the next chamber is aligned with the barrel. A pistol is any handgun that does not contain its ammunition in a revolving cylinder. Pistols can be manually operated or semiautomatic. A semiautomatic pistol generally contains cartridges in a magazine located in the grip of the gun. When the semiautomatic pistol is fired, the spent cartridge that contained the bullet and propellant is ejected, the firing mechanism is cocked, and a new cartridge is chambered. On the other hand, a derringer is a small single- or multiple-shot handgun other than a revolver or a semiautomatic pistol.

A rifle is intended to be fired from the shoulder. It uses the energy of the explosive in a fixed metallic cartridge to fire only a single projectile through a rifled bore for each single pull of the trigger. A shotgun is also intended to be fired from the shoulder. It uses the energy of the explosive, but in contrast to a rifle, it uses a fixed shotgun shell to fire through a smooth bore either a number of ball shot or a single projectile for each single pull of the trigger.

A semiautomatic firearm requires a trigger pull for each round that is fired. For example, if someone were to shoot 10 rounds in a semiautomatic firearm, they would need to pull the trigger 10 times (once for each round fired). Compare this with a fully automatic firearm (machine gun), which will continue to fire as long as the trigger is held or until it runs out of ammunition.

The types of ammunition used in today's modern firearms are identified using two classifications: caliber and gauge. The caliber is the size of the ammunition that a firearm is designed to shoot as measured by the bullet's approximate diameter in inches in the United States and in millimeters in other countries. In some instances, ammunition is described with additional terms such as the year of its introduction (0.30/06) or the name of the designer (0.30 Newton). In some countries, ammunition is also described in terms of the length of the cartridge case (7.62 × 63 mm). A shotgun's gauge is determined by the number of spherical balls of pure lead, each exactly fitting the bore that equals 1 pound. The most common gauges of shotguns in the United States are the 12-gauge and 20-gauge shotguns.

THE LAW AND YOUTH FIREARMS POSSESSION

Federal firearms laws supersede any firearms laws in state and local jurisdictions. Current federal minimum age regulations relating to firearms vary by type of gun and means of access. The Federal Gun Control Act of 1968 made it unlawful for federally licensed firearms dealers to sell handguns to people under 21. In addition, the Youth Handgun Safety Act of 1994 generally prohibited the transfer of handguns to people under 18. Exceptions include official military use and the following activities with the written consent of the parent or guardian: employment, ranching, farming, target practice, hunting, and handgun safety instruction. People between the ages of 18 and 21 may still acquire handguns from nonlicensed sellers.[17] There is no federal age restriction on the possession of long guns (including rifles and shotguns). Licensed dealers may only sell rifles and shotguns to people age 18 and older, and there is no age restriction on the transfer of shotguns and rifles by nonlicensed sellers.

The complexity of the firearms market poses a challenge for law enforcement officials who are seeking to develop strategies to attack the illegal market that supplies youthful offenders. The firearms market includes federal firearms licensees, unregulated sellers, and private transferors in what is known as the secondary market and the illegal gun market. The illegal market involves transfers from both federal licensees and from unregulated transferors. The market for guns in the United States is difficult enough that it is helpful to think in terms of several interdependent gun markets. There are both legal and illegal retail markets in guns. It was believed that theft was the main source of guns for the illegal market, but new evidence demonstrates that the legal market is the chief source of supply for the illegal market's crime guns. The intentional diversion of guns from the legal to the illegal market, a process known as "firearms trafficking," has been the subject of intense research and intervention.

The legal gun market is divided into a primary market, comprising all transfers of guns by sources such as federally licensed retailers (gun dealers and pawnbrokers), and a secondary market, consisting of transfers involving less formal sources, such as private parties, collectors, and unlicensed vendors at gun shows. The split between primary market sales by licensed retailers and secondary market sales by other sources is approximately 60/ 40.[18] Gun violence is facilitated when firearms are inadequately secured by licensees; common carriers such as the United Parcel Service (UPS[TM]); and gun owners, especially parents with children at home.

THE PROBLEM OF GUNS IN AMERICA

There are approximately 44 million gun owners in the United States.[19] This means that 25 percent of all adults, and 40 percent of American households, own at least one firearm. Of the 192 million firearms that are possessed, 65 million are handguns.[20] Every day there are approximately 37,500 gun sales, which include the sale of 17,800 handguns. This statistic alone elevates the danger of firearms reaching the illegal firearms trafficking market through robberies and burglaries. Yet, this figure does not provide an accurate representation of the number of individuals actually purchasing a firearm. Although 37,500 firearms sold per day is an astonishing number, it should be pointed out that this figure also includes those firearms that are sold during multiple sales transactions. Federal law requires that an official record be kept and documentation is forwarded to the ATF detailing the sale of more than one handgun to an individual during a five-day period. There is no limit on the number of firearms that an individual can purchase at any one time. The firearms multiple sale issue has become a significant issue in the border states of Texas and Arizona. Federal firearms licensees in those two states have a large number of multiple sales transactions because of the proximity to Mexico. A firearm that costs $50 in the United States can be sold for $300 in Mexico or the firearm can be traded for illegal narcotics.

In 1994, it was reported that a quarter-million households had a theft of one or more firearms, which accounted for an estimated 600,000 guns stolen during burglaries.[21] This is another figure that is deceiving because no one truly knows how many guns are stolen each year from both official (FFLs) and unofficial (private individuals) sources. As stated, 600,000 is only an estimate, but some estimates show an even greater theft rate.

In Houston, Texas, there have been recent reports of firearms thefts from a local sporting goods chain. The thieves committed a well-orchestrated "smash and grab" during work hours of numerous firearms. Because of the similarity to past thefts in New Orleans, it is thought that evacuees from New Orleans during hurricane Katrina in 2005 played an important role in these thefts. The disruption caused by several major hurricanes during this period also provided opportunities for guns to be stolen in both store looting and thefts from abandoned homes, to be transported between states, and to be made more accessible to children during periods of transient living.

Since 1993, the number of youth who report that they carry a gun has risen.[22] In 1997, it was reported that 14 percent or one in seven male juveniles reported carrying a gun.[23] Sheley and Wright[24] report that 22 percent of inner-city youth carry weapons. This same report states that 88 percent of convicted juvenile offenders carry guns. However, in a 1999 survey of high school students, the National Youth Violence Prevention Resource Center determined that 9 percent of all male students carried a gun at least once during the 30 days preceding the survey. This figure was down from 13.7 percent when the survey was conducted in 1993.[25]

Firearms are readily available on the illegal gun market and those who are likely to possess guns are young males who are drug sellers and gang members.[26] In one study, 23 percent of arrestees who owned a gun said that they used one to commit a crime. Among juvenile drug sellers who owned a firearm, 42 percent reported using a gun in a crime; among gang members, 50 percent reported using a gun.[27]

In 2004, the ATF received more than 251,000 requests from police departments for gun trace information involving firearms used in crime. Three-fourths of the guns traced were handguns and one-third of the guns were less than three years old. Revolvers and semiautomatic guns are the most frequently used.[28]

In their research, Decker, Pennell, and Caldwell[29] reveal that being a juvenile male, gang member, or a drug seller means a greater involvement in using a gun while committing a crime. Their research found that 23 percent of those who owned a gun also said they used one to commit a crime, but that figure was higher at 33 percent for juvenile males, 50 percent for juvenile gang members, and 42 percent for drug dealers.

Youth Gun Culture

It is widely known that there has been a change in the weapons used by young people. Over the last decade, the weapons involved in settling juveniles' disputes have changed dramatically from fists or knives to handguns. That change in the weapons of choice of juveniles is reflected in the homicide rate for juveniles.[30]

Juvenile and youth gun violence can be attributed to three separate and distinct areas of discussion. The first area is gun violence in schools. School gun violence became a serious public issue with the extensive media coverage of shootings in places like Jonesboro, Arkansas; Pearl, Mississippi; and West Paducah, Kentucky. There were 40 school shooting deaths during the 1997–98 school years.[31] According to the National School Safety Center, school homicides and suicides declined in the 1997–98 school year. According to a study conducted by the Centers for Disease Control and Prevention, there is a less than one in a million chance that there would be a school-related death.[32] From this statistic, it appears that school shootings are rare, but carrying a gun to school is not. During one school year, a survey of 12th-grade males revealed that 1 in 17 carried a gun to school.

Second, guns and drugs contribute a great deal to the U.S. homicide rate. With the introduction of crack cocaine in the 1980s, the homicide rate skyrocketed among juveniles and youth. Other drugs such as methamphetamine have found their way into the urban and rural areas of the United State.[33] Because of the violent nature of the illegal drug business, firearms have become the weapons of choice among drug dealers. It has been known for a long time that firearms are the tools of the trade for the violent narcotics trafficker. Historically, firearm investigations have crossed the lines into narcotics investigations. More than 80 percent of all the firearms recovered in the United States are those typically used by drug dealers or are firearms used in drug-related crimes. Sheley concluded, "involvement in drugs leads one to possess, carry and use firearms,"[34] but Sheley also states that involvement in illegal narcotics activity does not necessarily lead to illegal gun activity. Sheley's research has revealed that nonusers of illegal narcotics were heavily involved in illegal criminal activity involving a firearm.

Third, in the 1980s, the involvement of youth gangs in drugs became a major concern. In 1980, there were approximately 2,000 gangs in the United States consisting of approximately 100,000 members. In 1996, there were 31,000 gangs consisting of approximately 846,000 members.[35] Gang members are more likely to own guns for protection than nongang members. Gang members are at a higher risk of being killed than the general population. In a 1998 survey of gang members, most of them acknowledged that they owned guns. Ninety percent of the gang members commented that they preferred more powerful handguns.[36]

The firearms study by Ruddell and Mays[37] classified 1,055 firearms that were confiscated from juveniles (those under 17 years of age) in St. Louis, Missouri, from 1992 to 1999. The authors used the National Institute of Justice (NIJ) body armor threat-level scale to classify the lethality of each confiscated firearm. Body armor also known as "bullet-proof vests" are rated on a scale of one to five that designates the ability of the vest to withstand the penetration of various calibers of gun ammunitions. The authors modified the NIJ scale by adding one additional level that would classify weapons that have a very low capacity for injury, such as BB and pellet guns that were also confiscated by police. The authors recognized the fact that the lethality of wounds is related to such factors as the design, velocity, and weight of the bullet. To account for the wide variation of bullet types, the authors presupposed that the most lethal types of cartridges were used in each firearm contained in the data set. The authors also considered the muzzle velocity and the stopping power of the bullet.

Ruddell and Mays concluded that handguns (pistols and revolvers) made up 77 percent of the firearms that were confiscated during the study period. The authors further concluded that 61 percent of the handguns were factored in at Threat-Level 2, which represents low-caliber weapons (0.22, -.25, 0.32) or the so-called Saturday night specials (a term synonymous with small, cheap handguns or "junk guns"). In contrast, 12 percent of the handguns recovered by the police had the greatest threat level. This group of firearms consisted of the 9 mm, 0.40, 0.357, 0.45, 0.41, and 0.44 calibers.

Ruddell and Mays pointed out that the portrayals in the media about juveniles using sophisticated firearms are not supported in this study. The authors found that "youths are more likely to have pellet guns, 0.22 caliber firearms, and Saturday night specials recovered by police."[38] Finally, the authors made two interesting observation because of their study. The first is that juveniles were not likely to have an assault weapon confiscated and, secondly, a high amount of sawed-off rifles and shotguns were confiscated by police. Although it is often difficult and ill-advised to make any conclusions as to the lethality of the weapons simply from their caliber, the NIJ Threat-Level Scale can be used, with caution, as an indicator of firearm lethality.

Sources of Firearms

In the tragic 1999 Columbine High School shootings, teens Harris and Klebold used a Tec-9 semiautomatic and a 9 mm high-point carbine rifle, both of which had originally been legally purchased from a gun dealer in Denver 18 months before the mass murder/suicides. Tracing the history of those firearms, officials found that they were then sold through various nonregistered transactions until they fell into the hands of the youths plotting the violent attack. The Tec-9 was a modified version of a handgun outlawed under the federal assault weapons ban. It is cheap, light, and potent, as authorities explained, firing 32 rounds in seconds. It is designed to kill many people very quickly and is popular with gangs. Investigations following the incident led to charges against the dealer who eventually sold the weapon to Harris, 17, who was underage at the time of the purchase. The other weapons were given to Klebold by a female friend who was old enough to acquire them legally, and technically, it was not a crime for her to allow the rifle into the possession of someone underage.[39]

Youths arrested with firearms often claim that it takes little time or effort for them to obtain such weapons illegally. And it was found that those who belong to a gang and those who sell drugs are more likely to have easy access to guns. This revelation figures strongly into the association between guns and youth. Among male juvenile arrestees, gun ownership and use is higher than among arrestees in general.[40]

Before seriously studying the firearms trafficking phenomena, it was believed that there were two sources of illegally supplied firearms: old guns that were stolen and new guns that were trafficked. If was further believed that the trafficking occurred in large volume and primarily across state lines. It was also thought that youths and felons always committed firearm thefts. After the implementation of extensive firearms tracing, however, multiple sources of illegally trafficked firearms emerged.

The trafficking in new firearms, interstate and intrastate, results in firearms moving quickly from retail sale into the hands of youths. As many as one-third of the guns used by juveniles and up one-half of those used by people ages 18 to 24 were purchased within the last three years from an FFL, which indicates that a large amount of new guns are being sold to youth illegally.[41] This type of illegal firearms trafficking can best be illustrated in the following example: In March 1996, a gun was recovered from a Washington, D.C., youth and was traced after its obliterated serial number was successfully raised by a crime laboratory. The firearm's trace information led to a licensed gun dealer in Missouri and later to a

Nashville, Tennessee, gun trafficker who sold 200 to 300 guns on the streets of the nation's capital. Through this investigation, 138 semiautomatic firearms originally sold by the Missouri dealer were recovered in crimes in the Washington, D.C., area. These crimes included murder, kidnapping, robbery, and armed assault. In June 1997, the Nashville gun trafficker pleaded guilty to federal charges and was sentenced to serve a term of confinement in federal prison.

The trafficking in used firearms, interstate and intrastate, is brought about by licensed firearms dealers, pawnbrokers, straw purchasers, and straw purchasing rings. This type of firearms trafficking can be accomplished through unlicensed sellers, including at gun shows, at flea markets, or through newspaper ads, gun magazines, Internet sales, and personal associations. The illegal trafficking of used firearms accounts for a significant source of crime guns, and these guns are more likely to show up in the hands of youths.[42] People prohibited from purchasing firearms under federal law because of felony convictions or other prohibitions often use "straw purchasers" with clean records to obtain their firearms. Straw purchasers falsely represent that they are the actual buyers of the firearms; in reality, they are paid to purchase them for prohibited people from outlets, stores, pawn shops, flea markets, and other firearms dealers. Straw purchasers are the second most common way that firearms end up in the hands of criminals. As an example of this type of illegal firearms trafficking, it has been reported that during a four-month period, two traffickers transported approximately 90 firearms from Georgia to New York. Investigators conducted surveillance on the subjects as they transported 11 firearms from Augusta, Georgia, to New York City. The two suspects were charged with illegally transporting firearms interstate, unlicensed dealing in firearms, and conspiracy.

Trafficking in new and used stolen firearms involves firearms that are stolen from federally licensed dealers, pawnbrokers, manufactures, wholesalers, importers and common carries (e.g., UPS), and residences. These firearms range from new to old. The time to crime for new firearms is relatively fast in this type of firearms trafficking.[43] In 1996, investigators in Wilmington, Delaware, arrested a defendant for receipt of a large quantity of firearms stolen by another defendant, who had been arrested for the theft of 390 Llama firearms from an interstate shipment. Interviews with the thief yielded information regarding the identity and role of the recipient of the guns, who was subsequently arrested. The recipient pleaded guilty to possession of stolen firearms and was sentenced to prison.

The final method of illegal firearms trafficking that contributes to youth gun possession is individual thefts of firearms by criminals and juveniles for their own purposes. This simply describes individuals who steal firearms, mostly from residences, for their own criminal purposes. In this case, no trafficking occurs.[44] In one example, a group of young men, the defendants, committed commercial and residential burglaries. The defendants stole entire gun safes out of homes and cut them open inside a small storage unit they had rented. The suspects became increasingly bolder and more violent, ultimately committing a home invasion in which the female victim was tied up and her house robbed. During the investigation, 200 firearms were recovered. All the defendants were prosecuted and served lengthy prison terms.

In 2002, it was estimated that approximately 250,000 firearms existed in the United States. In a 1996 survey of 10th and 11th graders, 50 percent of the respondents reported that obtaining a gun would be no trouble.[45] This same survey pointed out that family and friends were the primary sources of guns. Few surveyed had asked someone to purchase the gun for them from a legal or an illegal source. It is also reported that 14 percent of the firearms used in crimes by juveniles were sold by private sellers without an FFL, and 10 percent were sold at gun shows or fleas markets.[46]

In a study of guns recovered from youth in Houston,[47] it was found that the majority were sophisticated (semiautomatic) and high caliber (0.38 caliber and above). These findings refute some of earlier results by Ruddell and Mays in their study of crime guns recovered in St. Louis, Missouri. Perhaps surprisingly, only 18 percent of the guns taken from Houston youth were classified as Saturday night specials. Most guns were confiscated by authorities before official charges were developed so the records were more likely to reflect "weapons offenses" than any other charges.

PROBLEMS IN RESEARCHING JUVENILE GUN USE

Generally, data obtained from government and private agencies before 2003 were grossly incomplete or nonexistent or came from ungeneralizable sources. One of the major problems in analyzing firearms trend research is that few jurisdictions have collected such data over time, and fewer have divided these data into categories of youth, juveniles, and adults. Another research problem is the subjective nature of some gun classifications, particularly regarding the lethality or sophistication of the firearm, because all are potentially lethal regardless of caliber or sophistication. Furthermore, a wide variety of ammunition can be used in the various calibers of firearms (i.e., 0.22 short versus 0.22 long rifle ammunition, hollow point versus lead versus full metal jacket or Teflon-coated ammunition). For example, a 0.38 caliber cartridge can be fired in a 0.357 caliber handgun, thus in some minds it has a lower-level lethality. All of these cartridges have a certain muzzle velocity (stopping power)—for example, 300 to 400 feet/second for a well-made pellet gun (which can kill with a well-placed shot to the head) to an excess of 2,500 feet/second for a military M-16. All of the other calibers—0.380, 0.38, 0.357, 0.40, 0.44, and so on—fall somewhere in between. In addition, both cheap and expensive ammunition are available and some is even made at home. A 0.44 magnum handgun is a powerful weapon (some say, "the most powerful handgun in the world") and is capable of killing an elephant. In contrast, a 0.22 caliber handgun is a significantly less powerful weapon, but still it can incapacitate a human being. Between 1985 and 1996, of the 599 police officers killed in the United States, 75 were killed with firearms with a caliber of 0.32 or less (the so-called Saturday night specials).[48] As far as sophistication goes, a Glock Model 22 0.40 caliber semiautomatic handgun is a lethal, sophisticated, and expensive weapon as compared with a homemade, much less sophisticated zip gun, but both weapons will kill.

Finally, drawing any conclusions as to lethality cannot be accomplished if a data set does not report the type of ammunition used with the firearm. In addition, many data sets do not identify a "short-barrel shotgun" (sawed-off shotgun) or a "short-barrel rifle" (sawed-off rifle) or firearms that have been converted to fire fully automatic (machine gun).

PROGRAMS TO COMBAT YOUTH GUN VIOLENCE

To address citizens' fear of gun violence, many communities are adopting strategies that are tailor-made for a specific gun-violence problem. This problem-solving approach requires the community to participate in implementing a gun-violence reduction plan. In many cities, local and federal law enforcement are working with the community to combat gun violence. Many of the violence reduction programs are specific to youth gun violence. Below are a few of these enforcement initiatives aimed at reducing youth and violent crime.

Project Exile, originating in the Richmond, Virginia, U.S. attorney's office, created an Exile Task Force composed of federal and local prosecutors, ATF agents, local police officers, state troopers, and a Federal Bureau of Investigation (FBI) agent. The task force reviews every local gun arrest to determine whether it should be prosecuted federally or locally.

As part of the Exile model, the U.S. attorney's office provided training to local police on federal firearms statutes as well as search-and-seizure issues. To expedite cases, the police firearms office was electronically connected to ATF to arrange immediate tracing of seized firearms. Both the Commonwealth attorney and the Virginia attorney general detailed a staff prosecutor to the U.S. attorney for assistance in firearms prosecutions.

A major component of the project has been the innovative outreach and education effort promoted through various media outlets to convey the Exile initiative's message. For example, the U.S. attorney successfully formed a coalition of businesses, community, and church leaders to promote the project. Additionally, a nonprofit foundation was established to fund the media efforts for this outreach program. Media efforts included television ads, billboards, bus wraps, and bumper stickers.

Exile was advertised as being very successful, reducing the number of homicides by 40 percent and armed robberies by 30 percent in its first year (mid-1998), with further decreases in the subsequent two years. The federal Virginia Exile program was successfully replicated in other federal districts, including the western district of New York (Rochester), the southern (Houston) and western (Austin) districts of Texas, the northern district of Indiana, and the district of Colorado. Each jurisdiction consulted with the U.S. attorney in Richmond and implemented the same, or similar, task force approach, referral process, training, and coordination. Denver's Exile program also includes an intensive focus on prosecution of gun dealer violations, Brady denials, comprehensive gun tracing, and identification of violent crime hot spots.

Similar to Exile, Project I.C.E. (Project Isolating the Criminal Element), which originated in the northern district of Alabama, bases its success on its vigorous prosecution of federal firearms offenses in partnership with the Birmingham police department, ATF, and local district attorneys' offices. Project I.C.E. included a training program for local law enforcement as well as a community outreach component. The project was complemented by a comprehensive crime-gun tracing program under ATF's Youth Crime Gun Interdiction Initiative and the Department of Housing and Urban Development's (HUD's) Operation Safe Home, a task force targeting violent crime in public housing.

The Kansas City Gun Experiment focused on reducing crime by seizures of illegal guns. This 1992–93 project targeted directed patrols to an 80-block area where the homicide rate was 20 times the national average. Patrol officers utilized stop-and-frisk methods and plain-view sightings during vehicle stops. During a 29-week experimental period, it has been reported that drive-by shootings dropped from seven to one in the target area, overall crimes dropped 49 percent, and homicides dropped 67 percent.

Project Exile, Project I.C.E., and the Kansas City Gun Experiment are just three of the gun-crime reduction programs that have been implemented across the United States. The Boston Gun Project's Operation Ceasefire is a program that been written about extensively and one that has received the most publicity as the premier youth-crime reduction program in the country. During a five-year period, Boston experienced 155 youth homicides. Most of these homicides occurred by gun. In an effort to contain gun violence in Boston, a National Institute of Justice problem-solving project was launched. It took approximately two years (from 1994 to 1996) for Boston to develop its plan, during which time "Gun Project participants approached the problem in supply and demand terms."[49] The illicit gun markets were targeted by law enforcement. These illegal gun markets supplied guns to the youth in Boston. Using firearms tracing, law enforcement was able to determine the sources of the firearms and have these firearm traffickers prosecuted in federal court.

Through the use of crime-gun analysis, it was determined that Boston's youth had a taste for new guns: 33 percent of the guns associated with gang members were less than two years old.[50] This analysis also proved that the southern states were not the largest source of the firearms. Crime-gun analysis revealed that 33 percent of the traceable guns were sold in Massachusetts and that the next largest source state was Georgia at 8 percent. As Kennedy and colleagues said, "Boston had a large problem in its own backyard."[51]

The Boston Gun Project was meaningful in that it united police, practitioners, and researchers to assess the youth violence problem in Boston. The outcomes from the assessment were responsible for a substantial reduction in youth homicide and youth violence in Boston.[52]

Federal authorities in Camden, New Jersey; Baton Rouge, Louisiana; Memphis, Tennessee; High Point and Wilmington, North Carolina; Stockton, California; and the District of Columbia have replicated Ceasefire by emphasizing deterrence of youth gun violence in selected hot-spot neighborhoods. For example, the Memphis Operation Ceasefire locates gun-crime hot spots with the assistance of researchers from the University of Memphis and emphasizes its zero tolerance policy for firearms possession in school zones. The Stockton Ceasefire targeted street-level youth gang violence, and it has been reported that this initiative reduced the youth homicide rate by 75 percent in 1998. Conducting its own internal crime mapping, the District of Columbia found success by focusing efforts on youth gang violence and prosecuting large cases as "organized crime" matters involving gun violence. Operation Target in the western district of Pennsylvania obtained the assistance of Carnegie-Mellon University to secure gun-tracing data and crime mapping. The U.S. attorney and the ATF use this information to work with FFLs to detect illegal trafficking and deter straw purchases. Emphasis is devoted to suppressing the use of firearms by probationers and parolees.

Many of these profiled communities have collaborated on issues of juvenile violence and illegal firearms trafficking. Not only is law enforcement involved in these crime protection efforts, but also community residents. Other public and private agencies were also included in the development of these plans. None of these programs comes from a cookie cutter; all are different in that they are shaped to the makeup and the direction of the community. All of these programs, however, do have one thing in common: the goal to attack youth gun violence in the community.

In 2001, President Bush unveiled Project Safe Neighborhoods (PSN), a comprehensive, strategic approach to gun-crime enforcement. PSN targets crime guns and violent offenders in an effort to make streets and communities safer. The plan calls on each U.S. attorney to implement this national initiative, working in partnership with communities and state and local law enforcement agencies. The plan calls for an invigorated enforcement effort that builds on the successful programs already in place or, through new resources and tools, assists in creating effective gun-violence reduction programs.

The human and resource costs of gun violence are enormous. Although some programs have attempted to provide services and compensation for victims of gun violence, most programs are becoming more restrictive and the forms and amounts of assistance are growing smaller. New policies have placed restrictions on who may receive compensation and under what conditions, and caps have been placed on the amount of victim compensation. There are new limits on access to mental health counseling and assistance with medical expenses. In most cases, victims must cooperate with law enforcement investigators and time limits are imposed for filing for aid. This makes it difficult for the poor and those who live in fear in violent neighborhoods to benefit from resources that might help needy victims.[53]

NOTES

1. Federal Bureau of Investigation, hereafter FBI, 1998.
2. Kennedy, 1997.
3. U.S. Department of Education, 2002.

4. Grunbaum et al., 2004.
5. Braga, Kennedy, Piehl, & Waring, 2000.
6. Mokdad, Marks, Stroup, & Gerberding, 2004.
7. Fingerhut, 1993.
8. Office of Juvenile Justice and Delinquency Prevention, hereafter OJJDP, 1999.
9. Fingerhut, 1993.
10. Kennedy, 1997.
11. Moore & Terrett, 1996.
12. Cook & Ludwig, 1997.
13. Bureau of Alcohol Tobacco and Firearms and Explosives, hereafter ATF, 2000.
14. ATF, 1997.
15. ATF, 1993.
16. Giannelli, 1991.
17. Department of Justice, hereafter DOJ, & U.S. Treasury Department, hereafter USTD, 2005.
18. DOJ & USTD, 1999.
19. Cook & Ludwig, 1997.
20. Cook & Ludwig, 1997.
21. Cook & Ludwig, 1997.
22. Moore & Terrett, 1996.
23. Centers for Disease Control and Prevention, 1997.
24. Sheley & Wright, 1993.
25. Grunbaum et al., 2004.
26. Decker, Pennell, & Caldwell, 1997.
27. OJJDP, 1999.
28. Zawitz, 1995.
29. Decker et al., 1997.
30. Blumstein & Rosenfeld, 1998.
31. Donohue, Schiraldi, & Ziendenberg, 1998.
32. Kaufman, Chandler, & Rand, 1998.
33. Decker et al., 1997.
34. Sheley, 1994.
35. Moore & Terrett, 1996.
36. Huff, 1998.
37. Ruddell & Mays, 2003.
38. Ruddell & Mays, 2003, p. 243.
39. Olinger, 1999.
40. Decker et al., 1997.
41. ATF, 1999.
42. ATF, 1999.
43. ATF, 1999.
44. ATF, 1999.
45. Sheley & Wright, 1998.
46. "Illegal trafficking," 1999.
47. Hardy, 2006.
48. Ruddell & Mays, 2003.
49. Kennedy, 1997, p. 451.
50. Kennedy, Braga, Piehl, & Waring, 2001.
51. Kennedy et al., 2001, p. 19.
52. Braga et al., 2000.
53. Bonderman, 2001.

REFERENCES

Blumstein, A., & Rosenfeld, R. (1998). Explaining recent trends in U.S. homicide rates. *Journal of Criminal Law and Criminology, 88*(4), 1175–1216.

Bonderman, J. (2001). *Working with victims of gun violence.* Washington, D.C.: National Institute of Justice, U.S. Department of Justice.

Braga, A. A., Kennedy, D. M., Piehl, A. M., & Waring, E. J. (2000, May). *The Boston Gun Project: Impact evaluation findings.* Washington, D.C.: National Institute of Justice, Office of Justice Programs, U.S. Department of Justice.

Bureau of Alcohol, Tobacco and Firearms. (1993, September). *Firearms and explosives tracing guidebook.* Washington, D.C.: Bureau of Alcohol, Tobacco and Firearms.

Bureau of Alcohol, Tobacco and Firearms. (1997, October). *Guide to investigating illegal firearms trafficking.* Washington, D.C.: U.S. Department of the Treasury.

Bureau of Alcohol, Tobacco and Firearms. (1999, February). *The youth crime gun interdiction initiative crime gun trace analysis reports: The illegal youth firearms markets in 27 communities.* Washington, D.C.: U.S. Department of the Treasury.

Bureau of Alcohol, Tobacco and Firearms. (2000, July). *Crime gun trace reports (2000), National report.* Washington, D.C.: U.S. Department of the Treasury.

Centers for Disease Control and Prevention. (1997). *Youth risk behavior study.* Washington, D.C.: Centers for Disease Control and Prevention.

Cook, P. J., & Ludwig, J. (1997). *Guns in America: Results of a comprehensive national survey on firearms ownership and use* (Summary Report). Washington, D.C.: Police Foundation.

Decker, S. H., Pennell, S., & Caldwell, A. (1997, January). *Illegal firearms: Access and use by arrestees* (Research in Brief). Washington, D.C.: National Institute of Justice, Office of Justice Programs, U.S. Department of Justice.

Donohue, E., Schiraldi, V., & Ziendenberg, J. (1998). *School house hype: School shootings and the real risks kids face in America* (Policy Report). San Francisco, CA: Justice Policy Institute, National School Safety Center.

Federal Bureau of Investigation. (1998, September). Pattern crimes: Firearms trafficking enforcement techniques. *FBI Law Enforcement Bulletin, 67*(9), 6.

Fingerhut, L. A. (1993). *Firearm mortality among children, youth, and young adults 1–34 years of age, trends and current status: United States, 1985–1990* (Advance data from Vital and Health Statistics). Washington, D.C.: National Center for Health Statistics.

Giannelli, P. C. (1991, May/June). Ballistics evidence: Firearms identification. *Criminal Law Bulletin, 27,* 195–215.

Grunbaum, J. A., Kann, L., Kinchen, S., Ross, J., Hawkins, J., Lowrey, R., Harris, W., McManus, T., Chyen, D., & Collins. J. (2004). Youth risk behavior surveillance, US—2003. *Surveillance Summaries,* MMWR, *53,* 1–96. Washington, D.C.: Centers for Disease Control.

Huff, C. R. (1998, October). *Comparing the criminal behavior of youth gangs and at-risk youth.* Washington, D.C.: National Institute of Justice, Office of Justice Programs, U.S. Department of Justice.

Illegal trafficking in new guns. (1999, June). *Society, 36,* 4, 5.

Kaufman, P., Chandler, K., & Rand, M. (1998). *Indicators of school crime and safety.* Washington, D.C.: National Association for Education Statistics and the U.S. Department of Justice, Office of Justice Programs, Bureau of Justice Statistics.

Kennedy, D. M. (1997). Pulling levers: Chronic offenders, high-crime settings, and a theory of prevention. *Valparaiso University Law Review, 31*(2), 449–484.

Kennedy, D. M., Braga, A. A., Piehl, A. M., & Waring, E. J. (2001, September). *Reducing gun violence: The Boston Gun Project's Operation Ceasefire.* Washington, D.C.: U.S. Justice Department, Office of Justice Programs.

Mokdad, A. H., Marks, J. S., Stroup, D. F., & Gerberding, J. L. (2004, March). Actual causes of death in the United States, 2000. *Journal of the American Medical Association, 29*(10), 1238–1245.

Moore, J. P., & Terrett, C. P. (1996). *Highlights of the 1996 national youth gang survey* (Fact Sheet). Washington, D.C.: U.S. Department of Justice, Office of Justice Programs, Office of Juvenile Justice and Delinquency Prevention.

Office of Juvenile Justice and Delinquency Prevention. (1999, February). *Promising strategies to reduce gun violence.* Washington, D.C.: U.S. Department of Justice, Office of Justice Programs.

Olinger, D. (1999). Gun dealer surrenders firearms license: Tec-9 sale to teens to bring criminal charges. *The Denver Post.* Thursday Oct. 14, 1999, p. B7.

Ruddell, R., & Mays, G. L. (2003). Examining the arsenal of juvenile gunslingers: Trends and policy implications. *Crime and Delinquency, 49*(2), 231–252.

Sheley, J. F. (1994). Drug activity and firearms possession and use by juveniles. *Journal of Drug Issues, 24*(3), 363–382.

Sheley, J. F., & Wright, J. D. (1993). *Gun acquisition and possession in selected juvenile samples* (Research in Brief). Washington, D.C.: U.S. Department of Justice, National Institute of Justice, Office of Juvenile Justice and Delinquency Prevention.

Sheley, J. F., & Wright, J. D. (1998, October). *High school youths, weapons, and violence: A national survey* (Research in Brief). Washington, D.C.: National Institute of Justice, office of Justice Programs, U.S. Department of Justice.

U.S. Department of Education. (2002, October). *Gun Free Schools Act report, school year 1998–1999.* Washington, D.C.: U.S. Department of Education.

U.S. Department of Justice. (1999, June). *Gun crime in the age group 18–20.* Washington, D.C.: U.S. Department of Justice.

U.S. Department of Justice & U.S. Treasury Department. (2005). ATF P53004. Federal Firearms Regulations Reference Guide 2005. Washington, D.C.

Zawitz, M. W. (1995, July). *Guns used in crime.* Washington, D.C.: Bureau of Justice Statistics, Office of Justice Programs, U.S. Department of Justice.

CHAPTER 10

Juveniles in Cyberspace: Risk and Perceptions of Victimization

Marilyn D. McShane, Frank P. Williams III, and Ming-Li Hsieh

Over the past century, many technological advances in various forms of media have resulted in parental concern about their negative influences on youth. Among these technologies and adaptations, music lyrics, books, magazines, films, and video games seem to have systematically produced the greatest concern. In some ways, these concerns simply may be a product of generational conflict with reflections of long-held disagreements concerning popular culture and taste. Each new genre of media appears to be objectionable to previous generations and, in many cases, has been viewed as a "cause" of delinquency. Although, to some extent, the contemporary media played some role in inciting concern over the risk of these influences, it has not helped that research on and knowledge of the consequences has been mixed and inconclusive.

Regulating access to perceived threats to the safety and well-being of our children has long been recognized as a parental responsibility. In fact, parents today face increasing pressure over the growing body of legal measures instituted to clarify social expectations for raising children. There appear to be growing real, as well as perceived, expectations for parents to anticipate and proactively regulate the home environment so that their children are exposed to as little harm and risk as possible. The courts have, in many cases, found parents negligent and liable for the failure to maintain and support their children according to rapidly evolving standards in a number of areas, including medical care, gang membership, vandalism, and debts accrued for such things as long-distance phone calls, credit cards, and Internet activity. Increased focus on supervision and fears of child abduction, being reported to child welfare services, and exposing youth to Internet pornography has spawned a cottage industry of v-chips, AMBER Alerts, fingerprint and DNA kits, and even home urinalysis testing, as well as lead to sophisticated rating systems for video games, movies, and Internet sites.

e-KIDS AND e-RISKS

Today, we live in a cybersociety in which children spend considerable amounts of time alone in an electronic environment with computers, video games, and sophisticated downloaded music systems. Although most of us were raised with exposure to the effects of a growing mass media, the vastness of the Internet and its capabilities are still disconcerting to many parents. The perceived dangers of electronic entertainment creates new risks about child safety and motivates us to find the best ways to protect children, while still allowing them to enjoy the benefits of these technological advancements.

The Concept of Home and Parental Concern

One of the sources of parental fears is clearly the location of the perceived threat. U.S. culture and popular belief has always portrayed the home as a private sanctuary—a fact legally enshrined in our Constitution—and a safe haven for our families. This image affects how we think of the home and events occurring within it. In some cases, the image is so powerful that it becomes difficult to embrace reality. Nowhere is this more true than in the perception that child sex offenders are strangers who lurk outside the home, when most of them are, in fact, relatives and friends. To change this perception, however, runs the risk of destroying the cherished notion of the home sanctuary.

That this notion is so powerful is critical to an understanding of parental concerns about the connection between the Internet and child molesters. With child molesters outside the home, children can be protected in traditional ways: teach them to beware of strangers and keep them safe in the home. Conversely, imagine the implied threat if that stranger is "virtually" inside the home, making contact via the Internet with the child in her or his own bedroom. This, then, is the perceived threat of Internet sexual solicitation (in this case, by pedophiles). Under these circumstances, there is a double threat, one to both child and sanctuary, that magnifies fear beyond either individual threat.

Emergent Social Problems

In situations in which fear is magnified, social scientists have identified a systematic set of events, otherwise known as the construction of a social problem (sometimes called "moral panics"). Social problems are based on a real or perceived threat to social order, but they are not tied to the actual prevalence of the threat. Instead, the important factor is the degree of concern elicited by the threat, as brought to our attention by media and moral entrepreneurs (people or agencies who, for good reasons, have a vested interest in the threat). Claims-making by the initial moral entrepreneurs are universally exaggerated, and the claimed facts are almost never confirmed when they are first made. When the threat involves protected members of society, sacred ideas and images, or particularly heinous misdeeds, the claims are sensationalized and spread quickly through the media. Moreover, because the news is "terrible," these threats remain unquestioned by the public (and frequently even authorities).

All of this results in multiple calls to "do something quickly." In the heat of the moment, other claimed instances of the threat appear, thus illustrating that the threat is growing. Action and social policy, then, are not far behind. History has demonstrated time and again that the highlighted threat or problem is rarely "worse" than at other times, but our attention (and the attention of the moral entrepreneurs) makes it seem so. Moreover, record-keeping efforts of these threat events are always enhanced, resulting in an increasing number of the events. At some point in the future, the pubic usually loses interest or another problem catches fire and the social problem dissipates (in the process, it is possible that the frequency of the threat event itself has never changed over the course of time and, in some cases, was already declining at the point of initial attention).

Given this process, it would seem that the combination of nervousness about new Internet technology, societal protection of children, and the concept of home—in conjunction with an already existing social problem (sex offenders)—most likely precipitates the social problem. Indeed, we cannot imagine a greater perceived threat than that of a child, playing in his or her own bedroom, being solicited by a stranger intent on sexual molestation. This combination of ingredients is so powerful that it literally demands recognition as a social problem.

The Internet as an Emerging Social Problem

Rapid advances in technology and consumer demands have created greater access to cybercommunications. This access, as well as ways to control it, has opened debate about social control and reinterpretation of basic rights and freedoms in relation to the risks of potential victimization and other forms of criminal behavior. Controversial associated issues range from free speech and expression to commerce between consenting adults and the possibility of civil rights violations in the promotion of practices that subjugate, discriminate, and oppress groups protected by age, race, gender, and religion. With a drive toward controlling or banning certain violent or sexually explicit materials on the Internet, or at least attempting to regulate or control them, these issues are clearly taking the form of an emergent social problem.

According to the U.S. Census Bureau, 53 million children, most of them teenagers, use a computer at home and at school. Although many are just playing interactive games, most are accessing the Internet, particularly e-mail. The home is the most common station of computer access, but family income and parents' education are significantly and positively related to the proportion of children who use the Internet and also *how* they use the Internet. The Federal Bureau of Investigation (FBI) reports that children are more at risk online in the evening hours and predators often target children by specific activities, traits, or needs that they identify. Chat rooms are specifically indicated as high-risk environments and the FBI has recently established an Endangered Child Alert Program (ECAP) to combat the sexual exploitation of children online.

Arguably, cybersexual exploitation has been sensationalized by the media in a way that often misrepresents what is, in fact, a relatively rare event. This occurs when incidents are reported in a way that suggests people are surprised that offenders have somehow adapted to and are exploiting a new and apparently successful means of committing offenses. Accounts seem to give the impression that predatory behavior by sex offenders is increasing rather than simply changing in its modus operandi. This failure to clarify the context of crime, or compare its incidence with the likelihood of other forms of victimization when weighted for frequency of use, demonstrates the difficulty we have in seeing or understanding these new trends as routine functions of crime and lifestyle changes. Yet, this is precisely how behaviors change and adapt to new situations; it is an expected consequence. Offenders traditionally move to newer and less easily detected methods as potential victims alter the dynamics of their interactions and become available and suitable as targets. Meanwhile, law enforcement races to adapt to these changes and to prevent further victimization. To criminologists, this is a well-established and normal cycle of activity.

This chapter explores a few of the most controversial areas of youthful offending and victimization related to exploration and activity using some of the more popular modern technologies. Many of these products and services have resulted in parental, as well as governmental, attempts to regulate children's behavior and their access to these technologies. Many of these products have an ambiguous nature, particularly those related to Internet pornography, violent video games, and personal Web sites. These activities and products are frequently interrelated and, in many ways, have been subject to scrutiny in their earlier forms, such as television and movie violence, sexually oriented magazines, and the home video industry. We will discuss some of the things parents can do to address Internet safety more proactively.

TECHNOLOGICAL REVOLUTION AND ITS EFFECTS

The literature on television and movie violence supports the notion that exposure to material of a violent nature leads to more aggressive behavior, reported acceptance of violence, and desensitization to violence, particularly in younger children.[1] Studies of sexual violence seem to find similar results. There is some debate, however, about whether exposure to sexually explicit materials, in general, affects established attitudes or sentiments regarding sexual morality.[2]

Even from the early days of public access to the Internet and personal computers, some people were concerned about the fact that racist or hate groups, pedophiles, pornographers, and even Satan worshippers all have access to videos, cable television channels, and computer bulletin boards. For instance, in the summer of 1994, an embarrassed high-security nuclear weapons laboratory acknowledged that hackers were using its vast computer storage capability to warehouse more than 1,000 pornographic images in what might have been a profitable Internet sales scheme.

A number of the more notorious hackers and spammers have been young people. The ability to work from home in one's spare time has made some illicit market activities attractive to the underage compensation seeker. Other people simply delight in the ability to crack into secure Web sites and to brag to online groups of colleagues about their technological skills. Downloading music, films, and videos illegally is a common offense that worries business and criminal justice investigators. The pirating and illegal reproduction of copyrighted material amount to billions of dollars lost to the industry each year. This fact worries delinquency experts who argue that the benefits and lack of sanctions at this level not only encourage criminal activity, but also may cause crime rates to escalate and trigger more serious levels of offenses.

From Computer Bulletin Boards to the Dangers of MySpace

Computer bulletin boards (CBBs) were early versions of what today might be considered Web sites. Dial-up in nature, these sites required knowledge of a specific phone number and were located on a remote server, but not on the Internet. Some CBBs were general-purpose sites, others had specific purposes (such as information for special scientific fields), but few had free access. Most weren't available to just anyone, requiring payment or paid-up membership codes to enter. Those with sexually oriented content were among the latter and, on the whole, did not pose much threat to the nation's youth because the content couldn't be merely happened upon. Conversely, the specialized content of some CBBs included pedophilic materials. At this point, the World Wide Web (WWW) with its graphics-based content had not yet become available. Text-based content was the order of the day on the Internet and downloading graphic content required any of a large number of specialized viewing programs.[3] Thus, CBBs were the solution to accessing and transmitting most graphic content.

In the early 1990s, the Justice Department's Child Exploitation and Obscenity Section established "Operation Long Arm" to track and prosecute child pornography transmitted from personal computers to network bulletin boards. One official related that pornographic magazines were simply being scanned and sent to subscribers.[4] Officials in Mexico and the United States claimed to have broken a child pornography ring run through e-mail with a $250 subscription. The investigation involved sites in New Jersey, California, Chicago, and Tijuana and included 2,000 subscribers of hard-core pornography.[5]

State and federal agents in Florida shut down and seized the equipment from two bulletin boards suspected of transmitting obscene photos and selling pornographic CD-ROMs. A Florida schoolteacher was arrested by U.S. Customs agents for allegedly possessing and disseminating child pornography via CBBs. Videos were allegedly made as well.[6] Another couple, from California, was charged and convicted of distributing pornography via interstate phone lines that depicted, among other things, bestiality. In that case, the materials were on a members-only bulletin board and downloaded by a postal inspector in Memphis.[7]

Another instance of the availability of pornography, this time on the Internet, was reported in a startling 1994 report based on a research study published in the *Georgetown Law Journal* by a Carnegie-Mellon University scholar. Given nationwide coverage by *Time* magazine and ABC television, the report suggested that pornography was widely available with easy access to text and pictures. Moreover, pornography and erotica were a major part of Internet content (actually the study said it accounted for 83 percent of all Internet images). It was all untrue. The "scholar" turned out to be an undergraduate student who used adult-oriented CBBs for his "research" and only briefly accessed one of the newsgroups on the Internet. Although we do not know the student's motivation, it has the appearance of purposefully misleading people. Carnegie-Mellon University disowned the research, and it was officially declared a scandal. The damage implicit in misleading the public, unfortunately, had already been done. In the public eye, cyberporn was a critical problem and children were in harm's way. The author of the *Times* article on the study put the propitious timing this way:

> So I think any reporter would recognize that this is an interesting thing, to have first crack at what sounded like a definitive study out of Carnegie-Mellon, which is a university with a long tradition in the Internet. It is a study that triggered this controversial crackdown at Carnegie-Mellon. And as it happened, the issue of pornography on the Internet had grown and come to the front burner. The study was going to be breaking at the exact time Senators, goofball Senators, were introducing an amendment to give away our free-speech rights!
>
> You know, the Exon amendment had passed the Senate when I got this study, and it looked like it was headed to the house. Here we had Congressmen debating this issue, parents clearly concerned about it, and everybody talking about porn on the Internet, and nobody really knowing how much there was, how accessible it was, where it was, who was seeing it, and so forth, and in this national context, here comes this study that seems to answer those questions.[8]

Politicians were prepared to attack the cyberporn problem, Senator Grassley had already scheduled a hearing on the issue—the Carnegie-Mellon "scholar" was to be his star witness and had to be pulled at the last minute. Even the resulting scandal was not enough to slow the political wheels. Senators James Exon and Slade Gorton sponsored a bill (SB-314, Telecommunications Decency Act) that proposed censoring and restricting erotic materials on the Internet. Their approach was to have the Internet treated as a telecommunication device. The Exon bill treated Internet transmission of obscene materials like an obscene telephone call. The major difference between the two, however, is that obscene phone calls are not voluntarily received. Internet "receivers" intentionally seek out and download the erotic products. Thus, the Exon bill actually transcended existing telecommunications laws and attempted to legislate morality. A version of that bill, attached as an amendment to the Telecommunications Decency Act, subsequently passed into law. Federal courts later struck down that portion of the act, but support for the concept remained and several attempts have been made to pass anti-cyberpornography laws since then.

Children's Access to Pornography

The fact is that erotica is not hidden on the Internet. The initial moral panic over the availability of Internet pornography was primarily a CBB issue and this availability was scarce, even for adults. Since that time, the growth of the graphics-based Internet, the WWW, has made the technical abilities required to access materials rather moot. The focus of the WWW is a transparent use of the Internet, even for those who have no knowledge of the technology behind it. Thus, today's browsers require no knowledge of downloading and compiling techniques, no identification of the types of file formats, and no specialized software to access graphics or text. Furthermore, the growth and sophistication of search engines such as Google[TM] and Yahoo!® make expertise in locating information moot, as well. Rarity of an item or type of material is no longer a bar to locating it. A simple search term and a click of the mouse are all that is necessary to bring up virtually any subject, text, or graphic on today's browsers.[9] Today's children have unparalleled access to information and that includes erotic content.

Although sexual predators and potential kidnappers seem to represent the major thrust of media coverage, access to pornography is a much more common experience and, according to some surveys, a greater parental concern. According to the National School Boards Association parents fears included access to pornography (46 percent), meeting undesirable adults online (29 percent), and violent or other inappropriate content or contact (20 percent).[10] The pedophile or pornography-producing entrepreneur has developed a more sophisticated operation over the years from the use of the Polaroid camera to the home video. These advances have allowed better quality production while affording privacy and the appearance of common household technology. Pornography businesses have adapted various mainstream sale and distribution techniques that allow consumers convenience and anonymity. In a Canadian survey, 34 percent of children ages 12 to 17 reported having visited sites containing pornography, violence, or adult chat-room activity.[11]

Sexual Predators on the Internet

Reported cases of sexual predation on the Internet seem to attract more media attention than other more common crimes, and the effect is to make online socializing appear to be a high-risk behavior. The accounts reflect a diverse group of predators and methods, although, according to research, most Internet predators are older men and victims are young teenage girls.[12] There are reports of 20 percent of youth ages 10 to 17 having received a sexual solicitation on the Internet.[13] Some of these cases result in arrests. Dr. Thomas Dent, 40, posed as a teenager online to talk to real teens about sex.[14] Gregory J. Mitchel, 38, enticed underage boys to perform sexually in front of Web cams.[15] Douglas French, a sex offender, lured a 17-year-old girl into a relationship with offers of modeling work through the Internet.[16] Sam Levitan posed as a 16-year-old boy and raped a girl he met on the Internet.[17] The FBI, utilizing undercover agents lured Noel Neff into soliciting sex online from a chat room.

The common pubic image of Internet predators is exemplified by the abovementioned cases. Even individuals in positions of responsibility, however, have been among those caught in the act. Brian J. Doyle, deputy press secretary for the U.S. Department of Homeland Security, was convicted of soliciting who he thought was a 14-year-old Florida girl over the Internet. Congressman Mark Foley of Florida, ironically chairman of the House Caucus on Missing and Exploited Children and one of the House's most outspoken members on issues of child pornography and sex offenders, resigned after reports that he had sent sexually oriented e-mails to an underage congressional page. Subsequent reports suggested that e-mail and instant message solicitations may have been sent to other pages as well. It is likely that many of the more recent scandals in the Roman Catholic Church have involved the Internet.

Thus, there is much evidence that sexual predators come from all walks of life. Nonetheless, there are a few commonalities among cyberpredators. Internet monitors indicate that predators prefer chat rooms, personal Web sites, and instant messaging. Most offenders spend two to four weeks cultivating a potential victim before attempting to meet them face to face.[18] Although the rate of offending and range of offenders may be the same as the peeping toms and school-yard and shopping mall perverts of days past, the ingredient most unsettling to parents may be the thought of such acts occurring in the home.

Possibility for Victimization

Officials point to the fact that children more readily divulge personal information in their daily use of the Internet. It is not uncommon for children to display their full names, age, gender, cell phone numbers, pictures, birthdays, hobbies, neighborhood, home address, school, after-school job locations, and other details about their routine activities. For instance, 40 percent of American high school students have posted personal data on an Internet Web site and 12 percent have arranged a meeting with a stranger whom they contacted online.[19] Since MySpace was created in 2003 the number of users has grown to its current enrollment of 60 million members.[20] An overwhelming number of youths are using free Internet accounts, which is a factor sure to close the economic gap once found in both offending and victimization. Close to one-third of all children involved with online blogs and Web sites, such as MySpace, access it more than twice a week.[21]

According to the Pew Internet and American Life Project, approximately four million children have their own blogs, eight million young people read them, and 60 percent of those who go online have created content on MySpace.[22] Ironically, 60 percent of children surveyed in one Canadian survey related that they had posed as someone else online when contacting and making new friends with other people. The survey indicated that boys had a higher rate of viewing violence as well as accessing gambling sites and adult chat rooms.[23]

Although this is a new technological phenomena, it is not inconsistent with more than 100 years of delinquency research that indicates that youth seeking excitement and stimulation often engage in high-risk behavior despite warnings, cautions, and restrictions to the contrary. And, following principles of risk and benefit, if offenders find it more economical and practical to use these resources for tracking and stalking potential victims, then they will use these resources until we can develop the tools to make it ineffective for them to do so.

COMPUTER BULLYING, PORNOGRAPHY, AND THE LAW

Years ago, the typical bully was a school-yard menace who physically intimated children on the playground. Now the Internet has escalated that scenario on a global scale, causing some teens considerable embarrassment and emotional trauma.[24] Today, 27 percent of children report an experience of cyberbullying and 70 percent report being sexually harassed (different from sexual solicitation) online.[25] There is some indication that children may try to stay home and avoid school because of fears related to this form of intimidation.

In 1994 (*U.S. v. Baker and Gonda*), a student by the name of "Jake Baker" at the University of Michigan was arrested by federal agents under a warrant obtained by the U.S. attorney.[26] Baker was accused of communicating a threat to a fellow student as a result of three erotic-tinged stories he uploaded onto the Internet. The stories contained rape, torture, and murder. Baker also had been communicating to a friend via computer and those communications were instrumental in bring the charges against him. The judge in the Baker case ultimately determined that the charges were without merit and dismissed the case. However, the case itself was widely reported in the media as a real offense, but its dismissal was barely reported.

Because those uploading erotica often use anonymous services or even out-of-country servers to transmit their materials, an incident in Helsinki is also of interest.[27] Finnish agents raided the home of an individual who maintained the most popular "anonymity server" at the request of the Church of Scientology, who claimed that someone had stolen copyright materials from them. Although the owner of the server finally agreed to provide only the name of the individual in question, the Internet was quickly abuzz about the threat to anonymity posed by such actions. Anonymity on the Internet is highly prized by a wide range of people, ranging from people who simply do not want to receive spam or be tracked from site to site by various marketing cookies to people in law enforcement searching for pedophiles.[28]

Although detecting, investigating, and prosecuting crimes committed on the Internet has posed serious challenges for law enforcement, coordinated agency efforts and time-consuming undercover work has been beneficial. In February of 2006, New York police arrested more than a dozen MySpace users who were sex offenders posing as children on the social networking Web site.[29] Though it is unclear exactly how many offenders and potential offenders use a digital modus operandi, the FBI indicates that at least 50,000 predators are operating online at any one time.[30] The FBI's projections are inherently suspicious, however, because they have grossly overestimated the number of missing children, serial killers, potential school shooters, and, most recently, terrorists. Considering the grand tradition of social problems claims-making by people with vested interests, it is highly likely that the actual number is substantially smaller.

WHAT YOU CAN DO

Regardless of the actual number, it is best to remember that the Internet is effectively a database that can be searched quickly. Thus, information that children post on the Internet, prize forms they fill out, and spam they respond to are all potential sources of searchable data. If adults are victimized by the existence of such data, then children certainly will be. The fact that young people are heavier users of new technology than adults increases their exposure. Applying routine activities and lifestyles theories[31] to their behavior, an elevated frequency of such contacts is literally to be expected: they spend more time on the Internet, engage in riskier behaviors while online, and tend to access the Internet without adult supervision. Although something might be done about the first two elements, the latter is more critical. Lacking the sophistication that maturity usually brings, unsupervised youth run a higher risk of having contact with unsavory elements on the Internet. Thus, parents can have an effect on the relative exposure risk of their children.

Unfortunately, although parents may seem concerned about Internet safety, many are not sophisticated users themselves. They are often uncertain about the specific practices that may constitute illegal activity or high-risk communication, and they are often unwilling or unable to purchase and install software mechanisms that might filter or block inappropriate sites. This means that the Internet, like other youthful activities that parents do not understand, is subject to fears and misconceptions that might be more effectively managed if parents were aware of the context of the situation and its relative risks.

Despite the best intentions of parents to monitor Internet access, 48 percent of children surveyed in one study reported that they "never" use the Internet with their parents and 42 percent reported that most of the time they were alone when they used the Internet.[32] Networking services like MySpace attempt to regulate activity by posting a minimum age requirement, but these requirements often are circumvented and impossible to enforce. All a child need do is "certify" that they are at least 14 years old.

Officials recommend the following measures for promoting safe Internet use for families with children:

- Instruct children on ways to avoid the display or disclosure of personal details related to names and addresses, and how to avoid posting scheduled activities and what may be interpreted as provocative pictures or language.
- Make children aware that their "friend" may be an adult and that some strangers are not to be trusted easily.
- Keep computers in open areas, such as the living room, family room, or kitchen, where the content of regular use may be monitored.
- Check Web sites that children log onto and make children aware that you are able to track their activity and that you are doing that to protect them.
- Invest in software that will help you to track, monitor, and control Internet access and activities. Exercise your ability to block high-risk sites of which you are aware.
- Share your information and experiences with other parents and with the school. An alliance or network is much more effective and efficient than one person alone. Children need to see the unity of parents in consensus on this issue and they need to be encouraged to bring Internet problems and issues to the attention of adults.
- Arrange to spend quality time with children in meaningful activities, travel, sports, recreation, and leisure time away from the computer to offset their interest and preoccupation in this one form of social activity.
- Talk to your children honestly and in a nonthreatening way about their use of the Internet. Involve them in making up rules and setting parameters so that they are invested in the issues and feel some of shared power that is an important need in their lives as they develop a sense of responsibility and control over their lives.

Although these practices cannot guarantee a safe Internet experience for children, they do provide some surveillance techniques over Internet behavior and suggest a model of how to assess risky activity.

CONCLUSION

The difficulty in dealing with violent and sexually explicit material is the lack of consensus on what constitutes harmful or obscene material and high-risk behaviors online. Great variations exist among jurisdictions on the extent to which First Amendment protections cover the exchange of print and film between consenting adults, and the degree to which regulations of what children can access is the government's responsibility and what is the parent's responsibility. Over the years, various regulations, codes, laws, and ordinances have been promulgated in an attempt to control the distribution of violent and sexually explicit material (and to keep up with its changing themes as well as evolving technological mediums). These problems of defining and controlling not only the music and film industry but also all of its bootlegged, illegally recorded, and downloaded offshoots are magnified when the Internet is concerned.

Proposed answers to censorship are parent-controlled software, generic legislation (as with the provisions in the Telecommunications Decency Act), and hardware. Software exists to censor the Internet and continues to evolve to balance the needs of access and protection. The consensus of the legal community appears to be that absolute prohibition of "indecent" materials (for adults and children) is clearly unconstitutional. Whatever its direction, the final legislative solution no doubt will work only as well in limiting juveniles' access to violence and pornography as have solutions to the equally thorny problems of alcohol, drugs, and tobacco.

One of the solutions needed is illustrated by the advertising campaigns designed for the war on drugs. Exaggerated statements and stories were disseminated for scare purposes but were presented as fact. In one sense, they had the intended effect, but for the wrong audience—parents. Youth were able to draw on personal and word-of-mouth experiences to determine that the statements and stories were, indeed, scare tactics and in many cases laughably so. Information on Internet risk should be informed by this experience and bear a closer resemblance to reality. The fact is that children, youth, and adults are all going to use the Internet (actually, the Internet is now a commodity and necessity). Without exaggerating risk and creating fear, the task is to determine how to manage potential risk through reasonable behavior. Governments are not going to be in the forefront of this activity, but parents will have to be, and perhaps only after learning to manage their own Internet risk.

NOTES

1. Donnerstein, Linz, & Penrod, 1987.
2. Scott & Cuvelier, 1993.
3. Graphics format had not yet become standardized. Most of the viewing programs, which also had to be individually downloaded, were usable for only a single graphics format. Thus, much of the graphics content available on "newsgroups" was in multiple parts, time-consuming to download with slow dial-up speeds of 9.6–14.4K baud rates, and largely unusable. Because of the multipart nature (necessary because of file size limitations), frequently a special program was needed to piece the parts together in the correct order.
4. "Justice Department warns of porn networks," 1993.
5. Rotella, 1994.
6. "Teacher arrested," 1995.
7. "Couple guilty of sending porn," 1994.
8. Philip Elmer-DeWitt quoted in Brickman, 1995.

9. In doing some quick online research in preparation for this chapter, we can attest that once one defeats the "safe-search" feature on common search sites (usually requiring a click on the "yes" box next to "I am an adult"), there are few taboo topics and graphics not available. Before viewing this fact as an evil, it is wise to reflect on the reason these search engines exist (and why they have become hugely capitalized entities, as well)—that is, for access to information of all types, which has become the hallmark of the twenty-first century.

10. National School Boards Association, 2002.

11. Media Awareness Network, 2005.

12. Kornblum, 2006.

13. ClearTraffic, 2006.

14. Bunyan, 2006.

15. Eichenwald, 2006.

16. Snell, 2006.

17. Garcia, 2006.

18. ClearTraffic, 2006.

19. McNulty, 2006.

20. Clifford, 2006.

21. Braithwaite, 2006.

22. Campanelli, Lubinger, & Dealer, 2005.

23. Media Awareness Network, 2005.

24. Coleman, 2006.

25. Media Awareness Network, 2005.

26. "Student jailed," 1995.

27. Akst, 1995.

28. We note that an anonymity plug-in is a popular download at the Firefox® browser Web site.

29. Proudfoot, 2006.

30. Goodchild & Owen, 2006.

31. Cohen & Felson, 1979; Hindelang, Gottfredson, & Garofalo, 1978.

32. Media Awareness Network, 2005.

REFERENCES

Akst, D. (1995, February 22). The Helsinki incident and the right to anonymity. *Los Angeles Times*, p. D1, D6.

Bauman, A. (1994, July 12). Computer at nuclear lab used for access to porn. *Los Angeles Times*, p. A1, A18.

Braithwaite, T. (2006, July 17). Internet sites seek to head off paedophilia concerns. *Financial Times*, p. 3.

Brickman, G. (1995, July 4). HotWired interview with Philip Elmer-DeWitt. *Hot-Wired*. Retrieved September 23, 2006, from http://xenia.media.mit.edu/~rhodes/Cyberporn/dewitt-interview.transcript.html.

Bunyan, N. (2006, January 4). Doctor had online sex chats with teenagers. *The Daily Telegraph*, p. 5.

Campanelli, J., Lubinger, B., & Dealer, P. (2005, November 5). Teen's logs: Private thoughts go public: Do you know what your teen is blogging? *Sports Final Edition*, p. A1.

Clear Traffic. (n.d.). Keeping your kids safe on the Internet. Tips from the Clear Traffic. Retrieved September 10, 2006, from www.cleartraffic.com/keeping kids-safe.htm.

Clifford, J. (2006, April 22). Space invaders: With web predators and other dangers on the Internet, parents must actively monitor their kids' computer use. *The San Diego Union-Tribune*, p. E1.

Cohen, L., & Felson, M. (1979). Social change and crime rate trends: A routine activities approach. *American Sociological Review, 44*, 588–607.

Coleman, S. (2006, March 30). Cyberspace invaders: Internet harassment can be a kid's virtual nightmare. *The Boston Globe*, p. P1.

Couple guilty of sending pornography by computer. (1994, July 29). *Los Angeles Times*, p. A10.

Donnerstein, E., Linz, D., & Penrod, S. (1987). *The question of pornography.* New York: The Free Press.

Eichenwald, K. (2006, January 29). Virginia man pleads guilty in online pornography case. *The New York Times*, p. 16.

Garcia, A. T. (2006, April 19). Keeping predators from our kids. *St. Louis Post-Dispatch*, p. A4.

Goodchild, S., & Owen, J. (2006, August 6). The secret world of the net: Special report: Children and the netBebo, MySpace, MSN. *Independent on Sunday*, p. 6.

Hindelang, M., Gottfredson, M., & Garofalo, J. (1978). *Victims of personal crime: An empirical foundation for a theory of personal victimization.* Cambridge, MA: Ballinger.

Justice Department warns of new child porn computer networks. (1993, August 16). *Criminal Justice Newsletter, 24*(16), 1–2.

Kornblum, J. (2006, February 13). Social websites scrutinized: MySpace, other reviewed in crimes against teenagers. *USA Today*, p. 6D.

McNulty, T. (2006, January 15). Teens flock to MySpace: parents worry that personal data posted will lure predators. *Pittsburgh Post-Gazette*, p. A1.

Media Awareness Network. (2005). Young Canadians in a wired world, phase II: Student survey. Canada, Ottawa: Media Awareness Network.

National School Boards Association. (2002). Safe and smart: Research and guidelines for childrens' use of the Internet. Alexandria, VA: National School Boards Foundation. Retrieved September 8, 2006, from www.nsbf.org/safe-smart/full-report.htm.

Proudfoot, S. (2006, May 11). Taking back MySpace. *Ottawa Citizen*, p. E1.

Rotella, S. (1994, September 24). Computerized child porno ring broken. *Los Angeles Times*, p. A31.

Scott, J., & Cuvelier, S. (1993). Violence and sexual violence in pornography: Is it really increasing? *Archives of Sexual Behavior, 22*(4), 357–371.

Snell, J. (2006, August 17), Man arrested in online sex case involving teenager. *The Oregonian*, p. B3.

Student jailed, faces trial for his Internet tale of torture and rape. (1995, February 11). *Los Angeles Times*, p. A14.

Teacher arrested in computer porn case. (1995, February 25). *San Diego Union-Tribune*, p. A3.

CASES CITED

U.S. v. Baker and Gonda, U.S. Dist. Ct., Eastern Dist. of Michigan, Southern Div., No. 95-80106.

CHAPTER 11

Mother Blame and Delinquency Claims: Juvenile Delinquency and Maternal Responsibility

Bruce Hoffman and Thomas M. Vander Ven

"Mother blame"—attributions of maternal responsibility for juvenile delinquency—has been a major theme of popular and scholarly attention over the past several decades. Major changes in women's roles, the structure of the family, and the contraction of the welfare state, have been accompanied by public fears and scholarly explorations questioning the potential effects of working mothers, single mothers, and adolescent mothers on their children's behavior. Although extreme, the contemporary concern over unconventional mothers and the foregrounding of their behavior as responsible for delinquency is by no means unprecedented. Indeed, the familiarity of these claims raises questions about the historical construction of connections between motherhood and delinquency, and the interests such attributions have served.

In this chapter, we empirically review and assess recent social scientific literature that attempts to explore the connection between delinquency and the behavior of adolescent, single, and working mothers. We next place such studies into their relevant context through an analysis of influential historical and sociological accounts of the "invention" of delinquency during the Progressive Era of the late 1800s. It is our hope that the study of the transformation of family, motherhood, and the dependent nature of the child can help us further understand how contemporary maternal roles, responsibilities, and practices of mother blame for child neglect function as instruments of self-regulation and underlie practices of formal intervention.

DELINQUENCY AND "NONTRADITIONAL" MOTHERS

Research aimed at understanding the manner in which absent, single, or underfunctioning mothers contribute to crime and delinquency grew significantly in the 1990s. Scholars suggest that broad public concerns about the ill effects of maternal employment, family breakdown, and adolescent childbearing were driven, in part, by the culture wars surrounding the Reagan administration's "family values" rhetoric, the backlash against feminist advancements, the welfare reform movement, and Congressman Newt Gingrich's "Contract with America."[1]

Some social critics argued that social pathologies, such as crime, delinquency, and youth violence, were caused by the weakening of the American family and that survey research showed that policy makers had a mandate to reverse this unfortunate tide. Other social commentators and social scientists argued that the American family was not, in fact, declining, but rather changing to meet the demands of structural conditions. From this perspective, mothers have to work because the dual-earning family is an economic necessity, not because mothers are carelessly choosing work over family responsibilities.

Researchers have produced a large body of empirical findings to address these concerns. Although there is no question that maternal support and control influence child developmental and behavioral trajectories, it is not clear how much and in what manner adolescent childbearing, single mothering, and maternal employment affect delinquent outcomes. A brief review of the research centered on these topics is offered below.

Adolescent Motherhood and Delinquency

The U.S. teen pregnancy rate for teens ages 15 to 19 decreased 28 percent between 1990 and 2000. Despite these recent declines, more than 30 percent of all teenage girls get pregnant at least once before they are 20 years old, resulting in more than 800,000 teen pregnancies a year.[2] Furthermore, the United States has the highest teen pregnancy rate in the industrialized world.[3]

As the rate of teen motherhood has remained high, so too has public concern for the wide-scale social consequences of "kids having kids." According to Maynard, the perception of teen pregnancy as a social problem was largely driven by rising rates of poverty and welfare dependency in the 1990s.[4] Over the last two decades, child poverty rates have escalated along with teen pregnancy. Furthermore, adolescent childbearing is particularly worrisome to social commentators and legislators because it is seen as both a cause and consequence of the dramatic increases in welfare dependency in recent decades.[5] Because the general public and politicians alike have set reducing the welfare rolls as a high priority, teen pregnancy has gained importance as a social problem.

Adolescent motherhood is seen not only as a prelude to welfare dependency and, thus, a greater tax burden, but also is regarded as a contributor to the production of social ills, such as crime. As Grogger has pointed out, between 1950 and 1975 both teen pregnancy and national crime rose dramatically,[6] suggesting a possible link between the two. Although researchers have yet to clearly demonstrate a strong connection between teen pregnancy and crime, policy makers seem to be convinced that a relationship exists.[7] Specifically, it is commonly believed that the offspring of adolescent mothers have a greater propensity to engage in antisocial or criminal behavior.

Indeed, several researchers have found that the children of adolescent mothers are more likely to engage in various forms of crime and delinquency. The evidence, however, is not strong. The strength of association between early childbearing and delinquency has been shown to be moderate at best and the severity of child behavioral problems related to adolescent motherhood varies substantially across studies.

Moore, Morrison, and Greene reported that compared with children born to 20- and 21-year-old mothers, children born to 18- and 19-year-olds were more likely to run away from home. The authors found no association between having an adolescent mother and involvement in more serous delinquent acts such as assault, theft, or illegal drug use.[8] These findings are consistent with research that had suggested that early childbearers are more likely to have children who engage in less serious delinquency and status offenses, such as running away, stealing, and getting into trouble at school.

Other researchers have developed a somewhat tenuous link between adolescent childbearing and more serious criminal behavior in offspring. In an exploratory analysis of four data sets, Morash and Rucker found that the children of early childbearers were more likely to commit offenses against people and that the children of young mothers had penetrated more deeply into the juvenile justice system. The authors report, however, that in most cases mother's age explains only a trivial amount of variation in delinquency and that the association between maternal age and delinquency was significant for white youth but not black youth. Furthermore, the analysis showed that the often weak association detected between mother's age and delinquency depended on the mother's marital status during the child's adolescence: when fathers were present, many negative child outcomes associated with maternal age were ameliorated.[9]

Like Morash and Rucker, Grogger found an association between having an adolescent mother and more serious criminality. Specifically, the analysis involved an assessment of whether a mother's age affects the likelihood of her son being incarcerated. Although the results were modest in size, Grogger found that delayed childbearing on the part of adolescent mothers would significantly reduce the probability that their sons would be incarcerated. As the author acknowledged, maternal age alone is not likely to explain much variation in criminal behavior.[10] And even if maternal age is associated with delinquency, the relationship may be largely spurious, with maternal age and delinquency being caused by economic disadvantage. Younger mothers and their children are more likely to face a wide variety of disadvantages, including poverty, welfare dependency, unstable marital unions and female-headed families, and community disorganization. To understand the causal process linking adolescent motherhood to delinquency, then, such contextual factors as poverty, neighborhoods, and family stability should be considered.

Nagin, Pogarsky, and Farrington attempted to specify the relationship between an adolescent mother and criminal behavior. Their approach mapped the influence of adolescent motherhood through three competing avenues that were hypothesized to increase the probability of criminal involvement in the adult children of young mothers.[11]

The first explanation, the life course–immaturity account, predicts that younger mothers produce antisocial behavior in their children because of their inability to be mature, sensitive, and effective parents. Young mothers are depicted as being unprepared to meet the challenges of raising a child because of emotional and developmental immaturity. Parental effectiveness, then, is treated as a function of developmental progression; although most adolescents would be regarded as too young to raise a child, they should have the potential to be good parents as they age and gain maturity.

The second explanation, the persistent poor parenting–role modeling account, predicts that those who bear children in adolescence are likely to be those least suited to be good parents. Early fertility, it is assumed, is likely to be caused by a stable personality trait characterized by impulsivity, self-centeredness, and lack of foresight. Drawing from Gottfredson and Hirschi's theory of self-control,[12] teen childbearing may be seen as an "analogous act"—a noncriminal behavior that, like criminal behavior, can be explained by low self-control. According to this account, teen mothers make unsuitable parents because they are likely to be engaged in antisocial behaviors themselves, because they lack the patience and planning skills a good parent needs, and because they are likely to select mates or marital partners who also lack the skills or behavioral habits to be effective parents.

The final explanation, the diminished resources account, predicts that the children of adolescent mothers are more prone to criminal behavior because they are more likely to experience impoverishment. Because early childbearing is likely to fix mothers and their children in a socioeconomically disadvantaged status,[13] children may experience prolonged deprivation of financial resources and cultural objects.[14] Furthermore, because adolescent mothers are less likely to be stably married, children also may be deprived of personal attention and support and are more likely to be raised by a highly stressed parent.[15] Nagin and others found some empirical support for the diminished resources and persistent poor parenting–role model accounts but could not confirm the life course–immaturity explanation.[16]

Finally, Pogarsky, Lizotte, and Thornberry found that children born to early childbearers were more prone to violence and delinquency than children born to later childbearers. This effect is best explained by the unstable, highly transitional composition of the families in which early childbearing is most likely to occur.[17]

Single Mothers, Divorce, and Delinquency

More than one-third of all American children are born to single mothers and more than half of all children will spend some period of their childhood in a single parent–headed home.[18] Statistics like these might seem alarming to those concerned about the relationship between changing family structures and related consequences for youth behavior. The empirical research findings on the topic, however, are mixed.

One pathway to understanding the single mother–delinquency link is to examine the research focused on divorce/separation and delinquency. Dating back to the nineteenth century, delinquency scholars have consistently looked to the "broken home"—families disrupted by marital dissolution or separation—as one of the primary explanations for delinquency.[19] Although this line of inquiry has resulted in a large accumulation of studies, the findings have been equivocal.

In the most well-known study of its kind, Wells and Rankin attempted to bring clarity to this issue by performing a meta-analysis of 50 "broken homes" studies. They concluded that broken homes had a consistent pattern of association with delinquency. The prevalence of delinquency in broken homes, in fact, was found to be 10 to 15 percent higher than in intact homes.[20] It should be noted, however, that the great majority of children raised in fractured families do not take part in serious patterned delinquency. Although a child of divorce may have a higher probability of delinquency, divorce itself does not doom a child to a life of crime.

The Wells and Rankin study adds to our general understanding of the relationship between family structure and delinquency, but it does not attempt to explain the causal process. More recent research conducted by Rebellon suggests that marital breakdown early in the life course and remarriage during adolescence are strong predictors of status offending. According to Rebellon, much of the relationship between family fissures and delinquency can be attributed to the child's increased involvement with delinquent peers and a corresponding increase in favorable attitudes toward law violation.[21]

The broken home might affect child outcomes in a variety of other ways. A divorce, for example, may result in the prolonged separation of a child from one of his or her parents (usually the father). Although some studies have found that children benefit from paternal involvement after divorce, other investigators have found that the frequency of involvement with divorced fathers is not related to child adjustment.[22]

King argues that frequent child involvement with divorced, noncustodial fathers may carry negative effects because involved ex-spouses are forced to interact more regularly to plan and facilitate visitation. Increased involvement between ex-partners may result in greater parental conflict that could counteract the benefits of father involvement.[23]

Other researchers have found that parental conflict, rather than parental separation, is a more powerful link between family disruption and child behavior. Loeber and Stouthamer-Loeber, for instance, discovered that marital discord, especially overt fighting between parents, is a stronger predictor of delinquency than parental separation.[24] This finding is supported by studies that have found comparable levels of child behavior problems between children from unhappy marriages and children from broken homes.[25] Furthermore, there is consistent evidence that children in high-conflict, intact families show more behavioral problems than children in low-conflict, single-parent families.[26] Loeber and Stouthamer-Loeber argue that this effect may be attributed to the fact that children suffer emotionally as a result of witnessing parental discord.[27] Observing fighting between parents may cause emotional scars as well as serve as an antisocial model of conflict resolution.

The great diversity of family forms in America and the large number of stable single mother–headed families has required researchers to look beyond the broken homes question to consider the effects of other family structures. Although some research suggests that the offspring of stable single mothers are more likely to experience a host of negative outcomes, including delinquency,[28] other investigators have failed to find that being raised by a single mother is criminogenic.[29]

More recent research efforts demonstrated that teens living with single mothers were more likely to be delinquent and experience school failure[30] and that these effects were best explained by relational instability in the family[31] and the breakdown of parental supports and controls (e.g., supervision, involvement, monitoring, closeness) that may occur in the single-parent home.[32]

Working Mothers and Delinquency

Female labor force participation has increased radically over the last 50 years. According to census data, the proportion of women working in the paid labor market has grown from approximately 28 percent in 1940 to close to 60 percent in 1992.[33] Recent estimates show that more than 60 percent of those mothers with children less than 3 years old are employed outside the home and more than 79 percent of those with children between the ages of 6 and 17 are employed.[34]

Although the greatest increase in maternal labor force participation has occurred in the last 40 years, social commentators and political leaders have expressed anxiety about this trend for some time. Chira argued that that the negative focus on working women can be traced back to the Great Depression when women were depicted in the popular media and in government literature as taking "men's jobs." Even when women were briefly encouraged to work to support the World War II effort, Hollywood films celebrated the sacrificial housewife while denigrating the "working mom." Meanwhile, the post–World War II Congress held hearings about the potential negative outcomes associated with maternal employment and Freudian psychologists added authoritative warnings to the discussion, suggesting that maternal work threatens the sanctity of the mother-child bond. These widespread anxieties, however, were largely fueled by threatened cultural ideals and the tensions created by rapid social change. Empirical inquiries rarely supported rhetorical attacks against the working mother.[35]

Today, the putative effects of maternal employment continue to stimulate much public debate in the popular press,[36] controversial books,[37] talk radio, and prime-time news specials. Working mothers, themselves, often feel a tremendous amount of guilt related to their assumed preference of work over parenting and its effects on the life chances of their children. These concerns have been driven, in part, by claims made by social critics and childrearing "experts" who have argued that working mothers cannot offer children the support and discipline that they need, which is likely to result in an attachment disorder and severe behavioral problems.[38]

In a well-known examination of the behavioral effects of having a working mother, Belsky demonstrated that maternal employment during infancy is associated with insecure attachment and aggressiveness and noncompliant behavior in middle childhood.[39] These findings, however, have been criticized for being based on nonrepresentative samples and for failing to account for critical background variables such as a mother's human capital and social capital.[40]

More recent research has suggested that concerns about the developmental risks of maternal employment may be somewhat overstated. In numerous studies, Parcel and Menaghan have discerned relatively few negative effects of having a working mother on family functioning or child behavior.[41] The number of hours mothers spent in the paid labor force, for example, was found to have no impact on the emotional support, cognitive stimulation, or physical environment of children between the ages of 3 and 6 years old.[42] Similarly, the 10- to 14-year-old children of regularly employed mothers suffered no deficits in maternal warmth, maternal monitoring, or cognitive stimulation.[43] Furthermore, a similar pattern can be seen in the relationship between maternal employment and child behavioral problems. The number of hours mothers spent in paid employment had no effect on the behavioral problems of 4- to 6-year-old[44] or 10- to 14-year-old youth.[45]

Although few work and family issues have stimulated more empirical investigation than the impact of maternal employment on child development, research on the link between mother's work and delinquency is relatively scarce. Early researchers found positive relationships between maternal work and delinquency, which they typically attributed to reduced supervision.[46] By contrast, some later studies suggested that delinquency is actually less common among children of regularly employed mothers.[47] Yet other research, however, reports little or no effect of maternal work on delinquency.[48]

Most recently, Vander Ven and Cullen found that maternal work, alone, had little effect on delinquency but that children were at a greater risk for delinquent involvement when their mothers worked in coercively controlled jobs in the secondary labor market. These jobs were characterized by low pay, low occupational complexity, and shift-based work schedules. This research suggests that policy makers should focus on creating better access to complex, rewarding, and well-paying jobs for all women, rather than demonizing the working mother.[49]

HISTORICAL PERSPECTIVES ON DELINQUENCY AND MOTHERHOOD

The recent attention given to the effects of the behavior of single, working, and adolescent mothers and the delinquency of their children during the last two decades raises questions about the distinctiveness of such attributions and their relationship to social change. Has the connection between motherhood and the delinquent behaviors of their children always been apparent, or does it have an apparent origin? Have there been previous periods during which maternal responsibility for delinquency has been stressed? If so, whose interests were served by such attribution? In exploring these questions, we return to the pioneering work on the "invention" of juvenile delinquency, Platt's *The Child Savers* and recent historiography influenced by Donzelot's *The Policing of Families*.

Maternal Justice and Delinquency

Platt's history of the emergence of understandings of juvenile delinquency and contemporary juvenile justice institutions was an early and influential work of revisionist historiography. Running parallel to the countercultural movements of the 1960s and 1970s, revisionist historians sought to challenge orthodox accounts that interpreted the law and social control practices of Western liberalism in terms of humanitarian progress and the expansion of freedom, exposing these interpretations as myths that functioned to conceal the extension of social control in everyday life.[50] In Platt's analysis, the so-called child-saving movement of the Progressive Era, which mobilized juvenile justice reform, was in fact a "symbolic movement" of the middle class, fighting to preserve normative values and the "sanctity of fundamental institutions" in the midst of the breakdown of traditional ways of life that were concomitant with urbanization.[51] Women, as social reformers and mothers, were understood to be central to this movement. Just as the values they defended were the traditional values of the "nuclear family," "parental discipline," and "women's domesticity," Platt argued that the movement reflected the interests of middle-class women by preserving their traditional roles as moral guardians and social workers in the face of social transformation.

Although Platt's work provocatively argues that juvenile justice reform was advancing class interests, not humanitarian ideals, his focus on "rule-makers and rule-making"—which he shares with Howard Becker and other labeling theorists of his day—leads him to direct his attention to the reformers and their formal institutions rather than those groups being acted upon and more subtle processes of change. In a number of ways, Platt's attention limits his study. Platt focuses on the innovations in formal law and the development of juvenile justice institutions, but says little about how concerns over the welfare of children lead to extensive indirect forms of surveillance as well as direct intervention. Of particular significance, although Platt holds that the "nuclear family" was a traditional value to be defended, he only touches on transformations of the family during the Progressive Era and how new conceptions of the relationship between parents, children, and the state enable increased regulation of families and children. Additionally, little is said about the relationship between juvenile justice reform and other agencies and institutions, as well as about the increased importance of expert knowledge in social and political life.

Familization, Expertise, and Scientific Motherhood

Many of the limitations identified above have been addressed by a more recent scholarship critically exploring social control and state. Such works not only interpret the emergence of delinquency in terms of legislation and institutions, but also approach delinquency as one aspect of a complex process of transformation—and regulation—of the family in the late-nineteenth and early twentieth century. Of singular importance is French sociologist Donzelot's 1977 study connecting the transformation of the family to new forms of state governance, *The Policing of Families*. For Donzelot, the development of the liberal state is made possible by the discovery of the "social," a realm outside the direct control of the state that can nevertheless be indirectly governed. It is in this context that Donzelot approaches the transformation of the family. If government authority was once envisioned as directly controlling the family and reciprocally dependent on its compliance, liberal government posits a fundamental distinction between the public and private spheres—that is, a shift "... from a government *of* families to a government *through* the family," restricting the family from direct control but rendering it more susceptible to new forms of regulation.[52] These new strategies of regulation and control require the development of new agencies and institutions to socialize and monitor the family, a process Rose calls "familization."[53]

Such scholarship broadens our understanding of social control processes by approaching regulation not simply in terms of legislation and formal justice institutions, but also as the result of a multiplicity of state and extrastate actors and institutions that are involved in reshaping, redefining, and regulating the family, including education, medicine, philanthropy, psychiatry, religion, and social work. Moreover, each field possesses its own forms of scientific expertise, understood by Donzelot to be at the center of the new approach to governance, which depends on socializing "free" citizens to self-regulate their behavior in predictable and desirable ways. The plurality of overlapping knowledge together works to shape, normalize, and regulate behavior, challenging traditional practices with "scientific" advice of the proper, "modern," and "normal" way to behave.

The confluence of extrastate actors and expert knowledge acted on the families in ways that transformed conceptions of maternal roles and responsibilities as well as the meaning of domestic space. Consider, for example, some of the effects of the public health movement of the late nineteenth and early twentieth centuries.[54] The new medical "germ" theory of disease established a connection between illness and hygienic practices, and was employed to shift the attention of women and public health actors to domestic space and everyday hygienic practices. Such theories aided the professionalization of medicine and shaped what historian Apple has called the "ideology of scientific motherhood," that is, the belief "... that women require expert scientific and medical advice to raise their children healthfully."[55] Medical authority was used to justify changes in informal customs, such as handshakes and kisses; women's fashion (longer skirts that dragged in the mud were seen as carriers of disease—as were men's beards); and religious practices, such as the common communion cup.[56] Considerations of health and disease led to a fundamental reconception of the importance of housework and of responsibility toward the home; led to "social hygiene" supplanting "moral purity" as a basis of moral reform movements; and called into question the traditional practices of breastfeeding infants and the health of women's bodies.[57]

Scientific motherhood, which "exalted science and devalued instinct and traditional knowledge," came not only from the growing number of medical professionals, but also from childcare manuals, newspapers, advertisements, and, by the 1920s, home economics and domestic science classes.[58] In particular, the ideals and practices of scientific motherhood were circulated through new women's magazines, including the *Ladies' Home Journal* and *Good Housekeeping*, respectively founded in 1883 and 1885, whose names reflect the domestic hygiene movement.[59] Such magazines regularly included articles and advertisements connecting health and parenting practices, and, in the case of *Good Housekeeping*, developed "The Good Housekeeping Institute" to experiment and "test consumer goods and household appliances."[60] Through such messages, women's responsibilities to the home, as housekeepers and as caregivers, were elevated, as well as made a target for increased scrutiny. So, too, were they subject to new forms of scrutiny and targets for intervention—the elevation of women's responsibility as caregivers within the home was paralleled with making women "allies" of medical professionals, which took knowledge and control away from women.[61]

Single Mothers and the Emergence of Child Neglect

Although the discourses of scientific motherhood crossed class lines, they concentrated on self-regulation among middle-class families. The transformation of motherhood and the family, however, also allowed for new forms of philanthropic intervention in the name of the child. Gordon's groundbreaking study of the politics and history of family violence, *Heroes of Their Own Lives*, traces the development of concepts and policies of child mistreatment and intervention in its name. For Gordon, "child neglect" as a category and cause for intervention emerges as a response to the Progressive Era's newly defined norms of family and motherhood. In turn-of-the-century Boston, where "approximately 20 percent of ... families were female-headed ... concern about [single motherhood] as a social problem arose sharply. ..."[62] Deviating from the ideals of family and caught in social structures of poverty, single mothers were perceived as a special challenge for social workers and especially subject to charges of child neglect: "single motherhood and child neglect were mutually and simultaneously constructed as social problems, and many of the defining indices of child neglect, such as lack of supervision, were essential to the survival of female-headed households."[63] By foregrounding the mother's deviation as neglect, such constructions pushed to the background recognition of the circumstances of poverty, cultural differences, and other ways in which children were subject to violence, such as child labor practices.[64] A concern with delinquency as a consequence of child neglect—and of parental neglect as an explanation for delinquency—only "became one of the major themes in child protection" during World War I, when it was tied to a concern for healthy children as future soldiers.[65] This association between maternal behavior and delinquency strengthened in the following years, in part through the scientific arguments of sociologists such as the Gluecks.

Studies of the contemporary practices of child welfare social workers and of welfare surveillance reveal similar evaluations being made of the mother as Gordon discovered at the start of the Progressive Era.[66] Swift's study of case files of child welfare social workers found that workers assess a mother's parenting skills by drawing inferences based on her physical appearance and emotional demeanor. Significantly, domestic hygiene continues to be an issue of evaluation, as housekeeping skills are frequently referenced in ways that connect cleanliness and order to the degree to which a mother "cares" for her child. And while family violence and conditions of poverty may be incorporated into case workers' evaluations, they remain secondary to the evaluation of the mother, who is held to be singularly responsible for the production of the child.[67]

CONCLUSION

In this chapter, we have explored the construction of a key myth in popular and scientific literature on delinquency, that of maternal responsibility. We have explored the empirical basis for contemporary constructions, finding that the evidence is often related to broader structural conditions associated with maternal behaviors. We have seen, moreover, that the construction of maternal responsibility for juvenile delinquency is not simply a contemporary construction, but one that emerges out of fundamental transformations of the family and technologies of governance and social regulation. Far from being an unprecedented construction, conceptions of child neglect emerge in connection with households led by single mothers. Such findings seem to support the suspicion of authors who believe that recent attention to the role of mothers in relation to juvenile delinquency is in response to uneasiness about changing gender roles. Such attention calls into question the ways in which mothers are foregrounded as singularly responsible for the behavior of youth, in ways that obscure the broader social conditions in which they are situated.[68]

NOTES

1. Chira, 1998; Cohen & Katzenstein, 1988; Faludi, 1991; Maynard, 1997.
2. Henshaw, 2004.
3. Singh & Darroch, 2000; McElroy & Moore, 1997.
4. Maynard, 1997.
5. Geronimus, 1997.
6. Grogger, 1997.

7. Geronimus, 1997.
8. Moore, Morrison, & Greene, 1997.
9. Morash & Rucker, 1989.
10. Grogger, 1997.
11. Nagin, Pogarsky, & Farrington, 1997.
12. Gottfredson & Hirschi, 1990.
13. Morash & Rucker, 1988.
14. Nagin et al., 1997.
15. McLoyd, 1990.
16. Nagin et al., 1997.
17. Pogarsky, Lizotte, & Thornberry, 2003.
18. Demuth & Brown, 2004.
19. Wells & Rankin, 1991.
20. Wells & Rankin, 1991.
21. Rebellon, 2002.
22. Simons, Whitbeck, Beaman, & Conger, 1994.
23. King, 1994.
24. Loeber & Stouthamer-Loeber, 1986.
25. Loeber & Stouthamer-Loeber, 1986.
26. Tschann, Johnston, Kline, & Wallerstein, 1989.
27. Loeber & Stouthamer-Loeber, 1986.
28. E.g., Garasky, 1995; McLanahan & Sandefur, 1994; Thomas, Farrell, & Barnes, 1996.
29. Turner, Irwin, & Millstone, 1991; Watts & Watts, 1991.
30. Demuth & Brown, 2004; Manning & Lamb, 2003.
31. Manning & Lamb, 2003.
32. Demuth & Brown, 2004.
33. U.S. Bureau of Census, 1993.
34. Bureau of Labor Statistics, 2002.
35. Chira, 1998.
36. Dionne, 2002; Kristol, 1996; Strubel, 1996.
37. Flanagan, 2006; Steiner, 2006.
38. See Eyer, 1996.
39. Belsky, 1988.
40. See Harvey, 1999.
41. See Parcel & Menaghan, 1994a, 1994b.
42. Menaghan & Parcel, 1991.
43. Menaghan, Kowaleski-Jones, & Mott, 1997.
44. Parcel & Menaghan, 1994a, 1994b.
45. Menaghan et al., 1997.
46. Glueck & Glueck, 1950; Hirschi, 1969; Roy, 1963; see also Sampson & Laub, 1993.
47. Farnworth, 1984; West, 1982; Zhao, Cao, & Cao, 1997.
48. Broidy, 1995; Hillman & Sawilowsky, 1991; Vander Ven, 2003; Vander Ven, Cullen, Carrozza, & Wright, 2001; Wadsworth, 1979.
49. Vander Ven & Cullen, 2004.
50. E.g., Cohen & Scull, 1983; Ignatieff, 1978; Rothman, 1990.
51. Platt, 1977, p. 74.
52. Donzelot, 1977, p. 92, emphasis added.
53. Rose, 1987, p. 70.
54. Lupton, 1995, p. 42.
55. Apple, 1995, p. 90; see also Lupton, 1995.

56. Tomes, 1998, pp. 104–105, 157–159, 132–134.

57. Ehrenreich & English, 2005, pp. 155–200; Hunt, 1999, pp. 77–139; Wolf, 2001.

58. Apple, 1995, p. 95.

59. Tomes, 1998, pp. 140–41.

60. Tomes, 1998, p. 140.

61. Apple, 1995, p. 91; cf. Donzelot, 1977.

62. Gordon, 2002, p. 86.

63. Gordon, 1994; Gordon, 2002, p. 84.

64. Gordon, 2002, p. 117.

65. Gordon, 2002, pp. 136, 139.

66. Gilliom, 2001; Swift, 1995.

67. Swift, 1995, pp. 101–125.

68. A variety of other scholars argue that a number of emergent social problems can be analyzed as extensions of childhood regulation and maternal responsibility. For Ian Hacking, contemporary attention to child abuse differs from constructions of "child battering" in previous centuries because of the medicalization and normalizing (as abuse) of the discourse. As constructions of child abuse allow for unprecedented intervention in family life at a time when the welfare state is in decline, Hacking suggests that child abuse enables a variety of theses about the construction of familial problems as an alternative form of regulation with the decline of state welfare strategies (Hacking, 1991). For Malacrida, discourses of Attention Deficit Disorder—be they mainstream or alternative—construct and rely on discourses of maternal responsibility, regulating parental behavior far into their child's teenage years based on constructions of maternal responsibility for a child's potential "dangerousness" or being "at risk" (Malacrida, 2002). Anorexia is also grounds for medicalized intervention (Vander Ven & Vander Ven, 2003). Vander Ven and Vander Ven show how expert discourses, both psychological and sociological, are constructed from the 1950s on to problematize girl's deviant eating behavior in ways that invoke maternal responsibility. Finally, in some U.S. states, alternative birthing practices that seek to limit medical expertise, such as midwifery and the home birth movement, have been responded to as a form of negligence, going so far as to label it a form of child abuse (Beckett & Hoffman, 2005).

REFERENCES

Apple, R. D. (1995). Constructing mothers: Scientific motherhood in the nineteenth and twentieth centuries. In R. D. Apple and J. Golden (Eds.), *Mothers and motherhood: Readings in American history* (pp. 90–110). Columbus, OH: The Ohio State University Press.

Beckett, K., & Hoffman, B. (2005). Challenging medicine: Law, resistance, and the cultural politics of childbirth. *Law and Society Review, 35,* 125–70.

Belsky, J. (1988). The "effects" of infant day care reconsidered. *Early Childhood Research Quarterly, 3,* 235–72.

Broidy, L. M. (1995). Direct supervision and delinquency: Assessing the adequacy of structural proxies. *Journal of Criminal Justice, 23,* 541–554.

Bureau of Labor Statistics. (2002). *Employment characteristics of families.* Bureau of Labor Statistics News. Washington, D.C.: U.S. Department of Labor.

Chira, S. (1998). *A Mother's place.* New York: HarperCollins.

Cohen S., & Katzenstein, M. (1988). The war over the family is not over the rights and interests of children. In M. Strober and S. Dornbusch (Eds.),

Feminism, children, and the new families (pp. 26–45). New York: Guilford Press.

Cohen, S., & Scull, A. (Eds.). (1983). *Social control and the state: Historical and comparative essays.* Oxford, UK: Basil Blackwell.

Demuth, S., & Brown, S. (2004). Family structure, family processes, and adolescent delinquency: The significance of parental absence versus parental gender. *Journal of Research in Crime and Delinquency, 41,* 58–81.

Dionne, E. J. (2002, July 26). The motherhood issue. *The Washington Post,* p. A33.

Donzelot, J. (1977). *The policing of families.* Baltimore, MD: The Johns Hopkins University Press.

Ehrenreich, B., & English, D. (2005). *For her own good: Two centuries of the experts' advice to women* (revised ed.). New York: Anchor Books.

Eyer, D. (1996). *Motherguilt: How our culture blames mothers for what's wrong with society.* New York: Random House.

Faludi, S. (1991). *Backlash: The undeclared war against American women.* New York: Crown.

Farnworth, M. (1984). Family structure, family attributes, and delinquency in a sample of low-income, minority males and females. *Journal of Youth and Adolescence, 13,* 349–364.

Flanagan, C. (2006). *To hell with all that: Loving and loathing our inner housewife.* New York: Little, Brown.

Garasky, S. (1995). The effects of family structure on education attainment: Do the effects vary by the age of the child? *American Journal of Economics and Sociology, 54,* 89–105.

Geronimus, A. (1997). Teenage childbearing and personal responsibility: An alternative view. *Political Science Quarterly, 112,* 405–430.

Gilliom, J. (2001). *Overseers of the poor: Surveillance, resistance, and the limits of privacy.* Chicago: The University of Chicago Press.

Glueck, S., & Glueck, E. (1950). *Unraveling juvenile delinquency.* Cambridge, MA: Harvard University Press.

Gordon, L. (1994). *Pitied but not entitled: Single mothers and the history of welfare 1890–1935.* New York: The Free Press.

Gordon, L. (2002). *Heroes of their own lives: The politics and history of family violence—Boston 1880–1960.* Urbana, IL: University of Illinois Press.

Gottfredson, M., & Hirschi, T. (1990). *A general theory of crime.* Stanford, CA: Stanford University Press.

Grogger, J. (1997). Incarceration-related costs of early childbearing. In R. Maynard (Ed.), *Kids having kids: Economic costs and social consequences of teen pregnancy* (pp. 95–143). Washington, D.C.: Urban Institute Press.

Hacking, I. (1991). The making and molding of child abuse. *Critical Inquiry, 17,* 253–88.

Harvey, E. (1999). Long-term effects of early parental employment on children of the National Longitudinal Survey of Youth. *Developmental Psychology, 35,* 445–59.

Henshaw, S. (2004). *U.S. teenage pregnancy statistics with comparative statistics for women aged 20–24.* New York: The Alan Guttmacher Institute.

Hillman, S. B., & Sawilowsky, S.S. (1991). Maternal employment and early adolescent substance use. *Adolescence, 26,* 829–837.

Hirschi, T. (1969). *Causes of delinquency.* Berkeley, CA: University of California Press.

Hunt, A. (1999). *Governing morals: A short history of moral regulation.* London: Cambridge University Press.

Ignatieff, M. (1978). *A just measure of pain: The penitentiary in the industrial revolution, 1750–1850.* New York: Pantheon Books.

King, V. (1994). Variation in the consequences of nonresident father involvement for childrens' well-being. *Journal of Marriage and the Family, 56,* 963–972.

Kristol, I. (1996, March 6). Sex trumps gender. *Wall Street Journal,* p. A20.

Loeber, R., & Stouthamer-Loeber, M. (1986). Family factors as correlates and predictors of juvenile conduct problems and delinquency. In M. Tonry & N. Morris (Eds.), *Crime and justice: An annual review of research* (Vol. 7, pp. 29–149). Chicago: University of Chicago Press.

Lupton, D. (1995). *The imperative of health: Public health and the regulated body.* London: Sage Publications.

Malacrida, C. (2002). Alternative therapies and attention deficit disorder: Discourses of maternal responsibility and risk. *Gender and Society, 16,* 366–385.

Manning, W., & Lamb, K. (2003). Adolescent well-being in cohabitating, married, and single-parent families. *Journal of Marriage and the Family, 65,* 876–893.

Maynard, R. (1997). *Kids having kids: Economic costs and social consequences of teen pregnancy.* Washington, D.C.: Urban Institute Press.

McElroy, S., & Moore, K. (1997). Trends over time in teenage pregnancy and childbearing: The critical changes. In R. Maynard (Ed.), *Kids having kids: Economic costs and social consequences of teen pregnancy* (pp. 23–53). Washington, D.C.: Urban Institute Press.

McLanahan, S., & Sandefur, G. (1994). *Growing up with a single parent: What hurts, what helps.* Cambridge, MA: Harvard University Press.

McLoyd, V. (1980). The impact of economic hardship on black families and children: Psychological distress, parenting, and socioemotional development. *Child Development, 61,* 311–46.

Menaghan, E. G., Kowaleski-Jones, L., & Mott, F. L. (1997). The intergenerational costs of parental social stressors: Academic and social difficulties in early adolescence for children of young mothers. *Journal of Health and Social Behavior, 38,* 72–86.

Menaghan, E. G., & Parcel, T. L. (1991). Determining children's home environments: The impact of maternal characteristics and current occupational and family conditions. *Journal of Marriage and the Family, 53,* 417–431.

Moore, K., Morrison, D., & Greene, A. (1997). Effects on the children born to adolescent mothers. In R. Maynard (Ed.), *Kids having kids: Economic costs and social consequences of teen pregnancy* (pp. 145–173). Washington, D.C.: Urban Institute Press.

Morash, M., & Rucker, L. (1989). An exploratory study of the connection of mother's age at childbearing to her children's delinquency in four data sets. *Crime and Delinquency, 35,* 45–93.

Nagin, D., Pogarsky, G., & Farrington, D. (1997). Adolescent mothers and the criminal behavior of their children. *Law and Society Review, 31,* 137–162.

Parcel, T. L., & Menaghan, E. G. (1994a). *Parents' jobs and children's lives.* New York: Aldine De Gruyter.

Parcel, T. L., & Menaghan, E. G. (1994b). Early parental work, family social capital, and early childhood outcomes. *American Journal of Sociology, 99,* 972–1009.

Platt, A. (1977). *The child savers: The invention of delinquency* (2nd ed., enlarged). Chicago: The University of Chicago Press.

Pogarsky, G., Lizotte, A. J., & Thornberry, T. P. (2003). The delinquency of children born to young mothers: Results from the Rochester youth development study. *Criminology, 41,* 1249–1286.

Rebellon, C. (2002). Reconsidering the broken homes/delinquency relationship and exploring its mediating mechanisms. *Criminology, 40,* 103–135.

Rose, N. (1989). *Governing the soul: The shaping of the private self* (2nd ed.). London: Free Association Books.

Rothman, D. J. (1990). *The discovery of the asylum: Social order and disorder in the new republic* (2nd ed., revised). Boston: Little, Brown.

Roy, P. (1963). Adolescent roles: Rural-urban differentials. In F. I. Nye and L. Hoffman (Eds.), *The employed mother in America* (pp. 165–181). Chicago: Rand McNally.

Sampson, R. J., & Laub, J. H. (1993). *Crime in the making: Pathways and turning points through life.* Cambridge, MA: Harvard University Press.

Simons, R., Whitbeck L., Beaman, J., & Conger, R. (1994). The impact of mothers' parenting, involvement by nonresidential fathers, and parental conflict on the adjustment of children. *Journal of Marriage and Family, 94,* 356–374.

Singh, S., & Darroch, J. (2000). Adolescent pregnancy and childbearing: Levels and trends in developed countries. *Family Planning Perspectives, 32,* 14–23.

Steiner, L. (2006). *Mommy wars: Stay-at-home and career moms face off on their choices, their lives, their families.* New York: Random House.

Strubel, A. (1996, March 18). What's a woman to do, Mr. Kristol? *Wall Street Journal,* p. A19.

Swift, K. J. (1995). *Manufacturing "bad mothers": A critical perspective on child neglect.* Toronto: University of Toronto Press.

Thomas G., Farrell, M., & Barnes, G. (1996). The effects of single-mother families and nonresident fathers on delinquency and substance abuse in black and white adolescents. *Journal of Marriage and the Family, 58,* 884–894.

Tomes, N. (1998). *The gospel of germs: Men, women, and the microbe in American life.* Cambridge, MA: Harvard University Press.

Tschann, J., Johnston, J., Kline, M., & Wallerstein, J. (1989). Family process and children's functioning during divorce. *Journal of Marriage and the Family, 51,* 431–444.

Turner, R., Irwin, C., & Millstone, S. (1991). Family structure, family processes, and experimenting with substances, during adolescence. *Journal of Research on Adolescence, 1,* 93–106.

U.S. Bureau of Census. (1993). *Statistical abstract of the United States* (113th ed.). Washington, D.C.: U.S. Government Printing Office.

Vander Ven, T. (2003). *Working mothers and juvenile delinquency.* New York: LFB Scholarly Press.

Vander Ven, T., & Cullen, F. (2004). The impact of maternal employment on serious youth crime: Does the quality of working conditions matter? *Crime and Delinquency, 50,* 272–291.

Vander Ven, T., Cullen, F., Carrozza, M., & Wright, J. (2001). Home alone: The impact of maternal employment on delinquency. *Social Problems, 48,* 236–257.

Vander Ven, T., & Vander Ven, M. (2003). Exploring patterns of mother-blaming in anorexia scholarship: A study in the sociology of knowledge. *Human Studies, 26,* 97–119.

Wadsworth, M. E. J. (1979). *Roots of delinquency: Infancy, adolescence, and crime.* New York: Barnes and Noble.

Watts, D., & Watts, K. (1991). Impact of female-headed parental families on academic achievement. *Journal of Divorce and Remarriage, 17,* 97–114.

Wells, B., & Rankin, J. (1991). Families and delinquents: A meta-analysis of the impact of broken homes. *Social Problems, 38,* 71–93

West, D. J. (1982). *Delinquency: Its roots, careers and prospects.* Cambridge, MA: Harvard University Press.

Wolf, J. H. (2001). *Don't kill your baby: Public health and the decline of breastfeeding in the nineteenth and twentieth centuries.* Columbus, OH: The Ohio State University Press.

Zhao, J., Cao, J., & Cao, L. (1997, Spring). *The effects of female headship and welfare on delinquency: An analysis of five-wave panel data.* Paper presented at the Academy of Criminal Justice Sciences annual meeting, Louisville, KY.

CHAPTER 12

The Great Wall of China: Cultural Buffers and Delinquency

Hsiao-Ming Wang

Residents of the upscale southern California community were shocked when a 17-year-old honor student, Stuart Tay, the son of a prominent obstetrician was found bludgeoned, choked, and buried in a backyard. The victim's parents, Chinese immigrants, were horrified to find out during the investigation that their obedient and academically oriented teen was brutally murdered by five classmates, four of whom were also young Chinese Americans. They were led in the attack by Robert Chan, a youth slated to be class valedictorian but who was reputed to have ties to Wah Ching, a Chinese criminal society. The story grew more surreal for the families as it was uncovered that the youth, including Tay, had been trafficking stolen computer parts. The group was planning a burglary but had grown suspicious of Tay's loyalty, which resulted in his murder. The involvement of so many Chinese American youth in a crime of this nature seemed to contradict perceptions of a law-abiding or "model" immigrant population. Could it be that the values of success and achievement had been pushed beyond the limits of acceptable behavior for these youth?

ASIAN AMERICANS AND DELINQUENCY

Asian Americans as a group are underrepresented in all areas of the criminal justice system from arrest through incarceration. As 2004 data from the U.S. Census Bureau indicates, about 4.1 percent of the total population were Asian Americans who contributed to only 1.2 percent of the total number of arrests. In a closer state analysis, about 3 percent of the Texas population was Asian in 2003. However, Asians accounted for only 0.5 percent of all arrests in that state in that same year. An identical pattern also could be found in the juvenile justice system. U.S. Census data in 2004 indicated that 17.4 percent of all students in grades 9 through 12 reported carrying a weapon at least one day during the previous 30 days, while only 10.6 percent of Asian American students reported the same behavior. The *Sourcebook of Criminal Justice Statistics 2003* presented a similar picture. Although 3.7 percent of Americans under the age of 18 were Asians, they accounted for only 1.5 percent of incarcerated juveniles. In Texas, Asian youth accounted for only 0.6 percent of all incarcerated juveniles.

The above data inevitably led to stereotypes about the "model minority," a concept derived from the Middleman Minority Theory. This theory maintains that the socioeconomic stratum of Asian Americans, specifically Japanese, Chinese, and Korean Americans, is between European Americans and African Americans. Asian Americans represent a collective "model minority," and may serve as a buffer or interface between European Americans and African Americans.[1]

The concept of a Middleman Minority, however, has been criticized for its apparent biases. Opponents point out that "model minority" perhaps is a positive label, but the theory itself can be biased. First, Asian American males, on the whole, are underemployed, underpaid, or both. Second, a diverse group of Hispanics and Jews who may also serve as a buffer are totally ignored by the theorists. Third, the theory is an attempt to segregate Asian Americans into a category separated from other racial minority groups in the United States.[2]

From a criminological viewpoint, the model minority thesis may have some merit. To Asians, at least, it had correctly described their characteristics as thrifty, industrious, persevering, delaying gratification, and investing in and expending hard work.[3] Those depictions seem to remind one of Gottfredson and Hirschi's "General Theory of Crime,"[4] which addressed the human characteristics thought to be related to criminal conduct. Gottfredson and Hirschi maintained that those with low self-control are more likely to commit crime because they enjoy risky, exciting, or thrilling behaviors with immediate gratification. Gottfredson and Hirschi depicted people with low self-control as deriving satisfaction from "money without work, sex without courtship, revenge without court delays." If Middleman Minority theorists' description of Asian American characteristics were correct, in line with Gottfredson and Hirschi's theory, Asian Americans would be less likely to engage in crime and delinquency. Crime data seem to support this assumption.

Research on cultural aspects of crime are often complicated by the use of generic terms such as Asian American, which involves a wide spectrum of ethnicities ranging from Chinese to Indians. Each ethnicity has its own history and culture. It would be problematic to assume Asian Americans to be a homogeneous group. To avoid this problem, it is better to examine a specific issue within the context of a certain culture. To follow this line, this chapter selectively examines the relationship between Chinese heritage and delinquency. To shed some light on this issue, this chapter begins with an overview of some of the most prominent aspects of Chinese culture.

CONFUCIANISM AS THE THEME OF CHINESE HERITAGE

To understand Chinese heritage, one must appreciate Confucianism, a Latinized term traced back to the Jesuits of the sixteenth century. Confucianism roughly means "the doctrine of *rujia*" or the "School of Ru" in Chinese. The formation of *rujia* was in the early years of the Zhou Dynasty (1100–256 B.C.). *Rujia*, as a distinct school, recognized Confucius (551–479 B.C.) as their master and devoted themselves to the Six Classics: the Book of Poetry, the Book of History, the Book of Rites, the Book of Music, the Book of Changes, and the Spring and Autumn Annals.

Although Confucianism is not a theory about criminal behavior, Confucius' thesis indeed addresses human behavior and social disorder. Confucius believed that social disorder developed from the decay of ritual (*li*). To maintain the social order, social harmony and responsibility must be considered above individual freedom and rights, and the virtues of humaneness (*ren*) and righteousness (*yi*) must be emphasized through education at home and school.[5]

Confucius' followers are split in terms of human nature. Mencius (371–289 B.C.), on the one hand, elaborated Confucius' teaching to maintain that human nature is basically good. And, the purpose of education is mainly to keep that original goodness. Xunzi (298–238 B.C.), on the other hand, claimed that humans are originally evil. To maintain the social order, strict laws and harsh punishments must be exercised, and attention must be paid to ritual through education. The *Fajia*, the Legalist School, later adopted Xunzi's views.

Confucianism did not enjoy official patronage until the Han Dynasty (206 B.C.–220 A.D.). The emperor of Han recognized that the blend of Confucian idealism and Legalist pragmatism was a stabilizing force for society. The neo-Confucianism movement, developing during the Song dynasty (960–1279 A.D.), expanded Confucian concerns and established new methods to attain enlightenment. The impact of Confucianism spread well beyond Chinese territories. Because of China's political and cultural dominance in East Asia, Confucianism had a lasting impact in Japan, Korea, and Vietnam, too. The influence of Confucianism continues to the present day.[6]

Confucianism as a Form of Control Theory

Dr. Sheu, a criminologist in Taiwan, once tried to link Confucianism to criminological theory. Sheu found parallels between Confucianism and Control Theory,[7] and concluded that Confucianism was the earliest form of Control Theory. Sheu argued that both perspectives emphasize the

cultivation of human nature and control mechanisms.[8] First, the primary
focus of Control Theory is to explain why people "do not" commit crime,
while the main aim of Confucianism is to educate people into becoming
"gentleman." Second, Control Theory emphasizes external controls
(exerted by family, school, and peer group) and internal control of desired
restraint, whereas Confucianism emphasizes the virtues of humaneness
(*ren*) and righteousness (*yi*) through education at home and school.

To test his assumptions, Sheu analyzed a self-reported data set consisting of 1,185 youth across four ethnic groups in Taiwan. He found that
the difference in educational attainment among these four ethnic groups
was significantly related to delinquency (measured by gambling, smoking,
drinking, and so on). This finding suggests that educational attainment,
a value emphasized by Confucianism, is a protective factor against
delinquency.

Sheu further used a data set collected from 417 high school students in
an American Chinatown in 1983 to test the effect of "assimilation." The
sample group included American-born or foreign-born students. He found
that American-born Chinese youth are more likely to assimilate into American culture or lose their sense of Chinese heritage. As a result, they are
more likely to be individually oriented and less likely to be attached to
school. Even though Sheu's Chinatown data did not directly address delinquency, his findings indirectly implied that Chinese cultural constraints
could be an inhibiting factor with delinquency.

THE *THREE-WORD SUTRA*

Prior cross-cultural studies of delinquency point to Chinese heritage as
a protective factor, but the process of cultural cultivation is still not clear.
In line with Control Theory and Confucianism, the process of cultivation
should begin at an early age. To shed some light on this issue, the author
examined the *Three-Word Sutra*, the first textbook for almost all Chinese
children. If the value of education is essential to social stability, then the
ideas of social control should be easily found in the content of this sutra.

There are at least two reasons why the *Three-Word Sutra* is so popular
in Chinese societies. The first reason is that it is easy for children to learn.
The *Three-Word Sutra* has a total of 216 words, which are organized into
three-word clauses and four-clause sentences. It reads like a poem and
sounds like a chant. That is why this book is also called the "three-word
chant" in English. Children enjoy chanting, and can memorize the lyrics
even before they actually recognize the words. The second reason is educational. The content of the *Three-Word Sutra* is precise, addressing the
basics of Chinese literatures, mathematics, geography, history, and ethics.
Most contemporary educators believe that this book should be the first
that children read. Hence, although the *Three-Word Sutra* is not an official
textbook in modern education systems, many Chinese parents still want
their children to study this book at home.

The *Three-Word Sutra* is not criminology oriented, but the contents
of the first seven sentences may be interpreted from a criminological

perspective. The first sentence—"men at their birth are naturally good; their natures are much the same, but their habits might be widely different"—addresses the basic assumption of human nature. The *Three-Word Sutra* essentially reflects Mencius' view, and maintains that human nature is good. However, it also recognizes that human's habits, and the appearance of human nature, might be widely different.

The second sentence—"if there is no teaching, one's nature will deteriorate; the right way in teaching is to attach the utmost importance in thoroughness"—gives a social-process explanation for why human habits might be widely different. The benefit of persistent teaching is that it can preserve the original goodness of human nature. The influence of the second sentence is that Chinese parents always emphasize the value of education, which is indicated in almost all comparative delinquency literature. It is not difficult to find Chinese parents who are willing to save every penny they earn to support their children's education.

Both the third and fourth sentences provide illustrations of the second sentence. However, the third sentence—"the mother of Mencius chose a nicer neighborhood to live; and if Mencius did not learn, she would break a shuttle from the loom"— is more of a reflection of the Chinese view of teaching. It refers to the childhood story of Mencius. Most Chinese people believe that Mencius' success should be attributed to his mother's dedication.

Mencius's father died when Mencius was very young. The life of Mencius' mother was as hard as most single mothers in America today. She could make a living only as a weaver. Initially, Mencius' mother and Mencius lived near a cemetery. Mencius' mother decided to move to a better neighborhood when she found Mencius intensely preoccupied with imitating funeral services as a game instead of studying. Their second home was near a market where Mencius became obsessed with the practices of doing business instead of studying. Mencius' mother decided to move again. They finally moved to a home near a school where Mencius actively imitated school children studying.

Later on, Mencius actually went to school. One day, he came home from school earlier than his normal schedule. His mother asked the reason for this while she was weaving at the loom. Young Mencius replied, "I left because I felt like it." His mother took her knife and cut the finished cloth on her loom. Mencius was startled and asked why. She replied, persistence is the way of studies. Like weaving, only the finished cloth is marketable. Thus, she explained, the result of your truancy is much like my cutting the cloth. Mencius obviously received the message from his mother's teaching. He studied very hard from that moment and eventually became a famous Confucian scholar.

The fifth sentence—"it is father's fault to feed without teaching, whereas it would be the teacher's laziness if he/she teaches without severity"—identifies those who have responsibility for teaching. Traditional Chinese society is patriarchal. The father is responsible for his children's education at home. When the father is not available, then the mother assumes the responsibility (as Mencius' mother did).

Similarly, the teacher takes the full responsibility of teaching at school. Chinese teachers not only are expected to teach but also to exact discipline as necessary. Traditionally, Chinese teachers have the privilege of using corporal punishment on students. Confucius has been recognized as "the ultimate sage master of yore," the greatest Chinese philosopher and educator, because of his dedication to teaching. In memory of his great achievements in education, Chinese people like to erect a statue of Confucius at schools and town halls, including the one standing in front of the Chinese Cultural Center in Houston. If one takes a close look, one may find that Confucius carries a stick. It is said that the stick in the Confucius statue is a figure of a teaching rod. Chinese parents generally believe the adage "spare the rod, spoil the child." Many Chinese American professionals mention their childhood experiences of having their teachers punish them for misbehaving or not studying hard enough by using the teaching rod. In addition, if they dared to complain about this punishment to their fathers, they would most likely receive another punishment when they returned home. This experience highlights the essence of the end of the fifth sentence—"good kids can be taught, as long as parents and teachers work together."

The sixth sentence—"if the child does not learn, this is not as it should be; if he does not learn while young, what will he be when he gets old"—addresses the importance of learning in childhood. The seventh sentence—"if jade is not polished, it cannot become a useful device; if a man does not learn, he cannot know the appropriate behavior"—elaborates the sixth sentence by using the metaphor of jade polishing and points out that the purpose of education is to learn correct manners.

A review of the first seven sentences of the *Three-Word Sutra* presents several ideas related to contemporary criminology. These ideas are summarized below:

- Human behavior is learned.
- Education is a way to prevent delinquent behavior.
- A good environment is essential for a child's education.
- Persistence is the essence of a successful learning journey.
- Fathers and teachers both have a responsibility for the child's education.
- A successful learning journey starts from early childhood.

These ideas are similar to Sutherland's Differential Association Theory.[9] Sutherland identified that the learning process is primarily from intimate groups, but he failed to point out that parents and teachers have the full responsibility to teach children right from wrong. Hirschi, in his Social Bond Theory, mentioned that delinquency could be prevented through four bonds: attachment to conventional institutions (e.g., family and school), involvement with conventional activities, commitment to conventional goals, and belief in traditional values. Hirschi's thesis may be the closest one to traditional Chinese ideas, but it still does not directly point out parents' and teachers' full responsibility. Furthermore, these ideas seem to parallel Interactional Theory. Thornberry conceptualized delinquency in integrated terms and maintained that different variables affect delinquency at certain ages.[10] For example, lack of attachment to parents is a significant contributor to delinquency among those in "early adolescence" (11 to 13 years old), while a decrease in school bonds and associations with peers assume greater influence in the stage of "middle adolescence" (15 to 16 years old).

This unique idea about parents' and teachers' full responsibility led Chinese parents and teachers to dedicate themselves to their children's education for a thousand years. Chinese media frequently reported stories about successful people from poor families and attributed this success to their parents' dedication to their educations. Chinese media often report stories about criminals and condemns their behavior as bringing shame to their parents. This unique idea was introduced in the United States during several different periods of Chinese immigration.

CHINESE AMERICAN IMMIGRATION

The two major groups of immigrants who became today's Chinese Americans were foreign exchange students and laborers. Both groups can be traced back to the nineteenth century. The first recorded Chinese student studying in the United States was Yung Wing. He came to America in 1847 when he was 19 years old and returned to China with a diploma from Yale in 1854. Yung later led the first group of carefully selected Chinese youth to study in the United States. Many of these former foreign exchange students became leaders in China. With several disruptions and variations, this study-abroad movement continues today.

In the mid-nineteenth century, American businessmen began to import Chinese laborers for the transcontinental railroad's construction. These Chinese men worked long hours in physically dangerous jobs, which few white men were willing to perform. These laborers had few, if any, basic rights or protections. For example, they could not own real estate or bring their family members to the United States. In 1882, the Chinese Exclusion Act was passed, which limited the number of Chinese laborers (not students) entering the United States. This discriminatory law existed until 1943 when China and the United States became allies in World War II.

Chinese Americans are a diversified group in terms of their areas of origin. Before 1949, a majority of Chinese Americans were from Canton, a province in China first exposed to Western influences. The civil war between Nationalists (led by Chang Kai-Shih) and Communists (led by Mao Tzu-Dong) in 1945–49 forced many Chinese refugees from different provinces in China to the United States. In the 1970s and 1980s, thousands of study-abroad students from Taiwan joined the group of Chinese Americans.[11] In 1989, immediately after the Tiananmen Square Massacre, the U.S. government issued special green cards to foreign exchange students from China, which brought even more Chinese immigrants to the United States. The return of Hong Kong to the sovereignty of China in 1997 also resulted in many Chinese immigrants from the former British colony coming to America.

Regardless of where Chinese Americans originally came from, they have a wide range of educational backgrounds. Generally speaking, those who were foreign exchange students usually had advanced degrees, while Chinese laborers may be barely literate. Consequently, Chinese study-abroad students tend to work as professionals, while Chinese labors are more likely to be found in restaurants, laundries, or factories. Despite these differences in educational backgrounds, there seems to be no difference in the parents' perceptions of their responsibility to their childrens' education.

Houston, for example, is the fourth largest city of the United States with a population of more than two million. The Chinese American community in the greater Houston area is estimated at more than 100,000 people. Many of them are highly educated professionals working in the oil, medical, or computer industries. They are more likely to work in Houston but live in Sugar Land, a small city near the outskirts of southwest Houston. The reason for commuting daily between Houston and Sugar Land is mainly due to the quality of education in Sugar Land. Conversely, the Chinese community in Houston also consists of some less-educated immigrants. These immigrants are more likely to reside in the areas of southwest Houston and work in nearby restaurants or shops. When they save enough money to afford a more expensive home, they move to Sugar Land or similar areas for the same reason—to provide better education opportunities for their children.

Chinese American parents' perceptions of their responsibility to their children's education is not only evident in their search for better school districts but also in the form of financial support. Although most American youth depend on scholarships, loans, or part-time jobs for their college education, almost all Chinese American parents are willing to financially support their children through college and even graduate school. Furthermore, this financial support often includes housing costs. For instance, several Chinese American parents in Houston bought condominiums in Austin for their children attending the University of Texas. It would be a big mistake to assume that these Chinese American parents are rich. Most of them came to America with few assets. They worked very hard and lived in a parsimonious way. While other parents may prefer to spend on improving conditions for their children when they are young, the Chinese save for their children's education. They realize that higher education is the pathway to a better future in the United States. They also understand that, being Chinese Americans, it is their full responsibility to help their children fulfill the American dream.

In line with Chinese heritages, the other side of full responsibility for children's education is expectation. First-generation Chinese Americans, regardless of where they originally came from and their education background, tend to impose traditional expectations on their children. They are more likely to ask their children to maintain Chinese cultural traditions, which often means going to Chinese school on the weekend. The weight of these expectations can sometimes cause identity confusion among Chinese American children.[12]

IDENTITY CONFUSION

Erikson, a developmental psychologist and psychoanalyst, coined the term identity crisis.[13] He maintained that identity crisis is the most important conflict human beings encounter when they go through the eight developmental stages in life. Criminologists found that "adolescents undergoing an identity crisis might exhibit out-of-control behavior and experiment with drugs and other forms of deviance."[14]

Self-identity relates to the question, "Who I am?" It is largely based on the internalization of reflections and feedback from other people. People see themselves as others see them. This process starts from the moment we are born. Although most first-generation Chinese Americans see themselves as Chinese, their children are more likely to see themselves as Americans. A survey conducted by the author in 1999 indicated that Chinese American youth generally characterize their parents as being very traditional in the values and in the expectations they hold for their children. Many youth noted that their parents always ask them to study but not play. Some youth further noted that they want to be artists, but their parents wish them to be doctors or engineers. Many youth noted that they perceive themselves as Americans, but their parents insist that they go to Chinese schools on weekend. These different perceptions inevitably cause the issue of identity confusion among Chinese American children.

Chinese culture underscores the notion that children should study hard to earn academic achievements to honor their parents. Many Chinese American youth truly appreciate their parents' support but are often overwhelmed by the magnitude of their expectations.

There are differences, however, between the American-born and the foreign-born (including China, Hong Kong, and Taiwan) youth regarding self-identity. If migration takes place after the children's memory is stabilized, usually by 10 or 12 years of age, and if the Chinese language is maintained, the young immigrants may not suffer from identity confusion.[15]

CHINESE HERITAGES AND DELINQUENCY

When Erikson's theory and Tung's thesis are integrated, it is reasonable to assume that the memory of home country and the practice of the mother tongue may protect Chinese American youth from an identity crisis. Studies on Asian American delinquency in North America have found that Asian American youth, particularly those of Chinese heritage, tend to have lower rates of delinquency.[16] Those studies suggested that Chinese Culture, which emphasizes conformity, harmonious relationships, and respect for authority, might contribute to this unique phenomenon. Conversely, previous research indicates that as youth adopt American values, they may become more likely to reject their traditional heritage. Thus, while Chinese heritage seems to serve as a protective factor against delinquency, this proposition should be interpreted with caution from two viewpoints: the traditional measuring rod and economic advancement.

The Side Effect of the Traditional Measuring Rod

Most Chinese parents tend to use studiousness and academic achievements to measure their children's behavior. Studiousness is usually measured by hours spent reading textbooks, and achievements are measured by the accumulation of trophies and awards. This traditional measuring rod usually triggers considerable tension between Chinese parents and their children. This problem is not as obvious, however, in Chinese societies in which the emphasis is on the success of groups and the society maintains tight social controls. Chinese children tend to recognize that everyone is under the same system of values—everyone follows parental expectations. Thus, they are not the only ones who have to follow these controls, and this mind-set helps them adjust and perform.

In Taiwan, a child is expected, on any given school day, to get up at 6 A.M. and go to classes by 7 or 8 A.M. He or she will study Chinese, math, English, sciences, social sciences, and other subjects at school until 4 P.M. After school, he or she will be sent to "cram schools"[17] for strengthening academic subjects or training in the arts, such as drawing, dancing, or playing piano until 9 P.M. A quick and simple dinner is often consumed either at home, in the cram school, or on the way to the cram school. After the cram school, he or she needs to complete a number of homework assignments before calling it a day. Despite all their efforts, a child cannot evaluate himself or herself as an achiever in Taiwan. Under the traditional measuring rod, a child must be ranked in the top three in his or her class and earn many trophies and awards to honor his or her parents.

For the first-generation Chinese Americans, it would be a problem if they still used this traditional measuring rod. This problem becomes more significant when children begin to go to school, where they are exposed to a less competitive mainstream culture. Many Chinese American children gradually find that they are being asked to do extra homework (most likely by their parents) after school, while other American children just play in their backyards. Additionally, Chinese American children find that they need to go to Chinese school on the weekend, while other American children enjoy recreational and leisure activities at home and with their families. Chinese American children start to question why they do not have the same American experiences. Prior research has indicated that most Chinese American youth will drop their mother language upon entering school because of exposure and the desire to fit in.[18] This change implies a transition of the self-identity from being Chinese to being American. This transition, especially in the initial stages, shocks many Chinese American parents and causes conflicts between them and their children. It is not too difficult to imagine hearing the following conversation in many Chinese American families:

> Parents: Why do you always play on your computer but do not study?
> Child: I am not "playing on" my computer. I am "using" it to contact my friends by the Internet.

Parents: Why are you not practicing piano at home on weekend but instead fooling around with your friends?

Child: We just go to movies, we are not "fooling around."

This conversation specifically highlights the different expectations of children's behavior between the East and West. Traditionally, the Chinese vocabulary does not have an equivalent term for delinquency. Youth in traditional Chinese societies are measured by the standard of maintaining good behavior and studying hard. They are expected to look up to their parents and siblings at home. They are also expected to follow their teachers and study hard at school. Any child who does not meet this standard would be regarded as a "bad kid" who is incorrigible and a shame to the whole family. This concept is not common in Western societies.

In Western society, there is a big difference between "bad kids" and delinquents. This difference can be addressed by a behavioral continuum. The left end of this continuum represents delinquent behavior, while the right end refers to normal behavior. Between these two ends is a gray area in which certain behaviors are neither fully normal nor totally delinquent. Chinese American parents, under the influence of traditional Chinese culture, tend to stand at the right end to evaluate their children's behavior. When their youngsters do not meet their standards, they tend to label their children as "bad kids." Conversely, most Chinese American youth, under the influence of American education, are more likely to stand at the left end to measure their behaviors. As long as they are not involved in what is legally considered delinquency, they tend to consider themselves as not bad.

This different perception of delinquency causes another side effect of the traditional measuring rod—two-faced Chinese American youth. One summer, several Chinese American youth were found drinking alcohol in a camp and bullied other kids into either joining them or not telling. These youth all maintained excellent academic records at high school. Why did they develop delinquent behavior at the summer camp? A different perception of delinquency could be one reason. The Chinese American youth were not involved in any delinquency when their parents were monitoring them as they studied hard, because the concept of studying hard included the connotation of no bad behavior, which is a traditional Chinese perspective. Thinking creatively, however, the Chinese American youth claimed they were not guilty when they were caught because their parents did not expressly ask them not to drink and threaten others while at the camp. In fact, these youth all had learned that drinking and threatening are delinquent behavior at schools. Their excuse squarely recalls Sykes and Matza's neutralization theory, which maintains that youth know right from wrong; they just use excuses to justify their conduct as they drift between the two.[19]

The Impact of Economic Advancement

To fully explore the relationship between Chinese heritage and delinquency, one cannot ignore the impact of economic advancement in

Chinese societies. Economic reform in China in the 1980s and 1990s largely changed Chinese society. On the one hand, China became the world's third largest exporter, surpassing Japan and following only the United States and Germany. On the other hand, the crime rate in China increased to 163.19 per 100,000 people in 1998 from 55.91 per 100,000 people in 1978. There is an observed association between economic development and crime trends. Studies suggested that the increased crime rate is a result of, among other things, changing cultural beliefs and disruption of traditional social control mechanisms.[20]

Taiwan experienced a similar trend during the recent past. According to time-series data (1998–2005) from the Economic Affairs Ministry in Taiwan, the gross national product of Taiwan increased from $278 billion in 1998 to $355 billion in 2005. Another time-series data set (1991–2005) from the National Police Administration, the highest law enforcement authority in Taiwan, indicated an upward crime trend in this same time period. This data set takes 1996 as its base year and standardizes the crime index at 100, whereas the index of 1991 and 2005 are 67 and 122, respectively.

Currently, although not enough evidence exists to say that economic advancement causes the increasing crime trend, the experiences in China and Taiwan suggest a correlation between these two factors. Some scholars have attempted to clarify this issue from a social control perspective.[21] They maintain that economic advancement weakens the effects of Chinese heritage, and thus more crimes are expected.

Theorists argue that China has existed as a stable and organized society for at least 5,000 years. The need for formal law, courts, or law enforcement had never been as great as that of Western societies. The bedrock of Chinese society is the family, which facilitates informal social control. In addition, Chinese people adopt Confucianism as the guideline for their daily life. Thus, Chinese people sought to create a sense of order from within. The impacts of economic advancement on Chinese heritage are twofold. First, economic development inevitably takes parents away from homes for long hours. Second, economic development emphasizes the value of materialism, which conflicts with the values of Confucianism. As a result, contemporary Chinese children receive less supervision and education from their parents at home. Thus, the inner-directed effort—that is, searching for appropriate behavior—becomes less important than before.

CONCLUSION

A significant amount of research has been conducted on factors predisposing youth to delinquency, but less study has been completed on the variables that may insulate or buffer a child from becoming involved in crime. There is an even greater need for information that identifies prevention or deterrence features in the lives of minority and immigrant youth. Each individual culture may have prescribed values, attitudes, and traditions that create a framework to analyze the potential for involvement in delinquency.

This chapter maintains that Confucianism, the dominant theme of Chinese culture, can be found in the content of the *Three-Word Sutra*. The concepts presented by the *Three-Word Sutra* parallel several contemporary criminological theories, including differential association, social bond, and the interactional approaches. Adherence to the principles of Chinese culture is a protective factor or buffer against delinquency. In an examination of Chinese American youth behavior, it was found that the young immigrants who retain their Chinese language may be less likely to suffer from identity confusion. This may be related to the empirical finding that the youth who are steeped in the Chinese culture tend to have lower rates of delinquency. However, this finding should be interpreted with caution. The side effects of the traditional measuring rod and the impact of economic development, the global marketplace, and exposure to Western culture may weaken the function of Chinese heritage as a preventive factor.

Previous research on Chinese American (or, more generally, Asian American) youth seems to document comparatively lower rates of involvement in delinquency than their non-Asian peers, but little work uses self-reported information to assess what factors may be related to success in school and deterrence from criminal behavior. This may be a needed direction for future research.

NOTES

1. Wong, 1998.
2. Wong, 1998.
3. Wong, 1998.
4. Gottfredson & Hirschi, 1990.
5. Yao, 2000.
6. Oldstone-Moore, 2002.
7. Hirschi, 1969.
8. Sheu, 1999, p. 8.
9. Sutherland, 1947.
10. Thornberry, 1987.
11. Some of them claim themselves as Taiwanese Americans for political reasons.
12. Hune & Chan, 1997.
13. Erikson, 1968.
14. Siegel, 2004.
15. Tung, 2000.
16. Le, Monfared, & Stockdale, 2005.
17. Most Chinese parents both need to go to work. They usually cannot return home until 7 p.m. By doing so, their children are expected to be under no supervision for three hours. To fulfill this gap, many retired teachers or incumbent teachers (not openly) run a cram school to provide supervision for this group of children by a way of extra education. This utility makes cram schools a billion-dollar industry in Taiwan.
18. Tung, 2000.
19. Sykes & Matza, 1957.
20. Liu & Messner, 2001.
21. Liu, Zhang, & Messner, 2001.

REFERENCES

Erikson, E. H. (1968). *Identity: Youth and crisis.* New York: Norton.

Gottfredson, M., & Hirschi, T. (1990). *A general theory of crime.* Palo Alto, CA: Stanford University Press.

Hirschi, T. (1969). *Causes of delinquency.* Berkeley, CA: University of California Press.

Hune, S., & Chan, K. (1997, September 5). All things being equal. *Asian Week,* p. 11.

Le, T. N., Monfared, G., & Stockdale, G. D. (2005). The relationship of school, parent, and peer: Contextual factors with self-reported delinquency for Chinese, Cambodian, Laotian or Mien, and Vietnamese youth. *Crime and Delinquency, 51*(2), 192–219.

Liu, J., & Messner, S. F. (2001). Modernization and crime trends in China's reform era. In J. Liu, L. Zhang, & S. E. Messner (Eds.), *Crime and social control in a changing China,* (pp. 3–21). Westport, CT: Greenwood.

Liu, J., Zhang, L., & Messner, S. F. (Eds.). (2001). *Crime and social control in a changing China.* Westport, CT: Greenwood.

Oldstone-Moore, J. (2002). *Confucianism.* New York: Oxford University Press.

Sheu, C-J. (1999). Confucianism as control theory explanation of crime among overseas Chinese in Southeast Asia. *Journal of Central Police University, 55,* 211–236.

Siegel, L. J. (2004). *Criminology: Theories, patterns, and typologies* (8th ed.). Belmont, CA: Wadsworth/Thomson Learning.

Sykes, G. M., & Matza, D. (1957). Techniques of neutralization: A theory of delinquency. *American Sociological Review, 22,* 667–670.

Sutherland, E. H. (1947). *Principles of criminology.* Philadelphia: J. B. Lippincott.

Thornberry, T. P. (1987). Toward an interactional theory of delinquency. *Criminology, 25,* 863–891.

Tung, M. P. (2000). *Chinese Americans and their immigrant parents: Conflict, identity, and values.* Binghamton, NY: Haworth Press.

Wong, E. F. (1998). Asian American middleman minority theory: The framework of an American myth. *The Journal of Ethnic Studies, 13*(1), 51–88.

Yao, X. (2000). *An introduction to Confucianism.* New York: Cambridge University Press.

Epilogue

Although these articles have covered a broad range of topics related to delinquency, it is easy to see certain consistencies in youthful offending and in our responses to them. It may be argued that, appearances aside, a juvenile crime is a crime and should be treated accordingly. Over time, age seems to have less effect on mitigating the seriousness of charges and the circumstances of bizarre crimes now seem commonplace. An eight-year-old is arrested for choking a playmate, a six-year-old shoots his sister. We shake our heads in disbelief at teens hiding a body from an unwanted birth and then moving on to a movie or a party, or shooting a parent and then shopping at a mall. Ironically, we assess the demeanor of immature youth in terms of our expectations for normal adult behavior. And, as a consequence, we often stop and reevaluate the way we think about youth crime.

Unfortunately, the immediate news versions that seem to form the basis of our perceptions about youthful offenders and their offenses provide some of the most distorted images. Later, when interest in stories has waned and the public has moved on to the next tantalizing story, the facts of juvenile cases, the explanations, the background, and the historical significance of family dynamics, abuse, secrets, and lies play out in ways that would perhaps temper and mediate our original views of what juvenile crime is really like. Much can be learned from these more notable cases. Away from the circus-like atmosphere of television crime events, children break down, reflect, and talk about not only their hopes and dreams but also what went terribly wrong.

LISTENING FOR ANSWERS

For those who are interested in the accounts behind the media hype, some excellent works bring a much more detailed understanding and insight to these unique cases. The complexity of the juvenile justice system, the network of familial pathologies, drug and alcohol abuse, neglect, and other causes and consequences of delinquency stand ready to be examined from a multitude of perspectives and in a more instructive context than the emotional and sensational "infotainment" accounts. Consider researching some of these sources if you are truly interested in learning more about delinquents and the juvenile justice system.

In *Somebody Else's Children*, journalists John Hubner and Jill Wolfson explore the lives of youth who find their way into California's social service system and the progressive court of noted jurist Len Edwards. Both Edward Humes' *No Matter How Loud I Shout* and Mark Salzman's *True Notebooks* are based on the experiences of journalists who spent a year teaching creative writing to some of the Los Angeles area's most serious delinquents incarcerated in the city's detention facility. Face to face with these superpredators, the authors are able to draw out feelings, reflections, and insights that bare the souls of lost youths. Their toughness and hardened demeanor cracks from time to time, as when Salzman played Saint-Saens's *Swan* on his cello and told the boys that it reminded him of his mother. When he finished the piece, he found that most of the boys—the murderers and robbers—were sniffling and wiping their eyes. He was obliged to play it two more times before they were able to end the session.

Legislators should have to read the comments of the detainees as they ponder the latest government efforts to crack down on crime. When asked about a new law that would charge anyone in a car tied to a drive-by shooting with first-degree murder, not just the actual gunman, a young girl responded, "Well, then, I might as well be firing, too." Rather than deter crime, this jaded veteran of the juvenile system knew that her chances of being able to travel independent of her gang member friends, or to separate herself from their activities, was simply unrealistic. She did not see those options in her life.

Options are, you may argue, in the eye of the beholder. Three generations of African American men take on the issue of the environment, opportunities, and choices in books that paint vivid pictures of street life and juvenile pressures. In *Fist, Stick, Knife, Gun*, Geoffrey Canada recalls how, growing up in a matriarchal household, his activities were monitored closely by his grandmother and mother. The poverty and squalor of the tough Bronx neighborhoods in 1960 where fatherless boys congregated oozed potential violence and dead-end lives, but as Canada recalls, the kids still fought by rules, attended school, and feared the consequences of being late for dinner. This is different from the 1970s childhood of *Washington Post* journalist Nathan McCall, whose anger and resentment fueled his vicious attacks on society, both black and white, male and female, rich and poor. Only while serving a lengthy prison term did the stern direction and discipline of prison mentors turn his life around. Now, he thinks about young men like gangster author Kody Scott and fears that the rage they hold inside propels them into a violent tailspin of "nothing to lose." Scott's memoir of his gang exploits characterizes a late-1980s escalation of violence foreshadowed by Canada as he, too, watched young minority men grow more hopeless and lethal. Incarcerated, yet unrehabilitated, Kody changes his name to Sanyika Shakur, a tribute to the older Muslim prisoners he meets who try, unsuccessfully, to calm him. Mostly, he retains his street moniker "Monster" and remains true to his destructive calling. Is it another time? Or is it another, angrier, young man?

Although the family was a valuable source of strength for young men like Canada, for others, there is the realization that they are playing out some sort of predestined tragedy that the bonds of kinship cannot overcome. Some of the young men in detention write as if it were fate, an unknown force, that kept moving them in opposition to the pleas of their relatives to avoid trouble and obey the law. And for a few, the family is the source of the poison and the pain that inflicts permanent damage on them. Jennifer Toth tracks the case of *What Happened to Johnnie Jordan*, an abused and neglected youngster who survived a horrific childhood only to become a frighteningly violent young man. In conversations with Toth, he admits that he was never cared for by his drug-involved parents but seems to have suppressed the accounts his siblings tell of sexual torture and physical violence, always being hungry, and never being clean. If encouraged to talk about his life after that, of the 19 foster homes he was placed in from the age of 10 to 15, he reflects "I don't let things go.... I might let it slip but its going to come back and I don't know what brings it back ... something in my mind goes with a taste or smell ... and whoever is there just happens to be the victim." Johnnie even seems to detach himself from the murder of his elderly foster mother. He says he does not know why she died, and is reminded that he killed her. "Yeah," he says quietly, his head down, "I don't know why."[1]

Still, for every Johnnie Jordan out there, there is another who simply needs to be given a chance. In *There are No Children Here: The Story of Two Boys Growing Up in the Other America*, Alex Kotlowitz reminds us of the universal optimism of children, even those mired in drugs, poverty, and crime. He shares with us an account of two children chasing a rainbow through the projects, wanting to believe that there really is a treasure at the end. Despite being battered by the adult experiences of cynicism, the 11-year-old still has that naive wonder and hope.

"I was gonna make a wish," he said. "Hope for our family, like get Terence out of jail, get a new house, get out of the projects." When he disclosed his appeal, he had to stop talking momentarily to keep himself from crying. It hurt to think of all that could have been. Lafeyette too conceded that he's wondered about what they would have found at the rainbow's end. Heaped with disappointments, fourteen-year-old Lafeyette wanted to believe. He wanted to be allowed to dream, to reach, to imagine, he wanted another chance to chase a rainbow.[2]

The chances youth get represent hope for our future. More than reducing crime and creating healthier communities is the obligation we have not only to study but also to design, implement, and support those opportunities that will best allow children to thrive and realize their potential, to chase their rainbows.

NOTES

1. Toth, 2002, pp. 101–103.
2. Kotlowitz, 1991, p. 285.

REFERENCES

Canada, G. (1995). *Fist, stick, knife, gun: A personal history of violence in America*. Boston: Beacon.

Hubner, J., & Wolfson, J. (1996). *Somebody else's children: The courts, the kids, and the struggle to save America's troubled families*. New York: Crown.

Humes, E. (1996). *No matter how loud I shout: A year in the life of juvenile court*. New York: Simon & Schuster.

Kotlowitz, A. (1991). *There are no children here: The story of two boys growing up in the other America*. New York: Anchor Books.

McCall, N. (1995). *Makes me wanna holler: A young black man in America*. New York: Vintage Books.

Salzman, M. (2003). *True notebooks*. New York: Knopf.

Shakur, S. (1993). *Monster: The autobiography of an L.A. gang member*. New York: Penguin.

Toth, J. (2002). *What happened to Johnnie Jordan? The story of a child turning violent*. New York: Free Press.

Index

Adam Walsh Child Protection and Safety Act, 71

alcohol, 103–4; abuse of by parents, 30–31, 111–12, 121–23; and Drug Abuse and Resistance Education (D.A.R.E.), 101; and legal age limit, 21, 93, 105; and treatment for abuse of, 97–100; use of by adolescents, 17, 73, 92–97, 100, 103, 105–6

Alison, L., 111

Almighty Latin King and Queen Nation, 53 n.50

American Medical Association, 103–4

Ames, M. A., 28

ammunition, 132, 138–39

animal cruelty, 12, 64, 66, 110

Apple, R. D., 167

arson, 109–10, 124–25; and attachment disorders, 111, 113, 119–22, 124–25; and ecological approach, 123–24; and fire fascination, 118, 120–21; and maladaptive coping, 117, 121–23; and motivational typologies, 111–12, 114–18, 123–25; and parental substance abuse, 111–12, 121–23; pathways of, 118–25

assault, 17, 20, 48, 96, 113, 161

ATF. *See* Bureau of Alcohol, Tobacco, Firearms, and Explosives (ATF)

attachment theory: and arson, 111, 113, 119–22, 124–25; and Chinese, 182–83; and delinquency, 165, 183; and sexual offenses, 64, 68–69

Bachelard, G., 110

Baker, Jake, 153

Bartholomew, K., 68

Beccaria, Cesare, 13–14

Becker, Howard, 166

Belsky, J., 165

Berliner, L., 68–69

Blackstone Rangers, 53 n.50

Bloods, 52 n.18

Bolger, K., 31

Boston Gun Project: Operation Ceasefire, 140

Bourdieu, Pierre, 53 n.51

Boyz 'N the Hood, 47

Bronson, Charles, 8

bullying, 20–21, 113, 153

Bundy, Ted, 29–30

Bureau of Alcohol, Tobacco, Firearms, and Explosives (ATF), 129, 131, 133, 139–41

Burton, D. L., 64

About the Editors and Contributors

Marilyn D. McShane is a trustee-at-large member of the executive board to the Academy of Criminal Justice Sciences. She and Frank Williams have recently published the textbook *Step By Step Through the Thesis Process: A Resource Guide*. Their *Criminological Theory* book is in its fourth edition with the same publisher.

Frank P. Williams III is professor emeritus at California State University. He is author of *Imagining Criminology* and coauthor of four editions of *Criminological Theory*. He also is coauthor of the soon-to-be-released textbook *Step by Step Through the Thesis Process: A Resource Guide*.

Thomas Austin is professor of criminal justice at Shippensburg University and a graduate of Michigan State University. He has authored or co-authored more than 30 peer-reviewed articles on a variety of criminal justice topics, most recently with one of his current coauthors. His article entitled "The Effect of Legal and Extra-Legal Factors on Statutory Exclusion of Juvenile Offenders" appeared in *Youth Violence and Juvenile Justice* (2005).

Robert L. Bing III is an associate professor of criminology and criminal justice at the University of Texas at Arlington. He earned his doctorate in criminology from Florida State University. He is former chair of the department of criminology and criminal justice and the author of more than 25 refereed articles. His research interests include race and crime, juvenile justice, organizational politics in the courtroom, and issues in criminal justice education.

Alan I. Feldberg is a Pennsylvania-licensed psychologist employed by Cornell Abraxas to provide clinical programming and services for the Juvenile Firesetter Programs in South Mountain, Pennsylvania. He has implemented an ever-evolving clinical program that includes cognitive behavioral approaches focused on firesetting issues, filling in areas of deficit, and working with underlying dynamic issues within a unique juvenile firesetter program. In addition to work with juvenile firesetters, his professional interests have included the relationship between trauma and conduct problems, the integration of cognitive behavioral techniques with ego psychology, and family therapy.

Jeannine A. Gailey is assistant professor of criminal justice at Texas Christian University. Her current research interests include organizational deviance, attributing responsibility for wrongdoing, and masculinities. Her work has appeared in such journals as *Social Psychology Quarterly, Deviant Behavior*, and *Journal of Applied Social Psychology.*

Camille Gibson is an assistant professor of criminal and juvenile justice at Prairie View A&M University in Texas. Her publications include work on education and delinquency, law enforcement, child abuse, and Jamaican organized crime.

H.R. "Rudy" Hardy Jr. is an adjunct professor of criminal justice at the Houston Community College-Northwest. He earned his master's degree in criminal justice at the University of Houston-Downtown. Rudy retired in 2003 after a 30-year career as a federal criminal investigator. He is presently under contract as a firearms crime analyst in Houston, Texas.

Bruce Hoffman is assistant professor in the department of sociology and anthropology at Ohio University. His areas of research include criminology, sociolegal studies, and science studies. He is currently working on a book investigating law's power in shaping the consciousness and organization of midwifery and the home birth movement in California, Oregon, and Washington.

Ming-Li Hsieh holds a bachelor's degree in Japanese language and literature from the University of Chinese Culture in Taipei and a master's degree in security management from the University of Houston-Downtown, where she was recognized as the outstanding graduate student in 2006. She has presented research at several academic conferences and plans to continue her graduate studies in criminal justice in a doctoral program.

Lorine A. Hughes is an assistant professor in the School of Criminology and Criminal Justice at University of Nebraska, Omaha. She is coeditor of *Studying Youth Gangs*.

John H. Lemmon earned his doctorate in social work from the University of Maryland and is currently an associate professor of criminal justice at

Shippensburg University. He has more than 30 years' experience working in Pennsylvania's Children and Youth and Juvenile Justice Systems. His research interests include the effect of family life on youth deviancy and clinical treatment of antisocial behavior. His most recent publication, entitled "The Effects of Maltreatment Recurrence and Child Welfare Services on Dimensions of Delinquency," appeared in the March 2006 edition of *Criminal Justice Review.*

Richard McWhorter earned his doctorate in juvenile justice at Prairie View A&M University. He is a Licensed Professional Counselor, a Licensed Marriage and Family Therapist, and a Certified Hypnotherapist. For nine years he has taught graduate courses in the Marriage and Family Therapy Program in the Human Science Department at Prairie View A&M University and currently he is the Graduate Human Science Program Coordinator. In addition, he has more than 15 years of clinical experience working with victims and offenders of violence and sexual offenses.

Ariane Prohaska is an instructor at the University of Alabama. She earned her doctorate in sociology from the University of Akron in December 2006. Her research and teaching interests include gender, work, and family, masculinities, research methods, and statistics.

Frances P. Reddington is a professor of criminal justice at the University of Central Missouri in Warrensburg, Missouri. She earned her doctorate in criminal justice from Sam Houston State University. Her research interests include all aspects of juvenile justice. She has published articles in the areas of juvenile law, juveniles in adult jails, transfer of juveniles to the adult court, juveniles and the age of criminal responsibility, training of juvenile probation officers, the use of charter schools, and the role of Guardian ad Litems in abuse and neglect cases in juvenile court.

Thomas M. Vander Ven is associate professor and director of criminology in the Department of Sociology and Anthropology at Ohio University. His research interests include delinquency and the social control of youth, work, and family; the sociology of social problems; and criminological theory. His publications include articles in *Social Problems, Criminology, Human Studies, Deviant Behavior,* and *Crime and Delinquency.*

Hsiao-Ming Wang is associate professor of criminal justice at the University of Houston-Downtown (UHD). Before beginning his academic career, he was assistant special-agent-in-charge at the Investigation Bureau, Ministry of Justice in Taiwan. He has published articles in several refereed journals such as the *Law & Society Review.* He is the director of Bayou Connection, an international academic cooperation program at the UHD.